Espionage

Books by Ernest Volkman

Legacy of Hate

Warriors of the Night

The Heist
(*with John Cummings*)

Secret Intelligence

Goombata
(*with John Cummings*)

Till Murder Do Us Part
(*with John Cummings*)

Spies: The Secret Agents Who
Changed the Course of History

Espionage

THE GREATEST
SPY OPERATIONS OF
THE TWENTIETH CENTURY

Ernest Volkman

John Wiley & Sons, Inc.
New York • Chichester • Brisbane • Toronto • Singapore

For Eric, Michelle, Christopher, and above all, The Toad

This text is printed on acid-free paper.

Copyright © 1995 by Ernest Volkman
Published by John Wiley & Sons, Inc.

All rights reserved. Published simultaneously in Canada.

Library of Congress Cataloging-in-Publication Data:

Volkman, Ernest,
    Espionage : the greatest spy operations of the twentieth century
  / Ernest Volkman
      p.   cm.
    Includes bibliographical references and index.
    ISBN 0-471-01492-3 (acid-free paper)
      1. Espionage—History—20th century.   2. Intelligence service—
  History—20th century.   I. Title
  JF1525.I6V65   1995
  327.12'09'04—dc20   95-30638

Printed in the United States of America

10 9 8 7 6 5 4 3 2 1

Acknowledgments

A number of unseen hands were required to bring this book to fruition, but I owe a special debt of gratitude to two of them: Wiley editor Judith McCarthy, whose talented efforts made it a much better book, and my literary agent, Victoria Pryor of Arcadia, whose wise advice and support were essential.

*God hath given you one face,
and you make yourselves another.*

—*Shakespeare*, Hamlet

Contents

Introduction   *xi*

Glossary   *xix*

The Kingdoms of Espionage   *xxii*

Grand Deceptions

1 The Master Spy's Last Case   *3*
     The Trust Operation, 1921–1924
     The Soviets hoodwink the West

2 Our Man in Havana   *16*
     Cuban Double Agents, 1961–1987
     Fidel Castro stings the CIA

3 All Quiet on the Western Front   *26*
     Operation BODYGUARD, 1943–1944
     The Germans miss D-Day

4 The Descent of A3725   *37*
     The Double Cross System, 1940–1945
     A deception masterpiece

5 Long Island Calling Hamburg   *48*
     Operation TRAMP, 1939–1941
     The destruction of Admiral Canaris

Spies in the Ether

6 The Bronze Goddess   *61*
     Operation ULTRA, 1939–1945
     Looking over Hitler's shoulder

7 "By Guess and by God"   *73*
     Operation MAGIC, 1936–1945
     Tokyo laid bare

8 The Key to Rebecca   *83*
     Operation KONDOR, 1942
     The blinding of the Desert Fox

The Enemy Within

9 **The Hollow Tennis Racket** 95

Operation GRIFFIN, 1937–1945
Germany's secrets betrayed

10 **The Biggest Secret** 105

Operation CANDY, 1941–1945
The Russians steal the atomic bomb

11 **Black Tom** 116

The German Sabotage Operation, 1915–1917
Blowing up America

12 **A Bullet for General Polyakov** 126

Operation TOP HAT, 1959–1985
The CIA penetrates Moscow

A Wilderness of Mirrors

13 **The Mole War** 139

The CIA-KGB Struggle, 1961–1974
A death in Dallas

14 **The Mystery of a "Righteous Gentile"** 149

The Wallenberg Case, 1944–1990
Poison in Lubyanka

15 **The Lady at the Kiosk** 160

The Berlin Spy Carousel, 1966–1989
A triple agent

16 **Mr. Kent Comes to Tea** 167

The Theft of American Secrets, 1939–1941
The ambassador as target

Disasters

17 **East Wind, Rain** 179

Operation Z, 1932–1941
The Pearl Harbor catastrophe

18 **Defeat at the Iron Curtain** 193

The CIA's Underground War, 1947–1956
Tragedy in Eastern Europe

19 The Colonel and the Aviatrix   *205*
     Spying in The Mandates, 1922–1937
     An impenetrable paradox

Spectaculars

20 The Cambridge Comintern   *217*
     The Ring of Five, 1934–1951
     Stalin's Englishmen

21 The Family That Spied   *227*
     The Walker Spy Ring, 1967–1985
     America as an open book

22 The Pirates of Tel Aviv   *239*
     Operation PLUMBAT, 1965–1968
     The supreme Israeli triumph

Epilogue

Espionage as Opera Bouffe   *248*
     Operation CORNFLAKES, 1944–1945
     An OSS curiosity

Index   *256*

Introduction

To the officers of *Estikhabarat,* the Iraqi military intelligence service, the arrival of the American in Baghdad one day in 1989 must have seemed like something out of the *Arabian Nights.* The American, a satellite reconnaissance expert with the CIA (Central Intelligence Agency), had come bearing treasures to rival anything out of Aladdin's Cave: amazingly clear spy satellite photographs of the ground held by Iran, Iraq's enemy in a bitter war that had been raging for years. Even individual foxholes had been spotted by cameras capable of a ground resolution of 39 inches (meaning the cameras could get clear pictures of any object as small as 39 inches in diameter).

Spread out over a large table, the color photos showed an overview of the enemy that the Iraqis, without their own spy satellites, could only dream of ever achieving—front-line positions, armor concentrations, artillery batteries, ammunition dumps, and supply lines. The Iraqis could hardly conceal their delight, for they were now being afforded the kind of intelligence that could gain them a decisive advantage over the Iranians.

And if that weren't enough, the CIA man went on to provide a few handy tips on how CIA analysts had learned to detect attempts by some of their photographic subjects to evade those prying eyes overhead: artillery pieces hidden inside wrecked houses during daylight hours, elaborate camouflage schemes, special devices to mask heat emissions (and balk satellites that use infrared cameras), and concealment of missiles among piles of large drainage pipes to confuse a spy satellite's cameras. The Iraqis listened very carefully—as things turned out, only too carefully.

However impressed the Iraqis were with this espionage wizardry, the significance of the event was much more than a covert U.S. attempt to tip the odds in the Iran-Iraq War. The act of laying those American spy satellite photographs on a table in Baghdad represented one of the more colossal intelligence blunders of modern times. It was a multidimensional failure, composed in equal parts of the Bush administration's belief that covertly aiding Iraq would defeat, with minimal American investment, the danger of the radical Khomeini regime in Iran; a conviction that covert American aid to Baghdad would enhance so-called moderates in the police state of Saddam Hussein; and a conclusion that such aid would inhibit Hussein's territorial ambitions and draw him closer to American interests. So fervently did the Americans believe these fatuous assumptions that they secretly permitted a covert arms pipeline to be opened to Hussein; combined with a similar pipeline British intelligence opened (at the urging of Washington), this influx of arms allowed Hussein to build a first-class strategic threat to the entire Middle East while at the same time fighting his Iranian enemy to a draw.

But that wasn't the worst of it. By the time the Gulf War broke out two years later, the Iraqis had learned much from their helpful CIA contacts. Above all, they had learned how to hide Scud surface-to-surface missiles from prying eyes. Despite total Allied air superiority and round-the-clock coverage by spy satellites and reconnaissance aircraft, the Iraqis managed to hide most of their Scuds by clever camouflage and dispersal schemes. As a result, even overwhelming Allied superiority was unable to prevent the Iraqis from launching Scuds against Israel and Saudi Arabia. The scores of Israeli and American dead from those missile strikes underscore an old lesson: the price of intelligence failure is always paid in blood.

Early histories of the Gulf War make little mention of the chain of American intelligence failures leading up to Hussein's invasion of Kuwait, a lapse that is not surprising. Traditionally, historiography has tended to overlook the role that intelligence plays in the course of world events, especially during this century. Partially, that is due to a general failure to appreciate the role of perception in the affairs of state; intelligence, fundamentally, is all about perception. There is a tendency to portray history as strictly linear, with its key players influenced and moved by forces that are sometimes beyond their control.

But, to cite the example immediately at hand, there can be no real understanding of the Gulf War without understanding the kind of perceptions that moved its participants inexorably to the abyss. What led George Bush to conclude that he could con-

The Soviet-built Scud missile raised to its firing position. Thanks to the CIA, the Iraqis learned how to camouflage their Scuds, with significant consequences during Desert Storm. (*Department of Defense*)

vert a man like Saddam Hussein into a virtual American ally? What led Saddam Hussein to conclude that the Americans and their allies would not fight over so insignificant a piece of real estate as Kuwait? The answer is perceptions, and they in turn cannot be understood without learning of the intelligence that formed them (or, alternatively, how preconceptions were unaffected by intelligence to the contrary).

Admittedly, getting a handle on this process is not an easy task. As historians and journalists have found out the hard way, trying to understand the role of intelligence in world events is much like hacking through a dark, thick tangle of mystery, paradox, contradictory facts, missing or "weeded" (sanitized) records, self-serving memories, secrecy, "plausible deniability," and, occasionally, outright falsehoods, to say nothing of disinformation and misinformation.

The world of intelligence is unique, for there is no other field of human endeavor that operates permanently in the shadows. Regarded as essential (every nation in the world operates some kind of governmental intelligence agency), it nevertheless represents the dark side of the world political system—as befits what is at root a form of state-sanctioned voyeurism.

Espionage has suffered from an odious reputation ever since the days of Greek city-states, when special envoys called *proxenos* were sent from one warring city-state to another. As such, they were granted the honor of "guest-friend" and given the various privileges due honored guests "standing in place" of their clients. Unfortunately, it did not take long before their clients grasped the espionage potential of the *proxenos,* and state-run intelligence was born. But when several city-states discovered that the envoys had taken advantage of their hosts, the resulting scandal tarnished the reputation of such "official spies," and espionage was banished to the netherworld of political affairs as a necessary evil to be performed only by the dregs of society.

For the next dozen centuries, espionage was relegated to the "black arts," strictly segregated from political affairs. That changed in sixteenth-century Europe, where two warring states, England and France, were locked in a deadly struggle. Separated by only a few miles of ocean, the two kingdoms had long-standing political antagonisms that had spilled over into both overt and covert wars. Given the danger each represented to the other, they realized the vital need for organized, systematic collection of intelligence to keep track of what the other side was planning or doing. And only an organization directed and funded by the state could accomplish that task. In other words, a government intelligence bureaucracy.

By the next century, espionage had become an ingrained part of European statecraft, with nations running networks of "intelligencers" (to use the popular medieval term for spies) to keep tabs on actual and presumed enemies. Structurally, all of them followed the example set by Queen Elizabeth's spymaster, Francis Walsingham, whose innovations included compartmentalized networks to conduct foreign intelligence collection and a force of counterintelligence agents to balk the activities of enemy spies and keep tabs on domestic dissidents against the Crown.

By the late nineteenth century, the rapid pace of technological change—especially in military technology—combined with
growing political tensions in Europe to spawn a renewed effort
to find out "what's on the other side of the hill." Such intelligence was vital, for at a time when mass armies were wedded to
the telegraph and the railroad, wars broke out with sudden swift-
ness and overwhelming force. An unwarned nation could lose a
war in an afternoon.

For that reason, international diplomacy began to level the
playing field. International agreements on diplomatic relations
for the first time codified a system that overtly permitted official
spying. The agreements, which remain in force to this day, allowed nations to station so-called military attachés in their overseas embassies. Officially, these attachés were to represent their
nation's armed forces, but as everyone understood and diplomats
tacitly conceded, their real function was to observe and collect
intelligence on the armed forces of their host countries. At a time
when intelligence was almost exclusively concerned with the military power and potential of adversaries (government intelligence
agencies were largely run by the military), these attachés performed a vital intelligence function.

Implicit in these international agreements was a concession
that espionage, as the world's second-oldest profession, was so
ingrained in the body politic there was not much sense in trying
to ignore it. So the agreements sought to control espionage,
much as the Geneva Convention tried to control the conduct of
war, regarded as another inevitability. The practices of granting
diplomats immunity from arrest, deeming overseas embassies in-
violable sovereign territory, and setting up specific rules to be
followed in the event that an accredited diplomat broke the rules
of "official spying" were all part of an attempt to codify espionage
in the context of international relations. The effect was similar
to the Marquis of Queensberry's rules that made boxing a regu-
lated, "civilized" sport.

The gentleman diplomats could not have foreseen the dramatic transformation of intelligence in the twentieth century,
which featured not only a quantum growth in the size of government intelligence bureaucracies, but a transformation of at least
some espionage agents into what John Le Carré has called "geo-
political alchemists"—the subverters of governments, the de-
stabilizers of economies, the assassins of declared enemies. There
were not many nineteenth-century minds who perceived a day

when an intelligence agency could dispense with the governments of Iran and Guatemala like so much used tissue, and another intelligence agency could impose its will over the people of Poland and Czechoslovakia.

In part because of the high visibility of such operations in this century, there is a sense that history may have overlooked their real significance. A small, but growing body of historians has begun to concentrate on what it calls the "missing dimension" in modern history. There is much for these historians to consider. For example, what role did British intelligence perceptions (which turned out to be exaggerated) of a militarily powerful Germany play in the British government's decision to avoid confrontation with Hitler in 1938 and create the infamous Munich Agreement? What intelligence persuaded the European powers of 1914 that each of their military organizations could easily defeat their rivals in a major war, and that such a war would be short? (Or, as the French generals told their troops in August 1914, they would be home "before the leaves fall.") And what intelligence persuaded the Americans that a mere whiff of their military power would be sufficient to compel North Vietnam to abandon its aim of uniting Vietnam?

The effort to understand this missing dimension received a major boost in 1974 when the British government revealed an astonishing, decades-old secret: during World War II, in an operation code-named ULTRA, its codebreakers had managed to solve virtually all German coded communications, giving the Allies advance word of Hitler's military plans. This revelation has inspired a wholesale revision of the war's history, for now all Allied decisions have to be evaluated anew in the light of ULTRA.

Similarly, revelations during the 1970s in the United States about the vast power (and abuses) of the American intelligence community during the Cold War have inspired an entire cottage industry to reexamine much of recent U.S. history. The questions being raised as a result—how that community shaped the perceptions of policy makers, whether the intelligence agencies were "rogue elephants" who created their own foreign policy—have important implications in the context of the American democratic system, since they address issues of accountability, presidential power, and control of foreign policy.

Although these are exclusively American concerns, they are shared in some part with historians in other countries, especially those confronting the huge stacks of intelligence records left behind in the rubble of East European Communist regimes. In those piles of paper lurks much of Eastern Europe's own hidden history; it will take many years before those citizens fully grasp how pervasively the intelligence and secret police establishments of their countries shaped their lives and destinies.

But one important conclusion has already emerged, a recurring theme at the crossroads of history and intelligence. It is best summarized in Francis Bacon's famous aphorism, "Knowledge is power."

This book is an attempt to grapple with the "missing dimension." It takes the form of a number of case studies involving intelligence operations. They include glittering successes, abject failures, and, for dessert, an oddity that defies easy categorization. All of them, divided among several major types of intelligence operations ranging from counterintelligence to codebreaking, share a common thread: an impact on the course of twentieth-century history.

Glossary

Like many other fields of human endeavor, espionage has its own special language. Whenever possible, I have tried to avoid using the jargon of the espionage trade in this book, but unavoidably, there are some unique terms that have no ordinary language equivalents:

AGENT: A spy in the pay of a nation's intelligence service on a regular, salaried basis, with the status of government employee.

AGENT OF INFLUENCE: An asset (*see* Asset), usually in an important government, political, or business position, who is assigned the task of influencing policy, rather than collecting intelligence.

AGENT PROVOCATEUR: An asset, usually under control of a counterintelligence or police agency, assigned the job of infiltrating a political organization and instigating illegal acts or violent action designed to discredit that organization and justify extreme countermeasures.

ASSET: A person enrolled by an intelligence service—either for pay or because of political convictions—to serve as an intelligence source or to handle other, related tasks in his or her native country.

BLACK BAG JOB: Break-in or burglary to gain access to secret papers, which are photographed and returned, customarily in the same operation. Such operations are carried out by highly trained teams who must conceal any indication that the secret papers (often cipher keys or codebooks) have been compromised.

BLACK PROPAGANDA: Propaganda, apparently originating from dissident elements broadcasting from a "secret" radio station within their country (or just outside the borders), that is in fact created by a hostile intelligence service from a bordering country. It is most often designed to sow discord and confusion in the process of destabilizing that country's government.

BLOWN: An agent or asset revealed to counterintelligence. Also called "burned," most commonly in American intelligence parlance. Official notification from an intelligence agency's headquarters to its various stations warning that an agent or asset has been compromised is known as a "burn notice."

BRUSH CONTACT: Rapid, apparently accidental, contact between an agent or asset and a case officer or control agent to exchange material, most often in crowded public places to confuse any surveillance by counterintelligence agents.

CASE OFFICER: Agent assigned to supervise other agents or assets (or a network—"ring"—of them) in matters of pay, collection of intelligence, and other details. Also called "control agent."

CHIEF OF STATION: Agent assigned to head an overseas intelligence unit, normally part of an embassy staff (to provide diplomatic immunity in event of arrest). In Soviet intelligence, such an agent is known as a *rezident*.

CIPHER: A method of concealing secret messages by writing them in rearranged letters according to a specific system that dictates how the rearrangement (encipherment) takes place. Within the system is the "key" that unlocks the encipherment. An enciphered message can only be read by someone who knows the key.

CODE: A system of concealing secret messages that, unlike a cipher, substitutes plaintext with other words or numbers in an unvarying system. A coded message can only be decoded by someone who has access to the system—most commonly, a codebook that lists all the words or numbers used in the system.

COVER: Organizational or other kind of disguise under which an agent hides connection to an intelligence agency.

COVERT ACTION: Use of intelligence agencies to effect political change in another country through sub rosa efforts directed against the target country's political and economic structure. Most often utilized to destabilize a regime.

CRYPTANALYST: Trained expert who works to break ciphers by attempting to recover the "key" used in encryption. Given the complexity of modern cipher systems, most cryptanalysts today tend to be mathematicians who work with supercomputers to attack computer-generated ciphers.

DEAD DROP: Site, usually in a public area, where agents can leave material or exchange messages with their control without having to undergo the risk of meeting face to face. Typically, dead drops are in nooks or crevices unlikely to be used by the general public. Also known as *dubok*, from Soviet intelligence parlance.

DISCARD: Agent or asset deliberately sacrificed to deflect attention from other, more important, agents.

DISINFORMATION: Carefully falsified information, usually containing at least an element of truth, designed to mislead or confuse another nation's intelligence service.

FRONT: Legitimate-appearing entity created by an intelligence service to provide cover for agents and assets. It can take many forms, from a charitable foundation to a corporate entity.

ILLEGAL: In Soviet intelligence, an agent operating in a foreign country under an assumed identity or cover job.

LEGAL: In Soviet intelligence, an agent operating in a foreign country under diplomatic cover, which provides diplomatic immunity from arrest.

LEGEND: Faked biography of an agent to conceal real identity.

LETTERBOX: Asset used as a go-between to receive and pass on messages. Also known as a "cutout."

MOLE: Agent inserted into the political, intelligence, or military structure of a target nation with the specific objective of rising to a key position, at which point the agent is "switched on" to provide important intelligence.

ONETIME PAD: Cipher device that uses a pad with sheets of random numbers. Each sheet is utilized to encrypt one message, then discarded. Since each sheet is readable only to someone on the other end with the same pad, the system is theoretically unbreakable.

PLAYBACK: The technique of using a captured agent's radio to feed disinformation to the agent's control. Also known as *funkspiel* (radio game), from German intelligence jargon. To warn headquarters that they are operating under enemy control, agents are trained to insert a special "warn key" in their transmissions, usually a specific word or phrase.

SLEEPER: Agent planted in a foreign country with orders to carry out a normal life and conduct no espionage operations until ordered to do so, usually in the event of hostilities.

STATION: Chief office of an intelligence agency in a foreign country, most often located in an embassy.

WALK-IN: Asset who literally walks into the embassy or intelligence headquarters of a foreign country and volunteers to work as a spy, most often for money. Intelligence agencies on occasion will deliberately send an agent posing as a walk-in in order to penetrate the other side and plant disinformation. Such an agent is called a "dangle."

The Kingdoms of Espionage

The twentieth century has sometimes been called the "Century of the Spy," a time when government spy agencies became institutionalized. At no time in recorded history have so many people and so much treasure been devoted to pursuit of the one world commodity beyond price: information. Of the many thousands of such organizations, a few have achieved significant influence in the course of world history. Many will recur throughout this book, usually referred to by their acronyms. For the convenience of readers, a list of these organizations follows, including their full titles and national affiliations.

Australia

Australian Secret Intelligence Service (ASIS, also known as MO9), successor agency to the Australian Secret Intelligence Organization (ASIO)

Defence Signals Directorate (DSD), communications intelligence

Canada

Canadian Security Intelligence Service (CSIS), successor agency to the Royal Canadian Mounted Police Security Service

Communications Security Establishment (CSE), communications intelligence

China

Guojia Anqouanbi (Ministry of State Security)
Te Wu (Central External Liaison Department)
Quingbao (Military Intelligence)

Cuba

Direccion General de Intelligencia (DGI, Intelligence Service)

France

Directorate Generale de la Securite Exterieure (DGSE), successor agency to *Service de Documentation Exterieure et de Contre-Espionage* (SDECE)

Groupement de Communications Radioelectriques (GCR), communications intelligence

Direction du Renseignements Militaires (DRM), successor agency to the *Deuxieme Bureau* of the French General Staff; military intelligence

Direction de la Surveillance du Territoire (DST), counterintelligence

Germany

Amt Ausland Nachrichten und Abwehr (*Abwehr,* Foreign and Defense Intelligence Service), absorbed by *Sicherheitsdienst* in 1944

Sicherheitsdienst (SD, Secret Service), disbanded 1945

Gehlen Org, disbanded 1954

Bundes Nachrichten Dienst (BND, Federal Intelligence Service)

Bundesamt für Verfassungsschutz (BfV, Federal Office for the Protection of the Constitution), counterintelligence

Geheime Staatspolizei (Gestapo, Secret State Police), disbanded 1945; counterintelligence

Iran

Savama (Information and Security Service of the Nation)

Iraq

Al Mukharbarat (Department of General Intelligence)

Estikhabarat (Military Intelligence)

Israel

Mossad Letafkidim Meyouch-hadim (*Mossad,* Central Institution for Intelligence and Special Duties)

Aman (Military Intelligence)

Sherlut Bitachon Kalali (Shabak, General Security Service), counterintelligence

Japan

Kempei Tai (Military Police), disbanded 1945; counterintelligence

Naicho (Foreign Intelligence)

Libya

Mukhabarat (Central Security Bureau)

Russia

Foreign Intelligence Service (FIS), successor agency to Soviet KGB

Russian Federation

Central Intelligence Service (CIS), successor agency to assorted Soviet intelligence organs

Glavnoye Razevedyaltelnoye (GRU), military intelligence

South Korea

Agency for National Security Planning (ANSP), successor agency to South Korean Central Intelligence Agency (KCIA)

Soviet Union

Chrezuyehainaya Komissiya po Borbe s Kontrrevolutisnei i Sabottazhem (CHEKA, Extraordinary Commission Against Counterrevolution and Sabotage), eventually reorganized into KGB

Komit Gosudarstvennoy Bezopasnosi (KGB, Commissariat for State Security), absorbed into FIS in 1990

United Kingdom

Secret Intelligence Service (SIS), also known as MI6

Security Service (MI5), counterintelligence

Government Communications Headquarters (GCHQ), successor agency to Government Code and Cipher School (GCCS)

United States

Central Intelligence Agency (CIA)

National Security Agency (NSA), communications intelligence

Federal Bureau of Investigation (FBI), counterintelligence

Vietnam

Bo Cong An (SRGV, Vietnamese General Research Service)

GRAND DECEPTIONS

If, as has sometimes been argued, espionage is the black art of international relations, then deception is its highest art form. In espionage terms, deception is an elaborate effort—sometimes involving huge expenditures of time, money, and people—to mislead an enemy. It is an extremely difficult technique to pull off, for even one small mistake can alert an enemy that a deception operation is underway.

There are any number of reasons for mounting a deception operation: to conceal weakness and make an enemy believe phantom strength, to penetrate an enemy's intelligence service, or to warp completely an enemy's perception. Like much else about espionage, deception shares a technique from the criminal world, the "con" or "sting," an elaborate ruse to fool the "mark" (usually into parting with his or her money). And like a criminal sting, a deception operation relies most heavily on the credulity of the victim.

Credulity is a key factor in the five case studies that follow; in each case a deception operation was mounted to take advantage of the victim's propensity to believe what the operation was prepared to reinforce. In other words, as any good con artist will testify, marks essentially con themselves.

The case studies include the granddaddy of all deception operations, which occurred in the 1920s, three brilliantly conducted operations during World War II that hoodwinked Nazi Germany, and a modern operation that deceived the CIA—this latter study by way of proving that the more things change, the more they remain the same.

1

1

The Master Spy's Last Case

The Trust Operation
1921–1924

The Soviets hoodwink the West

O n a crisp fall day in 1921, Yuri Artamanov was pleasantly surprised to receive a visit from an old friend he had assumed he would probably never see again. In later years, he would come to regret that this visit had ever happened.

But for the moment, there was only the thought of renewing a long-standing friendship that had been interrupted by the forces of world politics. Artamanov, an officer in the Czarist army, had fled Russia in 1918 after the Bolshevik revolution and settled in Tallinn, capital of Estonia, where he was eking out a living working as a translator at the British diplomatic mission. Meanwhile, he served as the representative in Estonia of an anti-Bolshevik exile group known as the Supreme Monarchist Council (VMS). Like Artamanov, all its members were former Czarist military or governmental officials who had fled certain death in Lenin's regime. In exile, they were united by a common goal: overthrow the Bolshevik government and restore the monarchy.

Among the friends Artamanov had left behind in Russia was the ambiguous figure of Aleksandr Yakushev, who had been manager of the Exploitation Department of Waterways Administration. Yakushev had resisted pleas from Artamanov and others to flee as the Bolsheviks took power, insisting that his expertise in administering the country's waterways would be urgently needed. To flee, he argued, would mean that Russia's economically vital canal system would soon collapse. He could not bear the thought of a system that had taken a century to construct falling apart in the confusion of revolution and civil war. That would severely injure the country he loved. No, he would stay and somehow work out an arrangement with the new revolutionary government.

Artamanov considered his friend naive; no Russian could fail to understand that the Bolsheviks clearly intended to eradicate all vestiges of the hated Czarist regime, most especially the officers and government officials whom Lenin openly called criminals. Thus, Artamanov was all the more surprised when, having not seen or heard from Yakushev for several years, his old friend appeared at his office in Tallinn, apparently unscathed. He was even more surprised when Yakushev told him that he had been recruited by Leon Trotsky himself to serve as consultant to the new Soviet Waterways Department and tell the Bolsheviks how to run Russia's system of waterborne commerce. The need for his expertise was so acute, Yakushev said, that the Bolsheviks were willing to take the unprecedented step of hiring an "enemy of the people."

Artamanov had barely absorbed this startling news when Yakushev provided a further shock. He was permitted to travel to Western countries, Yakushev said, as a representative of the New Economic Policy (NEP), a drastic gambit by Lenin to save the new Soviet state from imminent economic collapse. Essentially an infusion of capitalist ideas into the disastrous failure of state collectivization of Soviet industry and agriculture, NEP allowed limited free trade and the creation of large private combines to negotiate foreign trade. Yakushev had been chosen to negotiate the sale of Soviet lumber to Western countries.

Yakushev made it clear he was not a Bolshevik and did not share Lenin's policies or aims. To buttress that assertion, he then made an astonishing admission to Artamanov: he was a member of an underground monarchist group inside Russia, composed of former Czarist officials and sympathizers who were biding their time until the inevitable fall of the Bolshevik regime. Operating under the cover name *Tres* ("trust" in Russian), Yakushev confided, it had members in all levels of Soviet society and was now seeking to establish links with monarchist exiles outside Russia—all the better to aid the goal of undermining and then overthrowing the regime in Moscow. Yakushev claimed he was sharing this information with Artamanov strictly because of their long-standing friendship; naturally, he assumed Artamanov would exercise the greatest discretion lest word of what he had revealed get back to the dreaded CHEKA, the Bolshevik intelligence/internal security agency. Yakushev did not need to remind Artamanov that the CHEKA was slaughtering Russians by the hundreds of thousands; any opponent of the regime could expect to be dragged into the cellars of the new CHEKA headquarters on Lubyanka Street in Moscow and dispatched with a bullet in the back of the head.

By the time the visit ended, Artamanov was in a state of high excitement. The idea that a monarchist underground had managed to survive in the Soviet state was astounding news, and the fact that one of his old friends was among the group's important figures was an extra bonus. As the two men parted, Yakushev promised further meetings during other trips abroad. They agreed on a series of passwords to be used so that Artamanov could recognize "special emissaries" Yakushev might send in his place in the event he would not be able to make a foreign trip.

With that, Yakushev departed. Artamanov immediately sat down and wrote a letter to Kirill Shirinsky-Shikhmatov, one of the leading figures in VMS in Berlin, conveying news of Yakushev's visit. Shirinsky-Shikhmatov shared Artamanov's excitement, and by return letter directed him to maintain contact with Yakushev and forge a link with the *Tres*. The letter was so important, he entrusted it to a special courier who had been handling such sensitive VMS correspondence for some time.

The VMS didn't know it, but the courier was in fact a CHEKA agent. He carefully steamed open the envelope of Shirinsky-Shikhmatov's message, copied out the message by hand, and delivered it to the Soviet trade mission in Berlin. Shortly afterward, a coded message reached CHEKA headquarters: the bait had been taken.

That message would mark the real beginning of what would turn out to be the greatest, and most successful, deception operation in all history. Eventually, it would virtually destroy the organized anti-Bolshevik opposition, deceive the infant Soviet Union's external enemies, expose its internal enemies, and create, for Soviet intelligence, a vaunting reputation that would last until the very collapse of the Soviet Union itself some seventy years later. For Western intelligence, what would become known as the Trust operation was a disaster of the first magnitude: as a direct result of the operation they were blinded for years in the Soviet Union. It is no exaggeration to say that the operation was most responsible for the survival of the Soviet state during the difficult and perilous years of its infancy.

Conceived and organized with consummate skill, the Trust operation was almost breathtaking in scope. Its aim, finally achieved, was to organize and then monitor all anti-Bolshevik resistance both inside and outside Russia. Among the operation's more interesting elements, judged strictly by the standards of espionage tradecraft, was the creation of the opposition the operation was seeking to destroy.

There were two contexts in which the Trust operation was spawned, and both of them represented very serious threats to the Bolshevik regime. Domestically, after a bloody civil war had left the country economically devastated and given it a "Red Terror" that sought to exterminate all opposition, Russia was seething with unrest. As the Bolsheviks were only too acutely aware, they had been compelled to fill thousands of jobs in the governmental and military bureaucracy with ex-Czarists, for the simple reason that there were not enough trained Bolsheviks to keep the machinery of government going. But that created an internal security problem, a potential counterrevolutionary force working right inside the government. Many of those ex-Czarists, professing loyalty to the new Soviet state, secretly had organized themselves into underground cells that met clandestinely and began formulating plans—not all of them realistic—to overthrow the regime that was causing Russia so much misery.

The CHEKA had infiltrated some of these cells, and it soon learned that among them was a group of die-hard monarchists who had created a secret organization grandiloquently called the Monarchist Association of Central Russia (MOTsR). Composed of government officials who concealed their political sympathies, the group planned to bore into the Bolshevik power structure from within, weaken it, and then restore the Romanov dynasty. Among the leading MOTsR activists was a government official named Aleksandr Yakushev.

This festering domestic threat was compounded by a potentially more dangerous threat from without. The several hundred thousand anti-Bolsheviks who had fled the country after the revolution and subsequent civil war were preoccupied with the goal of returning to Russia and destroying the Bolsheviks. Scattered among a dozen European countries—although concentrated in France and Germany—they amounted to an uneasy coalition of left and right factions under the leadership of Grand Duke Nikolai, the last of the Romanov royal clan. Seen from Moscow, the exiles represented a formidable threat: they had some 400,000 men willing to take up arms to recapture Holy Russia, and teams of exiles routinely crossed Russia through still-porous borders to meet with domestic dissidents, carry out sabotage operations, and generally make life miserable for the Bolshevik government.

It was no secret that many of the exile factions had signed up with assorted intelligence services (including Japan's) to gather intelligence. In return, they were receiving money, arms, and even more important, promises to support their efforts to topple the Bolshevik regime. The threat was growing with each passing month, creating the possibility of an ultimate nightmare: a joining of the exterior exile movement with the interior dissident movement. Early in 1921, Lenin ordered that both these threats be destroyed.

There was only one man Lenin believed capable of succeeding in so daunting a task: Feliks Dzerzhinsky. The creator and chief of the CHEKA, Dzerzhinsky had been a close ally and friend of Lenin's since 1903, when he abandoned the Mensheviks and joined Lenin's Bolsheviks. Born in Poland, Dzerzhinsky had been a revolutionary since 1897 when, as a twenty-year-old university student, he decided to dedicate his life to overthrowing the Russian oligarchy that had enslaved his native country (Poland was then a province of Russia).

At first glance, the man who would become history's greatest spymaster did not cut an impressive figure. Thin and balding with a little wisp of a beard, he was constantly wracked by coughs from tuberculosis, a disease he contracted while forced to work in a Siberian coal mine during a two-year imprisonment by the Czar's government. But Dzerzhinsky had a formidable mind, distinguished by organizational talent, ruthlessness, strength of character, and, as he was about to prove, an unrivaled talent for running intricate deception operations.

By 1921, Dzerzhinsky had already demonstrated his considerable talents. When the CHEKA was created in 1917, he was a revolutionary with no experience in the intelligence field. In terms of assets, he had at hand the grand total of a squad of agents and

Feliks Dzerzhinsky, the legendary head of the Soviet CHEKA, shortly before his death in 1924. Dzerzhinsky did not live to see the culmination of his greatest triumph, a massive deception operation known as the Trust. (*Komit Gosudarstvennoy Bezopasnosi*)

four cars. But within a year he built a powerful organization of thousands of agents, a flourishing counterintelligence service, and a ferociously repressive internal security apparatus that enforced Bolshevik control.

Dzerzhinsky's new assignment represented his greatest challenge yet, and he devoted several weeks toward thinking the problem through. He finally emerged with a plan that his deputies found somewhat curious: their chief was proposing that the CHEKA get into the dissidence business.

Like the opening moves in a chess game (Dzerzhinsky was a devoted player), the CHEKA's first actions appeared distinctly low-key. On Dzerzhinsky's orders, surveillance was tightened on the MOTsR, with more CHEKA agents infiltrated into its ranks. When the CHEKA had a complete picture of the organization and its members, Dzerzhinsky then ordered his next move: Aleksandr Yakushev was to be secretly arrested.

Yakushev assumed he was about to be shot, but to his surprise he encountered at Lubyanka a battery of CHEKA officials who conducted something of a group therapy session with their prisoner. Most of the discussion was conducted by one of Dzerzhinsky's most brilliant deputies, his counterintelligence chief Artur Artuzov. In tones more suggestive of a university seminar than a secret police interrogation, Artuzov went to work on Yakushev's mind.

In the process, Artuzov tore away his prisoner's pretensions. Yakushev claimed to be opposed to the Czar's more draconian policies. Artuzov scoffed: yes, but what did you do about it? He noted Yakushev's many extramarital affairs in the years prior to the Czar's overthrow, then demanded, "And so, Comrade Yakushev, while the Russian people sacrificed, what did you do? Play around?" Artuzov went on to note, darkly, that Yakushev had some contact with British intelligence in 1918, when the British were carrying out an extensive covert action operation to overthrow the Bolshevik regime. Shocked that the CHEKA had found out about the link, Yakushev sought to explain that he merely discussed the future of Russia with the British, but Artuzov cut him off: "Well, so we see that you were willing to sell Russia to the British. This is patriotism?"

A few more weeks of this sort of round-the-clock mental assault on Yakushev finally produced a shamed and penitent prisoner, who now freely conceded that he had been a dilettante all his life and a hypocritical supporter of a Czarist regime that he professed to despise, yet did nothing to change. Yakushev pronounced himself ready to be shot for his sins.

But Dzerzhinsky had bigger plans in mind. Entering the game in person, the CHEKA chief told Yakushev that he had seen his "good side," and that Yakushev struck him as a man who sincerely wanted to do something to atone for his past sins and help relieve the miseries of Russia. To accomplish that, Dzerzhinsky said, it was first necessary to solve the problem of the exiles— fanatical men who wanted only to overthrow the present regime and restore their privileges. These men had never demonstrated any concern for the plight of the Russian people; their sole concern was to regain power and repress the people in the same way they had repressed them for centuries. Surely, Yakushev didn't want that to happen.

Yakushev agreed, and Dzerzhinsky now played his high card. The CHEKA, he said, was among the "liberalizers" of the Bolshevik regime. Beset by enemies from within and without, the regime unfortunately was forced to use terroristic methods to

keep the revolution alive. But as soon as these threats were elim-
inated, peace and democracy would return to Russia; a government where all points of view were considered would be established. To fulfill this promise, the liberalizers of the CHEKA and
their allies in the Bolshevik hierarchy would need to dampen the
opposition that had inspired the Red Terror in the first place.
Ideally, Dzerzhinsky said, there should be one "loyal opposition"
group in Russia, composed of intelligent men (such as Yakushev)
dedicated to reform and progress. That group, Dzerzhinsky said
in his final flourish, was the MOTsR.

It is a measure of Yakushev's colossal naivete and equally
colossal ego that he bought the CHEKA's gambit unreservedly.
Asked by Yakushev how he could aid this worthy goal, Dzerzhinsky
had just the plan in mind for him. Simply, Yakushev was to travel
abroad as a commercial representative of the NEP, make contact
with the leaders of the exile community, and inform them that
the MOTsR was the only powerful and respected dissident organization in all Russia. As such, it should serve as the exclusive
contact and intelligence collection point for the exile movement.
No other dissident group inside Russia had anywhere near the
MOTsR's organizational clout and contacts across the entire government spectrum.

Yakushev then was dispatched to his fateful encounter with
the exile leader Artamanov in Estonia. Of course, once outside
Russia, Yakushev simply could have blown the entire operation,
but Dzerzhinsky had measured his quarry well. From the first
moment, Yakushev threw himself enthusiastically into the project;
all the while the CHEKA kept whispering in his ear how his work
was certain to win him a high post in the new "democratic" government of Russia that would ultimately emerge.

Following Yakushev's first encounter with Artamanov, Dzerzhinsky deliberately withheld Yakushev from any further contact
with the exiles. Like a chess grandmaster luring an unwary opponent into a trap that would be sprung twenty moves hence,
Dzerzhinsky waited as the delicate tendrils of Western intelligence began to vibrate. As his agents began reporting to him, a
half-dozen intelligence agencies were excited about news of the
MOTsR and were pressing their exile assets to find out more.
Such interest was an essential part of Dzerzhinsky's plan; as in all
good stings, it was necessary for the targets to work themselves
into the proper pitch of desire.

As Dzerzhinsky knew, his Western opponents had become desperate for anything they could get on the Bolshevik regime. The Communist coup in Hungary in 1919, the invasion of Poland in 1920, and Communist-led insurrections in Germany all contributed to that desperation. Lenin had openly talked of world revolution, and there was not a single Western intelligence agency unwilling to do just about anything to get information on a threat to their nations' very existence.

When Dzerzhinsky judged that eagerness had reached a fevered pitch, a man named Pavel P. Kolesnikov (actually CHEKA* agent Viktor Stetakiewicz) appeared at Artamanov's door in Tallinn. This happened some months after Yakushev's visit. Claiming to be an important representative of the Trust—as it was most commonly known—Kolesnikov gave the proper password, saying he was acting in place of Yakushev, who was ill with the flu. He then provided a lavish account of how the Trust's operations had grown inside Russia, and how it had infiltrated virtually every level of Soviet society. For good measure, he handed over a number of typed reports on conditions inside Russia that he said had been prepared by the Trust.

Dzerzhinsky, the man who concocted those reports, a mixture of truth, half-truth, and fiction, was aware that Artamanov was an asset of British intelligence. Sure enough, he immediately turned them over to his contact in MI6. Shortly, the intelligence services of Poland, Estonia, Latvia, France, and Czechoslovakia were asking for copies. Even the Americans got into the act: one of the local employees in the U.S. Mission in Tallinn was also the chief source on Russia for the small intelligence section of the State Department. From there, the reports wound up in the hands of both Army Intelligence and the Office of Naval Intelligence.

Taken as a whole, the Trust reports painted a picture of a Soviet Union undergoing dramatic political changes. According to the reports, Lenin was abandoning his idea of world revolution, and a liberal faction was gradually taking control of the reins of power. In the process, such notorious radicals in the ruling Politburo as Josef Stalin were being shunted aside in favor of more pragmatic men who wanted to make the Soviet Union a

---

* While Stetakiewicz was on his mission, the CHEKA was reorganized and renamed *Gosudarstvennoye Politicheskoye Upravleniye* (GPU).

respected member of the world community (translation: obtain Western credits, trade, and aid).

This was pure disinformation, designed to influence Western governments and at the same time reduce outside pressure. The Trust took credit for the dramatic transformation in the Soviet Union, further enhancing its posture as the single, true representative of all political dissidence inside Russian borders. As an added bonus, it quickly became virtually the single intelligence source on Soviet affairs. Indeed, the Trust managed to convince Western intelligence agencies that it should serve as the exclusive facilitator of infiltrations across (and out of) Soviet borders on the theory that it controlled safe "windows" in border areas totally under Trust sway.

Ordinarily, intelligence agencies would have been reluctant to entrust operations and intelligence to a single source that somehow managed to thrive in the face of the tight internal security of the CHEKA/GPU, but Dzerzhinsky carefully stage-managed a few dazzling demonstrations to remove any doubts. Aware that cautious intelligence agencies would send agents into Russia to check out Trust claims firsthand, Dzerzhinsky let them infiltrate across the border. Once inside Russia, they were taken in hand by Trust representatives, who seemed adept in the art of clandestine operations and spouted an impressive line of passwords and other espionage mumbo jumbo. The agents were taken to conferences of Trust cells in Russia, secret sites where Trust members exchanged vital intelligence on the workings of the Bolshevik regime, and even an "underground" Eastern Orthodox service using Trust priests who were defying the government's official ban on religion. Exiles who infiltrated Russia were shown a remarkably organized underground government that even managed to spring the brother of one prominent exile from prison.

Like a scene from the movie *The Sting*, it was all an elaborate facade. The visitors did not know that Dzerzhinsky had quietly rounded up and imprisoned all the real MOTsR members, then substituted his own agents. From the "secret Trust sympathizers" who worked as border guards to the priests who conducted the underground services, all were Dzerzhinsky's men playing out their carefully rehearsed roles. It was a tribute to his meticulous attention to detail that there was not one single slip in this charade.

The consequences were momentous. Within two years of the beginning of the Trust operation, Dzerzhinsky had managed to convert the Trust into the exclusive source of all Western intelligence on the Soviet Union. Additionally, the exile movement had become a wholehearted supporter of the Trust, a faith that was to prove costly: one of the main exile leaders, Boris Savinkov, was lured to Russia with promises of a prominent leadership role in the Trust. He was arrested and imprisoned, an event explained away by the Trust as a result of Savinkov's inattention to security. Even better, the operation managed to lure the legendary British intelligence agent Sidney Reilly, at that point a key operative for the exiles. Captured the moment he crossed the border, he was extensively tortured to reveal everything he knew about British intelligence operations—most importantly, identities of agents and assets. Then he was executed, his fate revealed by the Trust as an unfortunate "accident" that occurred when he used the wrong window to infiltrate Russia and was shot by a border guard.

The GPU managed to convince Western intelligence and the exiles that the fates of Savinkov and Reilly were accidents, largely attributable to their failure to follow Trust security arrangements. It was a clever little touch, since such an explanation portrayed the Trust as something less than omnipotent. As a number of Western intelligence agents concluded, such errors as the Savinkov-Reilly incidents mitigated in favor of the Trust as the genuine article. After all, if the Trust was a deception, such mistakes would not have happened. Similarly, Yakushev was accepted uncritically on his many trips abroad on Trust business; as a known Czarist sympathizer, there seemed no possibility that he was working for the Bolsheviks.

But one man was not so easily fooled, and his suspicions would finally bring the Trust deception to an end. Wladyslaw Michniewicz, an officer in Polish intelligence, had been assigned in 1920 to go to Tallinn and set up a network for Polish intelligence inside Russia. He recruited a number of assets, including a few members of the MOTsR. Michniewicz's experience with the group convinced him it was ineffective, composed of a few diehard Czarists who had neither the organizational nor the clandestine skills to overthrow anybody, least of all the Bolsheviks.

He was thus all the more surprised when his superiors only a year later were proclaiming the MOTsR as the answer to their prayers. Something was very wrong, Michniewicz decided, and he arranged a trip to Moscow via the Trust to see for himself. What he experienced only confirmed his worst suspicions: however impressive the Trust representatives appeared, they were oddly vague when he pressed for specific items of military intelligence. When he returned to Tallinn, Michniewicz investigated further, finally concluding that the Trust was an elaborate deception. To his fury, his superiors rejected his report, citing all the valuable intelligence the Trust was providing.

But in 1926 the new Polish minister of war, Marshal Pilsudski, also suspicious of the Trust, ordered a thorough review of Michniewicz's reports. Concluding that Michniewicz was right, he devised an elaborate test: the Trust was asked to provide a copy of the Soviet mobilization plan in the event of a Russo-Polish war. Unaware that Pilsudski already had a copy he obtained via a source on the Soviet general staff, the Trust finally presented him with its own copy of the plan. Comparing the two, Pilsudski concluded at once that the Trust version was a clever fake, full of disinformation. He ordered Polish intelligence to cut off all further contact with the Trust.

Pilsudski's warning to other Western intelligence agencies forced further reevaluations, and within two months there was no further doubt: they all had been victimized by a Soviet deception. Aware of the growing doubts, the GPU abruptly decided to close down the Trust operation.

News of the deception fell upon the exile movement like a thunderclap. All of their hopes and dreams now lay shattered, along with what remained of any dissident movement within the Soviet Union. The exiles never recovered from this blow; until the collapse of the Soviet Union some decades later, they played virtually no role in determining the future of their native country. The Trust disaster deepened the political cracks among the exiles and split them into ineffective factions. Unable to rely again on any dissident movement inside the Soviet Union, there never was any uniting of the external and internal dissidents—no small aid to the creation of the Stalinist police state.

In intelligence terms, the importance of the Trust operation cannot be overestimated. Essentially, the operation was a tribute to wishful thinking; it not only shaped Western views of the infant Soviet Union, but also served to neutralize a very dangerous threat to a regime that needed time to consolidate its power. Moreover, the Soviets had the breathing space to refine an internal security apparatus that made the country virtually impervious to any future infiltration. Above all, the Trust gave the Soviets an unparalleled entry into Western intelligence, allowing identification of operatives and assets. Western intelligence would never quite recover from the disaster.

The man who made it all possible, Feliks Dzerzhinsky, did not live to see the fruition of his creation. In 1924, at the height of the Trust operation's success, he died from tuberculosis. His deputies, who later went to work for the GPU (which eventually became the KGB), were consumed in Stalin's purges during the 1930s for reasons that remain somewhat unclear. And Aleksandr Yakushev, the slightly addled Czarist who was the key pawn in the game? He was dragged into the Lubyanka cellars one day in 1936, accused of being a "Trotskyite saboteur." His appointment by Trotsky had now borne terrible fruit in Stalin's merciless purge of anyone who had come into contact with his hated political rival.

Yakushev was befuddled by it all. He demanded of his tormentors how he could be so accused, considering his great contribution to the Trust operation. They professed not to know what he was talking about. Then they shot him.

2

Our Man in Havana

Cuban Double Agents
1961–1987

Fidel Castro stings the CIA

The paper equivalent of a bomb arrived at the headquarters of the CIA in Langley, Virginia, on a July day in 1987. It came in the form of a cable from one of the agency's leading enemies and said, in effect, you have been had. It read:

> ON BEHALF OF THE STATE SECURITY AGENTS AND OF OUR FIGHTING PEOPLE I AM SENDING THIS LAST MESSAGE. WE RATIFY OUR DECISION TO FIGHT NO MATTER WHERE AND HOW AGAINST THE ATTEMPTS TO ASSASSINATE OUR COMMANDER IN CHIEF, AGAINST MILITARY THREATS, AGAINST THE ATTEMPTS TO THWART OUR INTERNATIONAL SOLIDARITY, AGAINST EVERY MACHINATION AIMED AT DESTROYING OUR SOCIALIST REVOLUTION. VIVA FIDEL! PATRIA O MUERTE!

This bombast was clearly the product of the Cuban intelligence agency *Direccion General de Intelligencia* (DGI). But it was signed MATEO, the code name for one of the CIA's top assets in Cuba. The message was unmistakable: MATEO actually worked for the DGI.

The cable was not entirely unexpected. Only a month before, a Cuban DGI agent named Antonio Rodriguez had de-

16

fected to the CIA. During his debriefings, he dropped a hint that severely rattled his inquisitors. He didn't know the details, but according to gossip he had heard around DGI headquarters in Havana, all the Cuban assets the CIA had managed to recruit during the previous 26 years were in fact DGI plants. If true, that meant the CIA's assets had been working all along for the other side. The implications, obviously, were devastating: CIA operations in Cuba, an abiding American obsession, had been compromised.

Confirmation of the CIA's worst fears came only a few weeks later, when still another DGI agent defected, a man who had more direct knowledge. Florentino Aspillaga Lombard, DGI chief of station in Prague, tired of the privations of life under Castro, simply drove across the border into Austria with his girlfriend. He arrived at the American embassy in Vienna, announced his intention to defect, and immediately made it clear he was a defector with valuable goods to trade. While shocked CIA agents listened, Aspillaga revealed that he had formerly worked in DGI counterintelligence, in which job he helped oversee his agency's operations against the CIA in Cuba. The DGI, he said, had succeeded in turning *every single one* of the 38 assets the CIA had recruited in Cuba since 1961.

In other words, as an urgent message to Langley from the Vienna station made clear, everything the CIA thought it knew about Cuba was actually DGI disinformation. Any doubt CIA headquarters might have had about Aspillaga's claims were quickly removed when the DGI, aware of his defection and assuming he would reveal the compromise of CIA assets, decided to end the game. The bombastic cable to Langley was a final flourish, meant to rub the CIA's nose in the mess on the floor. A few days later, the DGI unveiled another embarrassment: Cuban state television began running an 11-part documentary series entitled "The CIA War against Cuba." It featured interviews with a dozen Cuban men and women the CIA believed had been its assets for decades, along with grainy videos taken by DGI agents showing CIA agents under diplomatic cover in Havana servicing dead drops.

The CIA didn't need Cuban television to tell it it had a full-fledged intelligence disaster on its hands. Extensive debriefings of Aspillaga resulted in a damage assessment report that was unreservedly bleak: the CIA had been completely outwitted by the DGI, compromising all CIA human intelligence from Cuba. Even

the dry bureaucratic language of the report conveyed the dimensions of the disaster: for 26 years, a total of 38 Cuban assets had
been working for the DGI, which allowed the Cubans to identify
at least 179 CIA agents (24 of them, under diplomatic cover in
the U.S. Interests Section in Havana, fled the country when the
CIA first learned of the disaster). For all that time, the DGI was
able to control CIA intelligence from Cuba, rendering the CIA
blind. There now remained no doubt why the CIA's intelligence
on Cuba had been so bad for so long.

How had the disaster happened? How had a small, Third
World intelligence service managed so completely to hoodwink
the huge CIA? How had it managed to carry out the deception
so long against a superpower's vast panoply of technology and its
armies of agents?

The answers, as it turned out, involved all the classic elements of deception operations: very effective work by those who
conceived and carried out the deception, deception agents who
played their roles well, and above all, a certain credulousness on
the part of the victim. In the Cuban case, there was plenty of
American credulousness, aided in no small part by some astonishing ineptitude from an agency that should have known better.

MATEO, the Cuban asset who sent that last, gloating cable to CIA
headquarters, was prototypical of the assets the CIA recruited in
Cuba. His real name was Juan Acosta, a fishing boat captain who
became a dedicated follower of Fidel Castro during the revolution. After Castro took power in 1959, Acosta decided to stay in
Cuba. He was rewarded for his loyalty by being named head of
Cuba's tuna fishing fleet, a collection of oceangoing boats that
fished international waters, ranging as far as the Canary Islands.

Acosta's knowledge of the world of espionage was limited to
a few spy movies he had seen, but he avidly agreed to become
involved in the spy game when the DGI came calling in 1966.
Acosta was told that the CIA was actively recruiting Cubans, especially any who worked overseas. Almost certainly, Acosta was
informed, he would be approached at some point. When that
happened, he was to play along and immediately inform the DGI;
they would take care of the rest.

Initially, Acosta assumed he would be sent to some sort of
spy school to learn the esoterica of the spy trade, but his DGI
contacts made it clear no such training was necessary. If approached for recruitment, he would claim to be politically disaf-

In this scene from a Cuban television documentary, a CIA agent services a dead drop in Havana, unaware he's being videotaped by Cuban DGI agents. The videotaping was part of an extensive sting operation by the Cubans, who controlled all CIA assets in Cuba. (*Cuban State Television*)

fected, only too happy to provide intelligence against Castro. Otherwise, he was to function normally, telling no one of this extra twist in his life. Whatever intelligence he would be asked to gather would be provided by the DGI.

As the DGI predicted, Acosta was approached one day during a trip to the Canary Islands. It was a standard enough recruitment: as per his instructions, Acosta played the part of political dissident. His recruiter said he would be paid $250 a month (later raised to $1,700 a month), most of it placed in a U.S. bank account. At some future date he would be extricated from Cuba by the CIA and given all the money that had accrued (with interest) in his account.

Acosta was puzzled by his recruitment, for he knew no deep military or political secrets. He soon realized that the CIA was most interested in some more prosaic knowledge: Acosta was close friends with several boat captains who piloted the boats used by Cuban leaders, including Castro, during periodic fishing trips or other nautical diversions. Acosta was instructed to collect the details of those trips, especially the precise times Castro moved off and on the island. Acosta dutifully provided reports on Castro's movements, but as concocted by his DGI handlers, they amounted to a mishmash, with all the wrong times and dates.

Acosta was concerned his CIA contacts would see through the charade, but to his surprise, he was complimented on the quality of the information—which, he was told, had led the CIA to conclude that Castro's movements were "erratic."

The CIA's recruitment of so dedicated a *Fidelista* as Acosta was a decided advantage for the DGI, an advantage trumped when the Cubans learned that the CIA did not bother to check out the backgrounds of the assets it was recruiting in Cuba. Consider, for example, the case of another CIA asset named Ignacio Rodriguez-Mena Castrillon.

Even a cursory check of Rodriguez-Mena's background should have set off warning lights, for no more typical *Fidelista* could be imagined. A baseball fanatic whose skills were enough to win him a slot on the Cuban national junior team in his youth, Rodriguez-Mena had inherited that passion from his father. Although the elder Rodriguez-Mena never had the talent to fulfill his dream of playing major-league baseball in the United States, he became a close friend of another baseball addict, a young University of Havana political activist named Fidel Castro. His son regarded Castro as a favored uncle and became his devoted acolyte a few years later when the revolution broke out.* Active in the student revolutionary movement, Rodriguez-Mena worked at Cubana Airlines, taking time off to participate in antiguerrilla operations in the Escambray Mountains against die-hard anti-Castro forces. Later, he was part of an air defense unit during the Bay of Pigs invasion.

By 1966, working on international flight operations for Cubana, Rodriguez-Mena was a fanatically devoted *Fidelista* who often proclaimed his willingness to lay down his life for Castro. One can only imagine his shock, therefore, when he was approached by a female Cuban exile one day during a stopover in Madrid and asked to work for the CIA. He immediately agreed and, when he returned to Havana, told the DGI.

The DGI was as puzzled as Rodriguez-Mena was as to why he had been targeted for recruitment, especially considering his background. But so much the better; the DGI enlisted him for its growing roster of controlled CIA assets and set about con-

---

* A better-than-average pitcher, Castro during his student days tried out for the Washington Senators, but was rejected. Speculatively, what would have happened if the Senators had signed the fiery Cuban left-hander and he had taken up baseball instead of politics?

cocting the kind of intelligence for which the CIA had agreed to pay him $2,000 a month. Basically, the CIA wanted anything Rodriguez-Mena knew about Cubana's overseas operations, especially any intelligence having to do with use of the airline to ship troops or arms from Havana. He provided a steady stream of disinformation, which climaxed in 1975 when he misled the CIA about Cuban arms and troop movements into Angola. It contributed to the CIA's poor intelligence performance in Angola; the CIA consistently missed or underestimated Cuban support for the eventually victorious faction in the Angolan civil war.

Nevertheless, Rodriguez-Mena was considered a star catch among the CIA's Cuban assets. He successfully maintained his facade as a Cuban patriot disillusioned with Castro, a cover that held up even when he committed a colossal operational blunder. Assigned the code name JULIO by the CIA, he was listed in the DGI under the code name ISIDRO. One night, sending a message with a special burst transmitter provided by the CIA, he forgetfully signed the message ISIDRO. Incredibly, the CIA didn't notice the error.

Rodriguez-Mena was also able to defeat the CIA's sole means of checking the bona fides of its assets: the polygraph. The CIA tended to rely too heavily on such technology and in Cuba would pay a high price for that error. The KGB, whose training regimen had long included instructions on how to beat a polygraph test, let the Cubans in on its secret, which actually was quite simple. Since a polygraph cannot detect pathological liars (defined as people who believe their own lies), agents can be trained to believe so fervently in their cover stories that there is no real deception for the machine to detect. The CIA's Cuban assets were subjected to polygraph tests, which almost all passed with flying colors. Those who failed tended to be protected by their CIA case officers, who did not like to lose face (and threaten their own careers) by admitting that one of their assets was a fake. Polygraph failures were most often explained away by assorted excuses; continued retests simply provided the assets with practice on how to deceive the machine.

Thanks in part to its KGB advisers, the DGI had a fairly comprehensive handle on the CIA's working methods, polygraph included. The DGI was aware that in the CIA culture, as with so much else in America, there was an obsession with numbers. In intelligence terms, that meant CIA officers were judged primarily by statistics—how many assets they had managed to recruit in a given period. In this primacy of quantity over quality there was a tendency to define success by numbers of assets recruited, with much less attention paid to whether an asset had anything valuable to contribute.

It was the CIA culture and operating methods that made the DGI's job that much easier. For one thing, the agency did not use Cubans as agent-runners, and so it missed many of the subtleties of Cuban culture and daily life in Castro's Cuba that were essential in evaluating what its assets were reporting. For another, as the Cubans discovered, there was an ethnic arrogance about CIA agents, who tended to regard their assets as Third World boobs to be treated like children. Both the DGI and the KGB concluded that judged overall, the quality of CIA case officers—most of whom did not have even the most rudimentary knowledge about Cuba—was low. To fill the gap, the CIA used assets it recruited among Cuban exiles in the United States for such tasks as making direct approaches to Cubans traveling overseas. But the exiles, long removed from Cuba, were badly out of touch with the realities of Cuban life.

Even espionage technology, a field in which the CIA believed it led the world, turned out to be something less than impressive. The general pattern was for the Cuban assets to be recruited overseas, then equipped with state-of-the-art technology for transmitting messages once they returned to Cuba. The favorite such CIA device was the CD-501 transmitter, a wondrous piece of electronics that featured automatic coding of up to 1,596 letters, a computer chip memory that could store data for up to 30 days, and a 21-second burst transmission that was plucked from the air by an overhead American FLTSATCOM (naval communications) satellite some thirty thousand miles up in space.

But CIA agents in Havana soon found themselves preoccupied with filling and servicing dead drops for repairs on the CD-501. The assets complained that the technology frequently broke down, and the batteries went bad in the hot, humid Cuban climate.

The assets were equally unimpressed with other CIA espionage technology, which also had a tendency to malfunction. These included an ordinary-looking Sony radio that had a secret receiver inside to record transmissions from Langley and store them in a special memory. On predetermined evenings between 7:00 and 8:00, the CIA would transmit orders and requests to its Cuban assets via shortwave signals. The messages were read by a female voice of nightclub timbre who became known as Cynthia to the recipients. Each message opened with a 10-digit number that told the listener how many 4-digit code groups would make up the message. The assets had a onetime pad they used to read the messages, a system that was secure and simple (assets needed only minimal instruction in how to use a onetime pad).

However, the radios consistently malfunctioned, as did other espionage gadgets: miniature microphones concealed inside fountain pens and cigarette lighters, briefcases with cunningly hidden compartments, radios sewn inside teddy bears, and microphone-transmitters hidden inside sanitary napkins. All the technology was turned over to the KGB, which paid the DGI hefty fees for the opportunity to get its hands on the latest American technology.

The DGI was also making a tidy profit on its deception operation because all the assets dutifully turned over their CIA pay to the government. With the money, the DGI purchased Japanese videotape equipment that was planted near various Havana dead drops to record CIA agents as they showed up. One such incident provided unanticipated comic relief. While the watching DGI agents nearly collapsed in hysterics, a CIA agent showed up with his wife and daughter and immediately encountered trouble finding the precise site of the dead drop. As time ticked by, an increasingly exasperated wife and daughter complained about sitting there in the heat. He snapped back at them, and a real domestic brawl developed. "Talk to your mama!" he shouted at his daughter when she asked, for at least the hundredth time, how much longer they would have to wait. Finally the wife screamed at him, "Well, it might not be here, you idiot!"

That particular agent operated under diplomatic cover of the U.S. Interests Section in Havana, which opened in 1977 (a Cuban equivalent was formed at the same time in Washington, D.C.). As the DGI anticipated, at least a fair portion of the more than a hundred American diplomats assigned to the Section were CIA agents. The DGI and their KGB allies made extensive efforts to spot the agents, a task made that much simpler by still another CIA error: the agency segregated its agents in the Havana station on the second floor of the building containing the Interests Section, then cemented the windows in a way that made the floor look like a bunker. It did not take long for Castro's watching agents to figure out that any person who worked on that floor was a CIA agent.

Meanwhile, the DGI's big sting proceeded apace. Judged from Langley, the recruitment operation in Cuba appeared to be a dazzling success, producing reams of intelligence. The roster included Eduardo Leal, an official with the Cuban communications ministry EMTELCUBA, who was to provide the frequencies that Castro and other top officials used to communicate with each other and with various overseas posts. Leal was considered such a valuable asset he was paid a total of $200,000 by the CIA, plus a special $10,000 bonus and a CIA medal personally pinned on his chest by CIA Director William Casey. But the National Security Agency (NSA), which was supposed to use Leal's intelligence to tap into Castro's conversations, was somewhat less impressed; mysteriously, neither Castro nor any of his deputies ever seemed to say anything of consequence over those frequencies. The NSA wondered aloud if Leal might be a double agent, but the CIA pooh-poohed the idea, noting that its star asset had passed several polygraph tests.

Ranked below Leal were the other assets, who collectively provided what the CIA believed was a comprehensive picture of what was going on in Cuban agriculture, industry, government, and economics. The roster included an official of the sugar industry, the head of the Cuban ammonia industry, an official of the Cuban sports federation (who was to induce Cuban athletes to defect), a businessman involved in government-sponsored overseas business ventures, and assorted other officials and experts.

By 1987, some of these assets had been reporting to the CIA for nearly 26 years, a remarkably long string for a deception operation. Such operations usually have a limited life span, for inevitably at some point a slipup exposes them, or the target's suspicions become aroused, or a defector blows the secret. How long the Cuban deception would have continued were it not for Aspillaga's defection can never be known for certain, but it is a fact that until that defection the CIA's Latin America Division did not have even a whisper of a doubt about its several dozen Cuban assets. (In 1976, the division ignored a warning from CIA counterintelligence that the intelligence from those assets was suspiciously voluminous, considering they were operating in a police state with DGI informants posted to every apartment house, residential block, and office.)

The end, when it came, arrived suddenly. Rodriguez-Mena, the baseball fanatic and Cubana official, had just been asked by one of his CIA case officers what he wanted from the Americans for his years of loyal service as a spy. As a joke, the Cuban said he wanted to live in America and become an umpire in the major leagues. Solemnly, the case officer said he would look into it. Two weeks later, he proudly announced that thanks to the CIA's influence with the Major League Umpires Association, Rodriguez-Mena was guaranteed a job calling balls and strikes during the baseball season of his choice. The Cuban tried hard not to laugh.

On that odd note, the DGI's great deception operation ended, followed by its television documentary. A fascinated audience saw, in living color, CIA agents arriving at dead drops, other agents surreptitiously collecting samples of Cuba's tobacco crop, brush contacts with assets on busy Havana streets, and an asset code-named ANGEL sitting on a park bench for meetings, wearing a different colored shirt for each assignation to signify whether he was "clean" (not under surveillance) or "dirty" (under surveillance).

Meanwhile, the Cubans and Americans played out the diplomatic end of the game. The Cubans demanded the recall of a long list of American "diplomats" from the Havana station; in retaliation, the Americans expelled two Cuban envoys in Washington. This latter move was regarded as the minimum retribution under diplomatic protocol, a clear signal that the State Department was not particularly thrilled by having so many Foreign Service slots at the Havana station filled by CIA agents—who in any event failed to achieve anything, other than to blind American perceptions and embarrass their country.

One permanent monument to the DGI's deception operation remains in Havana. It is called the Museum of the Organs of State Security, a catchy Stalinist title for displays of assorted CIA equipment obtained in various DGI operations. It includes several miniature transmitters. Visitors like to pick them up and try to reach the United States—but no one ever answers.

3

All Quiet on the Western Front

Operation BODYGUARD
1943–1944

The Germans miss D-Day

By day, Colonel Alexis von Roenne of the German *Wehrmacht* intelligence tried to project the image of a cool military professional unworried about the disasters that seemed to occur almost daily during that winter of 1943. But at night, unable to sleep, he tried to confront an even greater nightmare.

From a drawer in his desk, von Roenne would pull out a map of Europe, staring at the vast European land mass still occupied by Germany. To von Roenne, that mass, with its thousands of miles of open coastline, looked like the underbelly of some ferocious dragon. True, the dragon had formidable weapons, but a surprise attack would render those weapons useless, fatally penetrating the soft underbelly before the dragon had time to react.

Every instinct honed in a life devoted to the military arts told von Roenne the Allies were preparing to deliver a decisive blow against his country, the long-predicted great invasion that would bring Germany to its knees. But where?

Using a set of crayons, he drew arrows of different colors on the map, marking all the possible invasion points against German-occupied Europe. A green arrow denoted the Dardanelles, blue the Adriatic coast, yellow southern France, black northern Italy, and red northern France around the Pas de Calais area. Each of these possible invasion routes was militarily logical, but as von Roenne understood, there was no way Germany could defend against all of them. The solution was inescapable: the Germans must get advance word of the actual invasion site so that their still-considerable military power could smash it before the enemy got a foothold. That advance word represented the only hope of Germany winning the war—or at least fighting the Allies to a standstill.

Von Roenne felt the pressure of this intelligence requirement most acutely, for his job involved nothing less than telling the *Wehrmacht* precisely where the enemy was massing, where the units were located, and what their capabilities were (indicating probable intentions). He was chief of *Fremde Heeres West* (FHW, Foreign Armies West), the military intelligence unit of the *Oberkommandos der Wehrmacht* (OKW), the German High Command. FHW's brief was to keep track of the Allied armies in the West. Von Roenne was responsible for what the Germans called *Feinbild,* a "picture of the enemy" that enabled the *Wehrmacht* to know, at any given time, precisely where and in what strength enemy units were deployed.

Von Roenne had enjoyed a meteoric military career to this point, largely because of his spectacular performance during the German assault on France in 1940. Von Roenne, then a captain, had developed a complete picture of the French forces, including the crucial intelligence that the French had failed to deploy a sufficient number of antitank guns to cover their front against armored attack. German panzers later raced through those gaps and completely routed the French.

But three years later von Roenne faced a much more daunting task. Just beyond the horizon facing the German defenses on the shores of Western Europe, he knew, the Allied armies were massing, preparing for a great leap into the heart of German-occupied Europe. And this time von Roenne had little insight into those preparations; since there was no front line, he could not send his highly trained infiltrators into the enemy's camp to gather firsthand intelligence. Because of Allied air superiority, German aerial reconnaissance was spotty at best.

Even worse, the German intelligence establishment was providing very little help. Meetings with Admiral Wilhelm Canaris, head of the *Abwehr,* produced only boasts by Canaris that since he had 130 topflight agents in Great Britain (site of the headquarters for the Allied armies), Germany would receive plenty of advance warning of any Allied offensive. "Why, I have one agent who sends me 29 reports a day!" Canaris bragged. Ever the cautious military politician, von Roenne resisted the temptation to point out that two years before, the *Abwehr* had somehow managed to miss the Allied invasion of North Africa—including two invasion fleets that literally steamed past *Abwehr* observation posts north of Gibraltar.

Von Roenne had little faith in Canaris's ability to tell him anything about an impending Allied move. Similarly, he could expect very little from the *Sicherheitsdienst* (SD), the Nazi intelligence service. The SD, he noted, seemed to be preoccupied with a bureaucratic turf war in which it sought to take over all German intelligence. (The SD would achieve the goal only a month later, in the process subsuming the *Abwehr* and succeeding in getting Canaris dismissed.) In any event, the SD had demonstrated manifest incompetence in foreign intelligence operations and did not have even the slightest clue what the Allies were doing or planning.

The net effect was that von Roenne's situation maps betrayed great gaps of ignorance. Only a few units around the European periphery had been positively identified; ominously, many other units were disappearing from the Allied order of battle. Von Roenne suspected that they had been withdrawn to England in preparation for their participation in the upcoming grand assault. Von Roenne had no insight into when this growing force would go on the attack.

Above all, von Roenne had to contend with the mind of Adolf Hitler, the one factor that dominated all German military planning. All too often, von Roenne had learned the hard way that no matter what military logic dictated, it was the intuition of Hitler that would most often decide things. Interestingly, although von Roenne had privately scoffed, Hitler's intuition initially had been perilously close to the truth. In 1941, Hitler had written a remarkable directive entitled *die Grosslandung der Alliierten* (The Decisive Landing of the Allies), in which he forecast that the Allies would conduct a large-scale amphibious assault on the "protruding parts of Normandy and Brittany." He went on to outline precisely how the assault would take place, which turned out to be an almost perfect prediction of the D-Day assault some three years later.

But by 1943 Hitler had changed his mind; his intuition now told him that the Allied invasion would come elsewhere, probably at another site on the French coast or in the Balkans. If the assault came in France, Hitler said, it would probably strike in northern France near Pas de Calais. Von Roenne had never thought much of Hitler's theory of a Normandy landing, but he was more impressed with the idea of a landing near Pas de Calais. To a trained military mind like von Roenne's, such a target made perfect sense: it was only 30 miles from Allied staging areas in England; it provided the most direct invasion route into the German industrial heartland in the Ruhr; it had an excellent road and rail network; and, best of all, it offered an essential port at Le Havre for the armada of supply ships necessary to sustain an offensive across France and into Germany.

As the spring of 1944 began, von Roenne became ever more convinced that Pas de Calais would be the invasion site. He had heard rumors of invasion plans for Norway, the Balkans, and northern Italy, but all military logic dictated that Pas de Calais was it. Aside from a gut feeling, he had very little intelligence to back up that assumption. One rare clue had surfaced in Ankara, Turkey, where the valet to the British ambassador there had gotten a look inside his employer's locked dispatch box. He copied the papers and sold them to the Germans, who learned for the first time that the Allied invasion plan was code-named OVER-LORD. A specific site for the invasion was not named, but from other clues in the diplomatic dispatches it was clear OVERLORD referred to an invasion somewhere along the French coast. Meanwhile, the *Abwehr* station in Stockholm had managed to recruit several Swedish military attachés who served in Great Britain; they reported that the Allies were planning a massive amphibious assault on the Normandy coast of France sometime between May 15 and June 15, 1944.

Abwehr headquarters rejected this intelligence as probable disinformation by British intelligence, but von Roenne began to wonder: there were accumulating, persistent indications that OVERLORD was intended to invade somewhere along the coast of France. The problem was to find out which units and precisely where they planned to land.

Hitler was not convinced that OVERLORD was targeted against France and had ordered general preparations to repel assaults at a number of potential invasion sites around the periphery of German-occupied territory. For Western Europe, he decreed the building of a massive system of fortifications along the entire coast that would delay an invasion at the water's edge until German reserves could move up and crush it. Called *Festung Europa* (Fortress Europe), it stretched along the entire western coast of Europe from Norway to Spain—a wall of 15,000 reinforced concrete bunkers, artillery positions, machine-gun nests, trenches, millions of mines, and 300,000 soldiers to garrison it.

However convinced Hitler was that this wall would balk any invasion launched against the coast of Western Europe, von Roenne was not so sure. In 1940 he had seen how easy it was for his own army to breach the Maginot Line, and as a professional military man, he understood that there was no such thing as a fortification impervious to attack by a determined enemy.

In the late spring of 1944, von Roenne suddenly got an intelligence break. German communications intercept stations had managed to pick up some incautious radio messages from several U.S. units in southern England. The intercepts provided a peek into what clearly was a huge buildup almost directly opposite the Pas de Calais area of northern France. To von Roenne, this was final proof: OVERLORD was aimed at Pas de Calais. On his situation map, he began to sketch in the American infantry and armored divisions the intercepts had identified and drew a large red arrow directly across the English Channel to France.

And with that act, von Roenne set in motion an astonishing deception that was to cost his country the war.

Winston Churchill was the man who did the most to ensure that von Roenne's attention became fixated on Pas de Calais. "In war," he liked to say, "truth must always be accompanied by a bodyguard of lies," and it was BODYGUARD he selected as the code name for a large-scale deception operation to mislead the Germans about the invasion of France.

He had announced BODYGUARD to Josef Stalin in 1943 at the Tehran Conference, when the Soviets were promised the invasion of France—the final offensive to defeat Nazi Germany. When Stalin wondered aloud how the Allies proposed to prevent the Germans from learning of so conspicuous an enterprise as a mass amphibious invasion, Churchill replied that there would be a deception plan that would completely fool the Germans. "It will be," he vowed, "the greatest hoax in history."

Churchill turned out to be right, but in 1943 it did not seem that any deception plan could solve the very real military obstacles the Allies faced. Indeed, they seemed insurmountable.

Despite catastrophic losses in men and matériel, the German war machine in 1944 was still a powerful instrument in the hands of its talented tactical leaders. Among the more talented was Field Marshal Gerd von Rundstedt, the commander of all German forces in the West, and his deputy, the famed "Desert Fox," Field Marshal Erwin Rommel, who had the specific responsibility for defeating any Allied invasion. Von Rundstedt had at his disposal five field armies in France, Belgium, and the Netherlands, plus several other divisions in Norway and Denmark. All told, he had 1,500,000 troops at his command, along with several thousand tanks. Some 31 of his divisions were regarded as second rate, but 17 were first class, including 35,000 crack *Waffen-SS* troops.

Any first-year military school student could see the problem clearly. With such power at his disposal, von Rundstedt could checkmate any Allied move, since the Allies could land only on a narrow front: under the OVERLORD plan, some 150,000 troops would be landed with 10,000 armored vehicles on the Normandy beaches, which stretched for several miles in width. Once von Rundstedt learned of the landing site, he could simply move his reserves and wipe out the beachhead, even in the face of Allied air superiority. Under prevailing military theory, an amphibious attacking force needed anywhere from a 3-to-1 to a 6-to-1 advantage in manpower to be guaranteed any kind of success. The plain truth was that the Allies were badly outnumbered, most dangerously so on the landing beaches, where the Germans could concentrate overwhelming manpower.

The solution, as Churchill conceived it, was to devise a plan under which the German forces would remain strung out all along the European coast so they could never concentrate against an outnumbered Allied force on the beaches. In military terms, the Allies would have to devise a deception plan under which there would be two attacks—one real, one fake. The real attack must appear to be a diversion, and the diversion must be made to appear real.

This tricky double bluff became the province of an entity called the Joint Intelligence Committee, a coalition of British and American intelligence. It operated with two significant advantages. One was ULTRA, the highly secret British codebreaking operation that was reading all the high-level German military messages. That not only allowed the Allies to monitor German military moves, but also let them peek into how any deception plan might play with the German command.

The second was an even more closely guarded secret, the so-called Double Cross System, under which every German spy sent to Britain had been detected (thanks to ULTRA), and a number of them turned to feed disinformation to Germany.

The Allies mobilized both these priceless attributes to build the core of the deception plan: the Germans would be convinced that Allied strength was so great, they had sufficient force to carry out both a large-scale feint and the actual invasion. Simply, the plan was to persuade the Germans that the landing at Normandy was the feint, while the bulk of the Allied forces were being held in reserve for the real thrust, directly at Pas de Calais.

Within weeks, German intelligence, which had been starved of raw data for months, was suddenly awash in information. All of it, deliberately leaked, concerned the vast Allied military buildup in southern England. For the first time, the Germans began to hear of something called FUSAG (First U.S. Army Group), a mighty force that was to serve as the main thrust in the upcoming invasion. Even the *National Geographic* magazine was enlisted; it published a color layout of U.S. Army divisional patches that included 24 for divisions that did not exist. The spread, which ultimately made its way to von Roenne's headquarters, compelled him to list those divisions on his situation maps. As the deception planners hoped, von Roenne concentrated the mythical divisions in the area of southern England directly opposite Pas de Calais. And as he inked those divisions on his maps, the very real threat they represented began to harden in the minds of the Germans. Von Rundstedt ordered an entire army deployed in the Pas de Calais area with armor, under orders to move toward the nearby beaches and crush any landing attempt.

The controlled double agents also played their role, transmitting dozens of tantalizing reports about seeing a huge army forming in the area where von Roenne presumed they were concentrating. To checkmate the possibility that the Germans might conclude the agent reports were cooked as part of a deception plan, the British arranged for an unimpeachable source to see with his own eyes the kind of buildup other sources were reporting.

The chosen instrument was General Hans Cramer, the last commander of the *Afrika Korps,* who had been captured in Tunisia in 1943. He was ailing, and the British agreed to repatriate him to Germany in exchange for a British prisoner. He was taken from a POW camp in Scotland and driven south to an embarkation port. To Cramer's satisfaction, the route followed the coast, allowing him a plain view of the Allied military buildup. He could hardly contain his excitement; as a trained military expert, Cramer was able to count the tanks, artillery pieces, trucks, and tents (giving him a rough approximation of how many men were bivouacked there). At one point, he casually asked where they were, and his escort told him: East Sussex and Kent. Actually, they were in Dorset, some two hundred miles farther down the coast, a deception the British could get away with because they had carefully removed all street and village signs.

Once back in Germany, Cramer recounted what he had seen and where he had seen it. Although in fact he had been given a peek at the buildup for the Normandy invasion, Cramer assumed he was in East Sussex—the ideal location for a military force that was about to invade Pas de Calais.

Von Roenne's situation maps, filling up by the day with new Allied units, looked better with the receipt of the latest intelligence report from Britain. It all seemed to be working according to militarily correct assumptions: a major military force gathering opposite Pas de Calais, and a smaller one forming opposite Normandy. Clearly, then, the force gathering opposite Normandy was to serve as the feint; it would land on the Normandy beaches and draw the German reserves and armor gathered around Pas de Calais. Once the Germans moved, the main force would then assault Pas de Calais, with catastrophic results for von Rundstedt's defenses.

And that is precisely the way the Allied deception planners wanted the Germans to think. Aware from their ULTRA operation that the Germans had begun to accept the deception, the Allies sought to harden it further with a few clever twists. One was the idea of conspicuously positioning General George Patton, considered the Allies' best tactical commander by the Germans, in the area of southern England opposite Pas de Calais. Ubiquitous at ceremonies, morale-building visits, and other such events, Patton was as visible as a fireworks display. The Germans took the bait: obviously, they reasoned, a military operation as risky as a mass amphibious landing in the teeth of fortifications would be led by the enemy's best tactical leader. Ergo, Patton's presence in southeast England could only mean he was the commander of the main force attack. And given its location, his FUSAG clearly intended to attack Pas de Calais.

If that weren't enough, the deception operation created an entire fake army, complete with communications signals that were deliberately broadcast with poor security, making the job of the German intercept stations that much easier. The nonexistent army also had thousands of tanks, acres of tents, and a vast air armada that any air reconnaissance flight could spot without much trouble. The Germans did, although they failed to wonder why their reconnaissance planes were suddenly able to make flights over southern England despite total Allied air superiority, and why antiaircraft guns opened up on them only at the moment their reconnaissance planes tried to fly lower than 30,000 feet. Any lower, and they would have realized that all those tanks, planes, and guns were in fact cleverly prepared rubber dummies.

By May, the elaborate deception operation had borne fruit in the German High Command. According to von Roenne's situation maps, the Allies had somewhere between 85 and 90 divisions poised in southern England, along with an additional seven airborne divisions. (Actually, the real total was 35 divisions, plus three airborne divisions.)

Von Roenne's estimates were critical, because when the D-Day invasion began at dawn on June 6, 1944, the Germans immediately assumed—based on the battlefield estimate of some 100,000-plus Allied troops involved—that Normandy was a diversion, since only a fraction of Allied strength was involved. Accordingly, von Roenne at noon that day sent an intelligence bulletin to Hitler, noting that only about twelve Allied divisions had been committed; clearly, he reported, the main force was still to be committed—almost certainly at Pas de Calais. (That night, 127,000 Allied troops were ashore at Normandy.)

Von Roenne's conclusion was supported by agent reports flowing from Britain, one of which claimed to have seen firsthand the vast Allied army still poised on the southern coast. Consequently, while the Allies expanded the Normandy beachhead, an entire German army of nearly 300,000 men sat on its hands near Pas de Calais, waiting for an assault that never came. It was not until June 15, when the Allies had put 30 divisions ashore at Normandy, that von Roenne and the German High Command realized how badly they had been hoodwinked. Clearly, there was no "Patton FUSAG," for Patton himself suddenly appeared at Nor-

Men and supplies pour ashore on the Normandy beachhead in June 1944, unmolested by a German army of 300,000 men some two hundred miles away. Fooled by an Allied deception plan, the Germans believed the landing was only a feint. (*United States Naval Institute*)

mandy to take command of the very real Third Army that was already cutting the *Wehrmacht* to pieces.

By the time the German forces around Pas de Calais got their orders to contain the Normandy beachhead, it was too late. They stumbled into a huge envelopment in which some 200,000 of them were slaughtered or captured; the rest fled eastward, pursued by Allied armies that less than a year later witnessed the German surrender.

The success of the Normandy deception owed much to careful planning and the immense advantage the Allies enjoyed from their ULTRA codebreaking and double agent operations. Yet the one essential ingredient that ensured its success was common to all other similar deceptions: the willingness of the victim to be deceived. In the case of the Germans, they were victimized by their devotion to military logic, the prism through which they filtered what little intelligence they had. It amounted to a classic case of a preconception firmly held, with no attempt to consider any alternatives.

It was a mind-set perhaps best summarized by Berlin Radio, which at the height of the Normandy invasion admitted, in a rare moment of candor, that the *Wehrmacht* had been "caught napping." But the radio commentator went on to say there was nothing to worry about, since the army was poised and ready to defeat the "main thrust," soon to come in the Pas de Calais area. At the end of the war news, listeners were told to expect a brief interlude of pleasant music. The chosen selection was the song "And So Another Beautiful Day Draws to a Close."

4

The Descent of A3725

The Double Cross System
1940–1945

A deception masterpiece

Just before he was to jump, Wulf Schmidt was seized by an overwhelming sense of dread, a feeling that everything was about to go wrong, and that it would, inevitably, result in his own death.

A glance out the open door of the Heinkel bomber circling above the English countryside that night of September 17, 1940, had set off the first uneasiness. Although he was supposed to parachute on a dark night, he noticed there was a full moon out, lighting up the land below with what he feared was the illumination of a spotlight. This was not the ideal condition for A3725—as Schmidt was known on the roster of the German *Abwehr*—to infiltrate an enemy country in wartime.

Still feeling dread, Schmidt braced himself in the plane's doorway as the pilot warned it was time to jump. When the signal came to drop out the door, a sudden gust of wind rocked the plane, wrenching one of Schmidt's hands against the door frame, tearing off his wristwatch. As he silently descended toward English soil, Schmidt felt a searing pain in his hand.

Schmidt landed in a field near the village of Willingham, in Cambridgeshire. With difficulty, he managed to bury his parachute and the *Luftwaffe* flight coveralls that hid the ordinary suit in which he was dressed. Then he opened the suitcase that was tied to his body during the descent. Inside was a small radio, some clothes, a few thousand dollars' worth of English pound notes, and a fake passport made out to Harry Williamson, a Dane.

His hand was really beginning to bother him as he set off by foot toward the village. After a while he reached it and immediately noticed a public water pump. He settled down beside it and began soaking his throbbing hand. Concerned about the swelling, he kept his hand in the cool water. Before long, the hand felt better and Schmidt fell asleep, curling up behind the water pump.

It was dawn when he awoke. Some villagers, already up and about, were staring at him suspiciously. Trying to look like an inconspicuous traveler, Schmidt picked up his suitcase and strolled down the main street. Spotting a jewelery store, he went inside to buy a new watch. The shopkeeper squinted at him when he heard Schmidt's German-sounding accent, and Schmidt noticed two other men outside the shop staring at him.

It was time to move on, Schmidt decided, but as he left the shop, two Home Guard soldiers stopped him. "You better come with us," one said, as the other took the suitcase from Schmidt's hand. Schmidt had the impression they were waiting for him.

Schmidt's sense of dread was now complete. There was no doubt in his mind that once the authorities saw that shortwave radio, his goose was cooked. Assuredly, the following day at dawn he would be tied to a stake someplace and shot. His espionage mission had failed even before it began. The *Abwehr* would hear nothing from him and gradually would draw the logical conclusion that he had been caught and executed. A3725 would be no more, and Germany would have to find another spy, like Schmidt, who would parachute into England and collect the information Germany so vitally needed before it could unleash an invasion of the British Isles: what the strength of the defending British forces was, their armament, and where they were deployed.

But that is not what happened. In fact, A3725 would live, although with a new code name: TATE. And under that code name he would become one of the greatest spies of all time. For nearly five years he would provide Germany with a breathtaking range of intelligence on everything from the strength and disposition of British forces to plans for the Allied invasion of France. His feats were so extraordinary, a grateful Germany would award him the Iron Cross, much money, and promises of a comfortable life on a generous pension once the war ended. No spy ever served Germany so long and so well.

Or so the Germans thought.

Following his capture, a glum Wulf Schmidt found himself in an odd-looking prison compound at Ham Common, in Richmond. On entering, he noticed a concerted effort to keep the prison secret: it was hidden away from the main road among trees, and a nondescript dirt road led to the entrance. The only outside evidence of its existence was a small sign that read, mysteriously, "Camp 020" and the fact that several armed soldiers were patrolling the perimeter. Inside, civilians seemed to run the place. Odd, Schmidt thought; the soldiers outside led him to believe this was a military prison. He was put into a cell.

The next morning he was taken to a room where three civilians sat behind a table. "Good morning, A3725," one of them said affably enough. "Welcome to England."

Schmidt felt his stomach sink to his shoes; obviously, his captors somehow knew everything. He listened, dumbstruck, as they outlined his mission: he was to infiltrate England, get in touch with two other *Abwehr* agents who had been parachuted into the country some time before, and together they were to organize an intelligence-collection operation to discover the numbers and dispositions of British forces deployed to fight the anticipated German invasion.

At this point Schmidt could almost feel the blindfold being tied around his head and the firing squad chambering rounds. But the conversation then took a strange turn. Almost as if he were chatting with friends in a pub, Schmidt was encouraged to tell the men sitting at the table how he became involved with the *Abwehr.*

There wasn't much to tell, actually, Schmidt replied. Born into a prominent Danish-German family in Schleswig-Holstein near the Danish border, he had been a restless youth, constantly seeking adventure. At one point he was manager of a banana plantation in the Cameroons. Some of his friends and relatives had joined the Nazi party, and lured by their tales of the excitement they found in the brownshirted vanguard of the "New Germany," he signed up.

When the war broke out, he was approached by some men who recruited him for an even more interesting existence: espi-

Former MI6 chief Stewart Menzies in 1967, a year before his death. Thanks to the ULTRA cryptanalytical triumph, Menzies' agents, in conjunction with MI5, were able to penetrate the German *Abwehr* and double all the enemy agents sent to Great Britain during World War II. (*Author's Collection*)

onage. They were *Abwehr* officers, apparently interested in this short, thin adventurer who had picked up a fair command of English in his travels. Following a short training course, he was told he would parachute into England and help prepare the way for the German invasion, certain to come at any moment. "The rest you know," said Schmidt to the men of Ham Common.

Indeed they did, and much more besides, but they were not about to tell Schmidt that. What they did tell Schmidt was that they were prepared to offer him an option: work with them or be shot as a spy. Schmidt didn't hesitate a second; intrigued by the notion of opening still another interesting chapter in his restless life, he accepted. The decision did not surprise the three listeners, for they were in the business of evaluating men. And their evaluation of Schmidt told them that despite his Nazi background and enlistment in German espionage, he was at root a stateless adventurer in love with any daring enterprise, regardless of political affiliation, for the pure sake of it. His political convictions, if any, were veneer-thin. To be sure, his decision to switch allegiances to the British was influenced in part by the thought he would not be shot, but he clearly was excited to be back in the world of intrigue, albeit for a different employer.

Schmidt didn't know it at the time, but he had just finished the first stage in what became one of history's more successful counterintelligence operations. Known as Double Cross, its record has seldom been surpassed in the annals of counterespionage: of the 138 spies that Germany sent into the British Isles during World War II and the nearly two dozen other people recruited by the Germans to spy against the British, every single one was detected by the British Security Service (MI5). Some forty of these people were successfully converted into double agents who fed the Germans a steady stream of disinformation until the end of the war. The operation was so skillfully run, the Germans never suspected that all the intelligence they received from the British Isles was actually concocted by their enemies.

For German intelligence, the consequences were disastrous. During the entire war they were misled, bamboozled, and misdirected. Based on the cooked intelligence they received, the Germans got everything consistently wrong. Doubtless, Double Cross played a vital role in saving Britain in World War II. And none of this would have happened were it not for some questions asked by a few bright academics.

At the outbreak of war, British intelligence was forced to increase its ranks, an expansion that brought it a sudden influx of academics and professional people. The academics, particularly, had the habit of questioning prevailing wisdom, and while that sort of skepticism was unwelcome among the ranks of intelligence old-timers, it had the advantage of inspiring a fresh look at procedures and practices that had grown hoary with age.

Among the bright, young academics who joined MI5 was a twenty-five-year-old Oxford academic named Hugh Trevor-Roper, assigned to an obscure branch known as MI 8-C, which monitored German intelligence agencies' wireless traffic. For years, Trevor-Roper discovered, the agency had routinely recorded the coded transmissions and shipped them off to the codebreaking establishment of the Government Communications Headquarters (GCHQ) on the assumption they were transmissions from the German code-making machine known as Enigma. But Trevor-Roper (in later years a famed historian) advocated a closer look; after all, he argued, German spies infiltrating Great Britain wouldn't be carrying Enigma machines around, so the odds were good that they were using a different cipher system—probably a relatively easy one that spies could master quickly. Trevor-Roper devoted virtually all his waking hours to piles of intercepted German communications and soon realized the Germans were using an ordinary, so-called book code. Under that system, spies in the field had a book—usually a popular novel whose possession would not arouse suspicion—that they used to encode messages according to a predetermined system that specified which page and line of the book contained the words in the message. (A code group 1410, for example, would tell the recipient, who had the same book, that the word in the message was on page 14, line 10; further groups would specify the exact word.)

In a remarkable feat, Trevor-Roper single-handedly broke the German code. Thanks to his fluency in German and expertise in German linguistics, by Christmas of 1939 he deduced that the Germans were using the popular novel *Our Hearts Were Young and Gay* as the basis for encoding their espionage messages. Two months later, he solved the system completely.

MI5 officials wanted to use the break to pinpoint German spies, then arrest and execute them, but Trevor-Roper complained such a traditional approach was shortsighted. Suppose, he argued, that the British were able to use their knowledge of the German code to create their own German spy ring. In other words, they could take over the German espionage communications and turn them into channels for disinformation.

While Trevor-Roper was making his argument, another young MI5 officer, Thomas A. Robertson, was attending a lecture by French *Deuxieme Bureau* officials. The Frenchmen questioned the standard British counterespionage practice of immediately executing German spies they had caught (seven German spies had been shot since the beginning of the war), arguing that there was real potential in "turning" such spies into assets for the British.

Robertson, assigned to counterespionage operations against the Germans, was wondering the same thing. But, as he was to discover, the idea was firmly rejected by MI5's old guard. In their view, such operations rarely worked, for the other side inevitably caught on to the game. The problem was the very reason why the spy had been sent to Great Britain in the first place: if he sent faked intelligence, or material of very low quality, that was a virtual advertisement he had been turned by the other side. At that point, the turned agent's usefulness was at an end. On the other hand, the only way to maintain the spy's bona fides was to send genuine intelligence—thus injuring the very secrets the counterespionage agency was trying to protect. Summarily, counterespionage could not have it both ways. Besides, military agencies were traditionally loathe to reveal any secrets, even for the purposes of counterespionage.

True, Robertson thought, but suppose there was some sort of organization that would have the authority to turn enemy agents, then provide them with a stream of carefully prepared intelligence that contained enough genuine secrets to mislead the other side. By happy coincidence, two other young, bright MI5 recruits—Dick White and J. C. Masterman—had also arrived at the same idea. White (whose later career would include directorships of both MI6 and MI5) was able to talk MI5's senior leadership into a daring experiment: the formation of a committee of key intelligence and military officials that would "cook" the nation's secrets into seamless intelligence that could be fed into a pipeline of turned agents and captured radios to mislead the Germans.

The committee, when it was formed, was so highly secret it could not be given a conventional bureaucratic title. It was called the XX Committee, known among its participants, in a slight pun, as "double cross." The entire system soon became known by that name, the one by which it passed into espionage legend.

Double Cross went into operation just in time, for the Germans had unleashed a major intelligence offensive. Actually, the offensive was a mark of desperation; in 1937, *Abwehr* chief Admiral Wilhelm Canaris had been prohibited by Hitler from undertaking major spying operations in Great Britain. In Hitler's view, Nazi Germany soon would reach some sort of major accommodation with the British, and he did not want such an arrangement jeopardized by the scandal over a spying operation that might go bad and anger the British.

But by early 1940, already planning Operation SEA LION, the German invasion of Britain, Hitler changed his mind. Canaris was ordered to conduct a "maximum effort" to prepare the way for the invading forces. This order put Canaris in something of a dilemma, for without assets in Britain he was required to come up with an army of spies—and fast. The *Abwehr* went trolling all over Europe, recruiting a variegated collection of volunteers and giving them a crash course in espionage tradecraft for what the

Germans called Operation LENA, a full-court assault on Britain's secrets.

But Canaris did not know that the British had a fifth ace in the game, their knowledge of the *Abwehr* codes that enabled them to read the messages from *Abwehr* headquarters. Thus, MI5 had advance word of *Abwehr* orders dispatching agents to the British Isles, most often in the guise of refugees from German-occupied countries. The British also learned beforehand of agents who were being infiltrated via parachute or U-boat, or other assets who had agreed to work for German intelligence.

They were swept up like so much dust as they arrived and taken to Camp 020, where MI5 carefully evaluated them for use in the Double Cross operation. Those who refused were executed; others were jailed. Those deemed usable were turned over to Robertson of MI5, the system's chief agent-handler. Among them was Wulf Schmidt.

Code-named TATE (because, Robertson said, he looked like the popular English music hall star Harry Tate), Schmidt was moved into Robertson's house, where the MI5 agent's wife, Joan, was already serving as den mother to several other Double Cross assets. As Schmidt perceived, the operation was grooming him as its star asset. An MI5 radio expert worked with Schmidt to learn how to duplicate his "fist" (distinctive touch on the Morse key of his transmitter), while Robertson was busy formulating the kind of "intelligence" A3725 would transmit to Germany.

The Double Cross Committee baited the trap carefully. Schmidt's transmitter began sending extensive intelligence on British military dispositions, actually a skillful mix of the true (that which might be independently checked by the Germans using other means) and the contrived (mainly subtle exaggerations in British strength). As it would in all future Double Cross operations, ULTRA now played a crucial role, allowing British intelligence to monitor how this cooked intelligence was percolating throughout the German military establishment.

It percolated very well, and with Schmidt's performance established in Berlin, Double Cross moved to the next phase. That involved promoting TATE as a superspy, the indefatigable man who had an amazing ability to develop sources at every level of British industry and the military. With these mythical subagents, TATE gradually became the *Abwehr*'s guru on a wide range of intelligence matters. He was bombarded with demands from

Abwehr headquarters for answers to various questions the Germans needed to know about. The answers were formulated by the Double Cross Committee, with precise attention to making at least part of them absolutely true and plausible. For example, when TATE was asked one day to find out when a British warship would arrive in Gibraltar, the committee first checked via ULTRA whether there were any U-boats in the area where the warship was sailing. Told there were none, the committee then felt it safely could send accurate information about the ship to Germany— aware that *Abwehr* spotters near Gibraltar would know when the ship arrived. When that ship showed up at Gibraltar at the time TATE said it would, TATE's stock with the *Abwehr* soared.

It was Robertson's idea to enhance TATE's credibility further by creating the mythological superspy who was running all over Great Britain recruiting sources and collecting secrets by the bushelful. As an extra twist, he made sure that TATE had a human dimension: a short temper that did not suffer fools gladly. TATE was willing to tell off his bosses when they pushed too hard. When some halfwit in *Abwehr* headquarters one day asked him to find out how much clothing could be bought on a British ration card, TATE transmitted a blunt reply: YOU CAN KISS MY ASS.

Meanwhile, convinced they had a flourishing spy operation in Great Britain, the Germans continued to drop in agents. Conveniently enough, news of many of these impending arrivals was first transmitted to TATE, who was to take them under his wing and show them the ropes. At the same time, MI5 was busy doubling a number of important *Abwehr* assets who had been recruited elsewhere in Europe and assigned the job of penetrating the British government at a high level. Among the more prominent were BRUTUS (Roman Garby-Czerniawski, a former Polish army captain for whom Double Cross invented a post as liaison to the headquarters of General Omar Bradley); TREASURE (Lily Sergeyev, a French adventuress who supposedly had a high-ranking job at the British Ministry of Information); GARBO (Juan Pujol, a Spanish businessman who allegedly ran a large network of subsources that infiltrated British industry); and the most famous, TRICYCLE (Dusko Popov, a Yugoslavian banker who the *Abwehr* believed had a network of sources at the upper level of the British government).

All the Double Cross sources were being meticulously groomed for what MI5 believed would be the climactic battle in this war of wits, the great deception operation for the invasion of

France. The first shot was fired on January 14, 1944, when TATE transmitted an urgent message to the *Abwehr* announcing his sources had learned of the secret arrival of General Dwight Eisenhower in Britain to take command of the Allied Expeditionary Force. Eisenhower's arrival was announced officially two days later, but the fact that TATE had learned of it 48 hours earlier helped boost his reputation in the *Abwehr.*

That was but a prelude to the elaborate deception that now unfolded, the orchestration of cunningly faked intelligence to convince the Germans that a huge (actually nonexistent) Allied army was forming opposite Pas de Calais. To that end, GARBO provided snippets of tantalizing hints of that army, TRICYCLE provided a top secret order of battle he obtained from a military aide to Winston Churchill, and TREASURE provided copies of local newspaper stories complaining about a blizzard of condoms littering the countryside where American troops were bivouacked (the stories had been created by Double Cross).

TATE himself played a key role in this deception, providing a steady run of reports about nonexistent British and American army divisions on the move. Those reports were carefully coordinated with fake radio traffic from the units; aware that German communications intercept stations would pick up the signals, the Double Cross operation ensured they provided "proof" of what TATE was reporting.

As for the D-Day invasion itself, TATE transmitted news of the invasion armada, but only after it had arrived off the shores of Normandy. Then he complained how his "inefficient" *Abwehr* radio prevented him from sending this vital intelligence earlier.

German credulousness seemed to know no end; D-Day should have at least aroused suspicions that there was something not quite right about all those busy *Abwehr* assets in Great Britain, but Berlin continued to repose total faith in them. That faith had everything to do with human nature. The officers of German intelligence who had recruited, trained, and nurtured these assets were not prepared to admit they had been hoodwinked. With so much human capital invested in their assets, the Germans could not confess they had been fools. In a state like Nazi Germany, that would have been the kind of admission that could have very serious consequences.

And so, to the surprise of the British, Double Cross rolled on. Some months after D-Day, TATE was asked by the Germans to help adjust the aim of the V-1 and V-2 missiles that had begun to rain down on London. TATE obliged, but Double Cross made certain the corrections led the missiles to areas away from population centers. For good measure, TATE informed Berlin that the missiles were totally ineffective.

A grateful Germany informed TATE that in view of such stellar performances he was being awarded the Iron Cross, along with a hefty cash bonus; both were to be left in custody of his brother to be retrieved after the war was over.

But TATE never bothered to collect. After the war, he was secretly awarded British citizenship, and he settled down to a relatively humdrum life as a newspaper photographer under a wholly new identity. It was not very adventurous, but apparently life in the world of espionage had slaked his thirst for adventure. His friends and neighbors did not learn of his espionage background until 1990, when he agreed to cooperate with a British television documentary on the Double Cross operation. Afterward, he slipped back into obscurity.

As for his Iron Cross decoration, MI5 retrieved it from Germany after the war. It remains to this day somewhere in MI5 headquarters, a curious souvenir of a remarkable counterespionage operation.

5

Long Island Calling Hamburg

Operation TRAMP
1939–1941

The destruction of Admiral Canaris

From the moment the forty-year-old man walked down the gangplank, three sets of eyes never let him out of their sight. They watched as the stocky American in a brown suit was processed through Hamburg customs. When he was finished, three men suddenly materialized beside him.

"*Herr* Sebold?" asked one of the men, brandishing a small badge connected to a key chain. "Gestapo."

William Sebold paled. There were few people in the world that February of 1939 unaware of the odious reputation of the *Geheime Staatspolizei* (Secret State Police), Nazi Germany's infamous internal security agency whose acronym was the very symbol of unchecked police terror. Although Sebold was a naturalized American citizen who had emigrated to the United States 17 years before, coming face to face with these sinister-looking Gestapo men was a heartpounding experience. He could not imagine why the Gestapo was bothering with him; he had traveled to Hamburg for the purely innocent purpose of visiting his mother.

"What do you want of me?" Sebold asked, trying not to sound frightened.

"Just a conversation," replied one of the Gestapo agents as the two other agents grabbed Sebold firmly by the upper arms

48

and led him to a small office. There, a man in a business suit glared at him for a moment, then commanded, "Passport."

Sebold handed over his passport. There was no sound in the room as the man appeared to examine it carefully. Then he reached into a file on the desk and withdrew a sheet of paper. Sebold recognized it as the personal history form he had filled out in New York when he applied for a visa to visit Germany by ship.

"You work as a mechanic at the Consolidated Aircraft Company in San Diego?" the man asked, somewhat rhetorically. When Sebold nodded yes, the man said, "You can be of great service to the Fatherland."

So that was it. Sebold hardly listened as the man launched into a lengthy spiel about the necessity of all Germans helping the "New Germany."

"I have no interest in participating in such activities," Sebold said, making it clear he had no intention of becoming a spy for Germany.

The man gave him a tight little smile and pulled out another sheet of paper from the file. "Your attitude is unfortunate, Mr. Sebold," he said, then paused for effect. "Or should I say, Mr. *Dembowski?*"

Like an animal hearing the trap clang shut, Sebold instantly understood he was ensnared. The Gestapo obviously had done its homework, discovering that Sebold/Dembowski had fought in World War I and then drifted into petty crime in the chaos of postwar Germany. He had served a brief jail sentence for smuggling. Upon release, he got false papers under the name Sebold and emigrated to the United States, there to settle down into an ordinary middle-class life as an airplane mechanic. Life was good; as a highly skilled technician, Sebold commanded good wages, some of which he dutifully sent to his widowed mother in Germany. Meanwhile, he became a naturalized U.S. citizen.

"Perhaps you have forgotten U.S. immigration law," the Gestapo man was saying now. "You did not mention your criminal record when applying for American citizenship. And in any case, you gave them a false name. Should American authorities learn of this, *Herr* Sebold, they will revoke your citizenship. You will be deported to Germany, and here the Gestapo will take charge of your case. Of course, if you should decide to cooperate with us. . . ."

It was not necessary to finish the sentence. Sebold agreed to become a spy for Germany.

Judged strictly in intelligence terms, what happened to Sebold represents one of the classic techniques in espionage recruitment, the blackmail approach. Usually, such an approach is used only selectively, for human nature remains immutable: people do not like being blackmailed into doing something against their moral judgment—especially betraying their country. Such recruits tend to be angry and resentful, and a high percentage of them have the habit of running to counterintelligence agencies at the first opportunity. Those agencies can be remarkably understanding and sympathetic to human beings who have become traitors under threat of blackmail and now seek salvation.

German intelligence was about to learn that lesson anew, but in the case of William Sebold it would prove an especially bitter one. Eventually, the forced recruitment of a middle-aged aircraft mechanic with a past to conceal would lead to one of Germany's more significant intelligence failures. The cost to Germany was almost incalculable, for its intelligence operations in the United States would be destroyed at the very moment the Germans needed them the most.

There were any number of mistakes the Germans made in the course of that failure, but perhaps chief among them was misreading William Sebold.

Following his agreement to become a spy, Sebold, to his surprise, found himself taken not to Gestapo headquarters but to a nondescript three-story building at 72–76 Tirpitz Ufer in Berlin. This was the headquarters of the *Abwehr,* popularly known among the people who worked there as *Fuchsbau* (fox's lair).

However cunning the *Abwehr* people might have regarded themselves, they were in something of a panic at the time Sebold entered the building. With war believed imminent (it would break out that September), Hitler had ordered the *Abwehr* to mount a "maximum effort" against the United States in the belief that although the Americans probably would be neutral in the coming conflict, the United States almost certainly would serve as Great Britain's logistical lifeline. The *Abwehr,* tasked with finding out everything available on the output of American defense industries, the state of U.S. military technology, and any military aid agreements between Washington and London, suddenly needed to recruit a lot of agents for work in the United States. And, as Hitler made clear, everybody was expected to participate enthusiastically in this effort. Consequently, all arms of the German intelligence establishment were busily beating the bushes to round up new recruits for the *Abwehr*'s American operations. The recruiting approaches ranged from the subtle to the somewhat more direct approach to William Sebold by the Gestapo, which used the typical heavy-handed methods that so distinguished its reputation.

At the *Fuchsbau,* Sebold was taken in hand by Nikolaus Ritter, head of the agency's U.S. operations. A dapper, convivial man who worked as a textile company executive in civilian life, Ritter had spent much time in the United States on business and was fluent in English. He was regarded as among the brightest stars of the *Abwehr,* for although American operations for years had a low priority at the agency, Ritter had managed to score some impressive successes.

Ritter's forte was technical espionage. From the time the *Abwehr* began operations in the United States in 1927, he had gone trolling among the large German-American community, looking for people willing to "serve the Fatherland." Judged statistically, Ritter's recruitment efforts would appear to have been a failure, since the overwhelming majority of German-Americans he contacted flatly rejected his approaches. But he did succeed in recruiting a network of key assets who worked in various defense factories, including a Ford Motor Company executive whose extensive contacts throughout the American industrial establishment gave him access to a wide range of industrial and technical secrets. Ritter also recruited a source who infiltrated the circle around the American rocket pioneer Dr. Robert H. Goddard. (American authorities had no interest in his advanced liquid-fueled rockets, but the Germans did, with consequences that were to rain down on London some years later.)

By 1936 Ritter had constructed a flourishing pipeline of American industrial secrets, especially in aeronautical science, that flowed to Germany. In 1937 he scored his greatest coup, recruiting an engineer who worked on America's biggest secret at that time, the Norden Bombsight, a gyrostabilized technology that allowed bombers to drop their bombs accurately under the most adverse conditions. The asset stole crucial blueprints, which he passed to Ritter on one of Ritter's frequent "business trips"

Dr. Robert H. Goddard, the famed American rocket pioneer, with one of his early liquid-fueled rockets during test firings in 1931. The German *Abwehr* gained access to Goddard's technical data, giving Germany a big lead in the development of guided missiles. (*Clark University*)

to the United States. Ritter rolled them inside an umbrella and coolly waltzed past U.S. Customs on his way back to Germany.

The result was a gushing tribute from the *Luftwaffe,* which credited Ritter's technical spying with enabling it to come up to snuff in a remarkably short time. As the *Luftwaffe* generals freely admitted, their air weapon could not have been ready for war in 1939 without the American technological treasures stolen by Ritter's agents.

There were two reasons for Ritter's success in the United States. One was the country's sheer indifference to internal security. Tending to hold itself aloof from the dark side of world affairs, the United States seemed to feel safe behind the bastion of two oceans. Second, and more important, the FBI had demonstrated manifest ineptitude in the area of counterespionage, one of its more important mandates. It had very little grasp of foreign intelligence operations in the United States, and as a result, both Soviet and German intelligence had a virtual free reign. It was not until 1938 that the FBI, in the process of sweeping up a small *Abwehr* spy ring, learned there was an active German intelligence presence in America. But the FBI thought the ring was run by the Gestapo, the only German intelligence entity the Bureau knew about. (The Gestapo had no foreign intelligence functions.)

It was thus a confident Nikolaus Ritter who prepared William Sebold for his American operation. So confident, in fact, that he committed two very critical mistakes. The first involved Sebold.

Ritter informed Sebold that he would be sent to the *Abwehr* spy training school in Hamburg, following which he would return to the United States and collect whatever interesting material he came across in his job. At some point, he would attempt to get jobs at other aeronautical firms and widen his access to technical secrets. Sebold, apparently overcoming his early reluctance, now appeared enthusiastic. But, he told Ritter, he needed to go to the American consulate in Cologne to arrange for money to be sent to his wife while he was in Germany. Ritter agreed without bothering to check if his new asset was in fact married. He wasn't.

Sebold was no sooner out of Ritter's sight than he headed for Cologne. The American diplomats Sebold spoke to informed the FBI, which told him to go along patiently for the moment; they would be in touch with him when he returned to the United States.

The FBI now had a remarkable stroke of good fortune. Sebold demonstrated an unsurpassed ability for radio work at the *Abwehr* spy school, an ability that gave Ritter an idea. He was just then wondering how he was going to transmit the intelligence his assets in America were collecting back to Germany. For some time he had been using couriers recruited from among the staff employees who worked aboard the German ocean liners that plied the Atlantic. But so-called hot intelligence (such as news of ship convoys) that had to be sent to Germany as quickly as possible obviously needed a faster route. Then, too, in the event of war, it was certain that the German liners would no longer be able to make their runs in the teeth of a British sea blockade, another presumed certitude for the next war.

The solution was radio, meaning a very powerful set capable of transmitting across the Atlantic. It would require a highly skilled operator who could overcome the vagaries of atmospheric conditions and other hindrances. In German intelligence parlance, such a radio would serve as a *Meldekopf* (communications center). Ritter had already tried one operator, but the man proved unequal to the job. To Ritter, Sebold was the perfect substitute.

But putting the untested Sebold at the hub of a *Meldekopf* was a reckless gamble, for in Ritter's plan, he would set up such an operation in New York, and *all* German intelligence would flow through it. Aside from using Sebold, an unknown quantity at that point, such a procedure violated all rules of espionage tradecraft—most especially the principle of compartmentalization, the very sensible practice of keeping members of a spy ring from meeting or dealing with each other, so as to prevent one member from betraying all the others.

None of these concerns seem to have occurred to Ritter. Apparently confident that he could run operations in the United States without fear of the FBI, he made his plans for an enlarged *Abwehr* presence without any regard to tradecraft. Ritter's plan was simple: Sebold was to quit his aircraft mechanic job and set up an office at Broadway and 42nd Street in New York City known as Diesel Research Company. This was a front for what was to become a central intelligence collection point. Ritter's assets would come into the office and deliver their intelligence reports to Sebold, who would then radio them to Germany. As a backstop, Ritter set up a second radio operation in the Bronx, New York City's northernmost borough.

In May 1940, Sebold arrived in New York. Met at the dock by two FBI agents, he showed them a very interesting piece of microfilm Ritter had given him before leaving Germany: a list of all of Ritter's assets in the United States, complete with code names, home addresses, work sites, and intelligence specialty. It was a counterintelligence officer's dream.

Sebold dutifully set up Diesel Research Company with the lavish supply of American dollars Ritter had provided him, but he did so without bothering to tell his control of a few extra decorating touches: behind one wall FBI agents set up movie cameras to shoot through a one-way mirror, and around the room microphones were embedded in walls and furniture.

What happened next was to prove, to Ritter's cost, that it was now a very different FBI at work. An organization that had always demonstrated an ability to learn from its mistakes, the Bureau had gone back to the drawing board in 1938, realizing that it had no handle on German espionage operations. An expanded staff, recruitment of top agents, and new training programs had produced a pretty formidable counterespionage agency. The Sebold case would be its first big test.

Ritter, of course, had made that first test all the easier by his operational mistakes. Day after day, as the FBI cameras rolled, Ritter's star assets wandered into the Diesel Research Company and handed over their goodies. With Sebold having insured they sat in a chair directly facing the mirror, these assets were recorded by the cameras and microphones as they chatted with him about the material they had just handed over (while attempting to impress Sebold with their cunning in obtaining it), along with assorted problems of their espionage existences.

Later the basis for the quasi-documentary movie *The House on 92nd Street,* the Diesel Research Company operation was akin to watching ripe peaches fall in a basket. Into the plain office strolled the cream of Ritter's American assets: Hermann Lang, who had stolen the Norden Bombsight blueprints; Lily Stein, the beautiful femme fatale who seduced men of important secrets; Edmund Heine, the Ford executive and collector of American industrial secrets; and Carl Reuper, a warehouse inspector who used his job to peek into interesting-looking boxes.

All told, there were 37 of them, the very core of Ritter's American spy ring. To the FBI's dismay, they were collecting a remarkable amount of first-class technical intelligence. But from now on, none of it was reaching Germany. Working with FBI radio experts, Sebold set up a radio station in the Long Island community of Centerport, some 45 miles east of New York City.

Back in Berlin, Ritter was delighted with the first transmissions from Sebold. They arrived precise and clear, loaded with intelligence reports on a wide range of technical matters. Ritter happily turned them over to the German military, but instead of the customary congratulations, he began to receive snotty memos. There must be some mistake, he was told: some of the intelligence reports were hopelessly garbled, some didn't check out, some seemed technologically incorrect, some made no sense at all. Only a few were absolutely correct.

Concerned, Ritter then ordered his second radio operator to transmit intelligence, but as the operator later reported, he couldn't get his radio to work. He was puzzled by this failure because he had thoroughly checked out every part of the set and even replaced some parts he thought might be giving him trouble. However, no matter what he tried, the set's signals would not reach Germany. Perhaps there was something wrong with the *Abwehr*'s receivers? No there wasn't, Ritter snapped, so obviously the fault lay with the operator.

Finally, Ritter decided his second radio operator was an incompetent and ordered him to stop transmitting. Henceforth, the *Abwehr* would depend solely on Sebold, while at the same time try to find out if he was somehow mixing up the material he was sending.

The increasing desperation of the messages to Sebold from Germany was a source of great satisfaction to the FBI team working with him. Headed by one of the FBI's legendary counterintelligence agents, William K. Harvey,* the team had been skillfully concocting cooked intelligence for Sebold to transmit. Meanwhile, to forestall the possibility of that second transmitter going into action, Harvey had arranged for FBI technicians to blanket the man's transmitter with static, sufficient to balk any outward signal.

Harvey trumped these maneuvers with another triumph, recruiting a worker at the German consulate in New York who agreed to provide secret documents he encountered. He encountered many of them, for his duties included burning sensitive documents in the consulate's furnace. He carefully separated the more interesting-looking documents from the pile and threw them into one side of the furnace that he kept unlit, later retrieving them for the FBI. The point of this operation was to monitor the consulate for any requests from the *Abwehr* to check out Sebold, certain indication that Berlin had become suspicious of his bona fides. (The FBI was also delighted to learn that Ritter had not yet ordered a change in the *Abwehr* code for his American

---

* Harvey's later career would include a denunciation of Kim Philby as being a KGB mole 12 years before Philby's defection. He eventually left the FBI after a dispute with J. Edgar Hoover and joined the CIA, where he ran the operation that dug a tunnel to tap into Soviet communications in East Germany, and still later headed Task Force W, the CIA's spearhead against Cuba. Called "Pear" for his expanding girth, he was a heavy drinker noted for his habit of pointing a pistol at people who argued with him and slowly cocking it.

Admiral Wilhelm Canaris, head of the German *Abwehr* intelligence service. He was victimized by an FBI sting that destroyed his major spy ring in the United States, as well as his reputation. (*National Archives*)

assets, a book code based on the execrable best-selling novel *All This and Heaven Too.* Any change would indicate plans to replace Sebold with another agent; a code change would be standard practice in such an event.)

Nevertheless, as the FBI understood, the deception could not last forever. As Ritter bombarded Sebold with messages of growing irritation, wondering what was wrong with the intelligence he was sending, the FBI finally decided to close it all down. In June 1941, the 37 assets who wandered into Sebold's web were arrested; since Sebold was not among them, the assets assumed he had managed to escape somehow. But three months later, on trial in federal court for espionage, they were stunned when the government called its first witness: William Sebold, whose testimony, combined with those highly incriminating FBI movies, convicted all the defendants.

There is no exaggerating the disaster Sebold's betrayal represented. In one blow, the entire *Abwehr* network in the United

States was decapitated, a disaster for Germany that could not have come at a worse time. With America serving as the "arsenal of democracy," the Germans suddenly had no insight into the U.S.-British supply line, no intelligence on the conversion of the American industrial machine to war production, no knowledge of the laboratories and development centers that were beginning to develop the technologies that would finally defeat Germany. For 16 crucial months, everything Germany thought it knew about the United States was a fake, cooked by the FBI.

The *Abwehr* never recovered from the blow. Its chief, Admiral Wilhelm Canaris, tried to explain away the disaster by claiming that his men were onto Sebold's "treason" from the start and simply played along to find out how much the FBI knew. The story rang hollow; nobody believed the *Abwehr* would sacrifice 37 assets merely to find out what J. Edgar Hoover might know. The *Abwehr*'s slide began; less than two years later it was dissolved, and Canaris was fired. He was executed in 1945. Ritter managed to survive the war and later spent two exhausting years in debriefings by various intelligence agencies.

As for Sebold, he disappeared into obscurity under still another new identity, this one prepared by the U.S. government. According to some reports, he became a farmer in Texas.

SPIES IN THE ETHER

On the morning of August 26, 1914, General Yakov Jilinsky, commander of the Russian Northwest Army Group, radioed a series of orders to the First and Second Armies that had invaded East Prussia. Radio was a relatively new innovation in the Russian military, so Jilinsky broadcast his orders in the clear, unaware that the Germans had set up a radio interception operation.

Within minutes of the transmission, German commanders were aware of those orders, giving them a complete picture of the two invading armies and their plans. Equipped with that priceless intelligence, the Germans conducted one of the great military strategems, secretly moving the bulk of their forces from in front of one Russian army and falling upon the other near a small village named Tannenberg. Retreat turned into a rout; in the next two weeks the Russians lost some 250,000 men, beginning a chain of military disasters that was to end some three years later in the complete collapse of the Czarist empire.

The Tannenberg battle electrified the European military establishments, for the warning was inescapable: woe to the nation's army that could not protect its communications from prying ears. Modern armies were now mass armies conducting operations over fronts that sometimes extended for thousands of miles. The old days of couriers on horseback carrying written orders from headquarters to field commanders were dead; from now on, in a modern world of huge military forces maneuvering with unprecedented speed—thanks to the railroad and the internal combustion engine—communications would have to be virtually instantaneous. Only another new invention, the radio, was capable of that kind of speed.

And so a race was on: as fast as the military enciphered its communications to protect them, intelligence agencies devised cryptanalytic methods to break inside. Both sides became locked in a furious upward spiral, with one side evolving ever more complex systems and the other ever greater resources to attack those systems.

Ironically, despite the lesson of Tannenberg, the Germans during the war were to suffer the greatest defeats at the hands of the cryptanalysts. French cryptanalysts made deep inroads into German military cipher systems, and the British scored the biggest such coup of the war, breaking the German diplomatic cipher and thereby reading a message revealing German plans to foment revolt in Mexico. The British arranged to have that message made public, and it played a key role in changing American public opinion in favor of war against Germany.

The three case studies that follow grow directly out of this sequence of events. By the beginning of World War II, the warring nations had carefully studied the role of communications intelligence in the previous war and emerged with two conclusions: (1) to maintain the complexity of cryptographic systems and balk the cryptanalysts, cryptographic machines capable of superhuman feats of encipherment would be vital; and (2) large cryptanalytical establishments would have to be created, not only to keep a nation's cryptological ability technologically advanced, but to attack the crypto-machines of other nations.

The stage was set for a battle that raged in the ether during World War II, with fateful consequences for some of the nations involved. These case studies concern only that war, for that is when the "battle of the beams" reached its pinnacle—and demonstrated just how crucial a role communications intelligence had come to play in espionage.

6

The Bronze Goddess

Operation ULTRA
1939–1945

Looking over Hitler's shoulder

“And how much will this cost us?” a concerned Gustave Bertrand asked, aware that the 1931 depression-era budget of the *Deuxieme Bureau*, France's military intelligence agency, did not permit many francs to buy intelligence.

“A great deal, I'm afraid,” replied Henry Navarre, his chief agent in Germany. “ASCHE is an expensive proposition.”

As indeed he proved to be when Bertrand first met him at a secret meeting in Belgium. But that meeting also made up Bertrand's mind: whatever he had to do, somehow he would scrounge enough money to lavish on this thin man with rimless spectacles. As Bertrand understood at that first moment, the man was literally worth his weight in gold.

ASCHE, as Navarre had code-named him, was Hans Thilo-Schmidt, whose lowly position belied his worth. A clerk in the cipher section of the OKW (the German High Command), Thilo-Schmidt had access to something that to Bertrand was almost beyond price: Enigma.

Beginning in 1929, Bertrand, head of the radio intelligence section of the *Deuxieme Bureau*, had become aware that the Germans were overhauling their military communications system with a new cipher machine they had named Enigma. Bertrand's staff had intercepted some of the first signals, and one glance was enough to tell him they represented a very serious problem. His cryptanalysts were completely stumped, finally deducing that the machine produced ciphers so complicated, they were impervious to attack by all known conventional methods. Only one solution was possible: Bertrand had to get a look inside that machine so that the cryptanalysts could get an idea of how the system worked.

Easier said than done; as Bertrand was to discover, the Germans guarded Enigma as though it were the crown jewels. Every attempt to penetrate the tight security around the German military's communications facilities failed. By 1931 Bertrand was desperate, for the prospect of a newly rearmed Germany—France's traditional enemy—operating under total communications security was unthinkable.

Just when Bertrand had despaired of solving the problem, along came ASCHE. Hans Thilo-Schmidt, aware of the value of Enigma, decided to betray his country strictly for money. He simply approached Navarre, who was under cover as a French military attaché in Berlin, and offered to sell the secrets of the new German cipher machine. He didn't specify a price, but he made clear it would be high.

ASCHE set strict conditions: he would never meet with the French on German soil, would initiate contact only at times of his choosing, and would never leave anything in a dead drop. He also would meet the French only on weekends and holidays so his absences could be explained.

The first meeting, in a Belgian frontier town, coincided with Thilo-Schmidt's vacation and revealed ASCHE to be cynical and apolitical, concerned only with money. As Bertrand tried to conceal his excitement, ASCHE handed over an instructional manual and some technical papers concerning construction of the Enigma machine. Having taken a gamble by convincing his superiors his new German source would be worth it, Bertrand had brought along about $10,000, an extraordinary sum in 1931. He gave half of it to ASCHE for the first treasures, with promises of more to come for further material.

Even the worldly-wise Bertrand and his equally sophisticated colleagues were stunned by what happened next: Thilo-Schmidt spent all the money in the space of a week on wine, women, and song, to a degree even the Frenchmen thought impossible. With an appetite that defied description, Thilo-Schmidt bought women in batches, treated them to lavish dinners at three-star restaurants, then retired to expensive hotels for a night of sex and champagne. It was not uncommon for Thilo-Schmidt to take three or four prostitutes to bed at once and carry on until dawn.

With a Gallic shrug, Bertrand ascribed such astonishing feats to some sort of overactive gland and concentrated his attention on what Thilo-Schmidt had provided. It turned out to be worth every franc Bertrand had paid, for the Frenchman was provided with insight into one of the highest achievements in human ingenuity: a cipher machine so cunning, it more than justified its name of Enigma.

But as Bertrand and a number of other people would learn, what human ingenuity can devise, the very same ingenuity can undo. That was the essential first lesson of what would become one of the more extraordinary and momentous stories in the history of secret communications. It would also form an important chapter in modern espionage, dramatically altering the course of World War II.

Codes and ciphers have been an integral part of human politics since the dawn of recorded history, for there has always existed a need to hide communications secrets. But these two terms, commonly used interchangeably, are actually quite different.

A code is a system that substitutes plaintext with a codebook equivalent, readable only to someone with the same codebook. "Tomorrow," for example, might be 2031 or some other word; to read a coded message, the recipient simply looks up the number or word in the codebook and translates the message.

A cipher transforms plaintext into numbers by a specific, but variable, "key" that scrambles the plaintext letters into a series of numbers that is unscrambled by a recipient who knows the key. A simple cipher system looks like this:

	1	2	3	4	5	6	7
1	A	B	C	D	E	F	G
2	H	I	J	K	L	M	N
3	O	P	Q	R	S	T	U
4	V	W	X	Y	Z		

To encipher a message, read the left column, then match the letter with the vertical column. "Come at once" would be enciphered by the 1–7 "key" as 13 31 26 15 11 36 31 27 13 15.

Commonly, the encipherment is written in five-figure groups, so the message as transmitted would read:

13312   61511   36312   71315

To decipher such a message, the recipient would need to know the 1–7 key to allow construction of the very same grid shown here.

There are any number of refinements to make codes and ciphers that much more difficult to break. Numbers in codebooks can have "additives" (one- or two-digit numbers) that are routinely changed. Ciphers have even more tricks, among them the constant changing of the key, "transposition" (rearrangement of the letters), and "substitution systems" (replacing the letters in the plaintext with other letters).

But no matter how sophisticated, all codes and ciphers are vulnerable to attack. The problem is linguistics: all languages have distinct patterns that codebreakers and cryptanalysts can detect in coded or enciphered messages. As any solver of newspaper cryptograms knows, a cipher or code written in English reflects the language's preference for the letter *e*. In English, an average of 591 out of every 1,000 words contains that letter. In French, it is 850 per 1,000. Similarly, a message in Spanish will have a high proportion of the letter *q*, and German messages are dominated by the letters *e* and *n*. No matter how sophisticated the system, at some point an attack will gradually uncover these distinctive linguistic patterns.

The answer is ever more sophisticated systems to hide those patterns, but that creates a problem. In military communications especially, coding or enciphering has to be a process that is not only fast, but reliable and easy to use by code clerks.

The solution to this problem came in 1915, when an American engineer named Edward Hebern invented an encipherment machine—simply, a typewriterlike device whose internal mechanism automatically enciphers a message typed on an ordinary keyboard. The recipient of the message, equipped with a similar device, merely sets the machine to the same key as the sender, and the machine does the rest.

The first machines were pretty crude, but Swiss engineers in the 1920s made further refinements, finally emerging with a technological marvel they christened Enigma. Although the Swiss designed the machines for a commercial market, mainly for multinational corporations who wanted to encrypt their sensitive international communications, the Germans instantly grasped the military potential of the machines. They bought out the patent, then began building an improved version in 1929; by 1933 they had developed the world's most advanced encryption machine. Hitler ordered a ban on all commercial sales of Enigma machines as his military kept refining them further.

As Bertrand of the *Deuxieme Bureau* learned in 1931, the soul of the German Enigma machine resided in two rotors. When one of 26 letters was pressed on the machine's keyboard, the signal was sent electrically (via a battery) to spinning rotors, each of which contained 26 illuminated letters. As the rotors turned (not in unison), a light came on behind rows of letters in the back of the machine (always different from the letters pressed on the keyboard). That illuminated letter was transmitted to another Enigma machine, whose rotors had been set according to a predetermined key, matching the sending Enigma.

All of this meant that each message sent by Enigma was essentially random, since the rotors, each one of which had at least 26 contacts on one face that connected at random to a similar number of contacts on the other face, never spun precisely the same way. Further German refinements made to the machine included a system of plug connectors that added another layer of random electric signals.

Punching in a word on Enigma set off a process whose effect was something like a toy robot with flashing lights. But in cryptographic terms it was wondrous: mathematically, Enigma's complicated electrical wizardry could produce somewhere around 400 quadrillion possible combinations of letters at any given stroke. Even better, all this was entirely machine-produced; operators needed only minimal training in setting the keys (positions of the rotors) each time they used the machine. For further security, the Germans changed these settings periodically.

No wonder the French cryptanalysts told Bertrand that despite the material being provided by Thilo-Schmidt, they still were stumped. Even if Bertrand were to manage so great a feat as actually stealing an Enigma, that still wouldn't help much, because the cryptanalysts wouldn't know the settings. Bertrand got the same reaction when he discussed the problem with the topflight codebreakers at Britain's Government Code and Cipher School (later renamed Government Communications Headquarters, GCHQ), who pronounced Enigma unbreakable.

The German Enigma cipher machine. Although considered unbreakable by the Germans, it was solved by a remarkable operation code-named ULTRA that contributed greatly to Nazi Germany's defeat in World War II. The machine's secrets were unraveled by a collection of British eccentrics headed by a mathematician who developed a deciphering machine that led to the computer revolution. (*National Security Agency*)

But the next intelligence agency Bertrand approached was much more optimistic. *Biuro Szyfrow 4,* an obscure codebreaking unit attached to the Polish army general staff, was even more concerned about Enigma than the French; caught between the Russian colossus and Germany, Poland was on the precipice of disaster in the event of war between those two natural enemies. *Biuro Szyfrow 4* worked on cracking the German and Russian communications so Poland would have advance warning of impending military action. The Poles were enjoying remarkable success in reading just about everything the Russians and Germans were transmitting, but the introduction of Enigma suddenly cut off access to German communications.

Gwido Langer, head of *Biuro Szyfrow 4,* took one look at the ASCHE material Bertrand showed him and had a sudden inspiration: the mistake everybody was making, Langer decided, was in trying to attack Enigma by conventional methods. The solution was mathematical: divining the spin of the rotors and various electrical connections by mathematical means, and then reconstructing the movement of the rotors. Skull-cracking stuff, but Langer recruited the best mathematicians in the country to work in deepest secrecy. By December 1932, they had managed to replicate Enigma and began reading the first decrypts.

But Langer had a limited staff, and it was soon outpaced by German security measures, including the changing of keys on a daily basis and the adding of more rotors. To the frustration of Langer's brilliant mathematicians, they found themselves in a constant race: as they solved one version of Enigma, a new round of German security improvements would blind them again, setting off still another concentrated effort to solve it.

This went on for seven years until December 1938, when still another set of German improvements—chiefly, the addition of a fifth rotor—balked Langer's mathematicians. They went to work around the clock, but nine months later, before they could finish, Germany invaded Poland. Packing up their copies of Enigma, they fled to Paris.

In the French capital the Poles held a fateful meeting with Bertrand and representatives of the British GCHQ. Given the imminence of a German attack on France, the three allies jointly decided that the assault on Enigma would now shift to Great Britain, whose large communications intelligence establishment would have the resources to build on the Polish successes.* That decision would have important consequences.

In early 1940, Winston Churchill paid a visit to what he liked to call his "most secret source," his government's intelligence communications operation. Moved to a mansion in Bletchley Park outside of London to protect this jewel of the British espionage establishment from the German bombing of London, GCHQ was undergoing a rapid expansion, as experts of every description were being recruited to attack the German codes and ciphers.

---

* Bertrand fled to the south of France, where he ran a secret codebreaking operation against German occupying forces. Arrested in 1943, he escaped from a Gestapo prison and made his way to England. Hans Thilo-Schmidt, his randy German asset, was blown to the Germans in 1943 by a French traitor. Thilo-Schmidt confessed, then asked to be shot, since a long prison sentence without female companionship would be unbearable. The Germans obliged him in July 1943. Meanwhile, the Poles escaped to England, where they spent the war cracking German ciphers.

The recruits, among them university dons, the chess editor of the *London Times,* mathematicians, and an Anglican clergyman addicted to crossword puzzles, included a high proportion of eccentrics. Churchill took one look and whispered to an aide, "I told you to leave no stone unturned. I did not expect you to take me so literally."

Among the more eccentric was a brilliant Cambridge mathematician named Alan Turing, a man whose genius ultimately would prove crucial in the attack against Enigma and—although he didn't realize it at the time—would create the modern computer revolution. Before the war Turing had devised the idea of what he called a "universal automaton," a mechanical device that would solve any mathematical problem by reading symbols in binary code. (It was the mathematical breakthrough that made possible the handheld calculators so common today.)

But it was his eccentricities that made Turing so striking a character. Convinced that the pound was about to collapse at any moment, he spent his money on silver coins that he melted into ingots and buried on the Bletchley Park grounds—and then forgot where he buried them. He was also convinced that bands of thieves coveted his nondescript coffee cup, so he chained it to a radiator in his office. The classic picture of absentminded professor with rumpled clothes, long hair, and shoestring tie, Turing focused instead on the higher forms of abstract mathematics, a realm where only a handful of human beings could exist. That much was known about him; what was not known was a dark secret. Turing was a homosexual at a time when homosexuality was a serious crime in Britain. At night, he would slip out of the tight security perimeter of Bletchley and cruise the pubs, trying to pick up truck drivers.

During duty hours, Turing's considerable mental power focused on the problem of Enigma. Examining the Poles' mathematical approach, he noted their clever construction of a device called *bombi* (named after a popular brand of Polish ice cream), a very ingenious mechanism that aped the Enigma machine's rotors with a set of wheels in an attempt to mimic the encipherment process. One day a critical insight occurred to Turing: the *bombi* lacked a memory, so it was unable to recreate and use any information it had received earlier. Suppose, Turing speculated, a *bombi* could be built with some sort of stored memory. The cryptanalysts thus would have a machine that could hold all the possible combinations of settings, against which they could compare an intercepted Enigma message.

Turing built his own version of *bombi,* a copper-colored monstrosity measuring seven feet by seven feet, full of electromagnetic devices that, aided by an algorithm he devised, could shift through the many possible combinations of Enigma settings. He called it the Bronze Goddess. The Goddess's function was to work out the initial position of the rotors, a task aided by German code clerks, who had the bad habit of using easily remembered letter combinations—such as ABC or XYZ—for such settings.

Turing had built the world's first real computer; it would take the development of transistor technology to refine and reduce the Bronze Goddess in size to the machines that sit on millions of desks today. Meanwhile, Turing's invention soon led to an increasing number of decryptions of Enigma traffic. Within a year, the Bletchley Park staff—which had grown to ten thousand people—was solving Enigma messages almost as fast as they were dispatched.

Code-named ULTRA, the operation first proved its immense worth during the battle for France, when it detected the overwhelming German military superiority that was in the process of preparing to cut off the British and French forces. Forewarned, most of them were evacuated from Dunkirk.

From there, ULTRA went on to other spectacular successes: reading the German orders for the bomber and fighter fleets being unleashed against Britain to allow the outnumbered British fighters to concentrate at key points for maximum effect; solving the Enigma messages that gathered U-boat wolfpacks and coordinated attacks against convoys; reading German Field Marshal Er in Rommel's complaints about lack of supplies and tanks, allowing attacking British forces to hit him where he was weakest at El Alamein.*

ULTRA played a pivotal role in the winning of the war. For nearly five years, all high-level German military communications were open books to Germany's enemies. So were all German intelligence communications, allowing the Allies literally to peek

---

* And yet, ULTRA was no panacea. It detected the German preparations for the 1941 offensive in the Balkans, for example, but since the decrypts did not specifically mention the Balkans, the German attack caught the British unaware. Similarly, the German offensive in 1944 that became known as the Battle of the Bulge caught the Allies completely by surprise because orders for the attack were dispatched only via land lines.

inside Hitler's intelligence establishment. An added bonus was ULTRA's use in monitoring how effective Allied deception and double agent operations were, since German intelligence evaluations and reactions to such operations were communicated via Enigma.

The astonishing success of ULTRA raises the question of how the Germans could have been fooled for so long.

There were two reasons. To begin with, the British, later joined by the Americans, were able to maintain an extraordinary security that prevented even the tiniest leak. Each major ULTRA decryption was carefully considered in terms of any action that might tip off the Germans that their Enigma had been compromised, especially any military countermove to an anticipated German move. A group known as SLU (Special Liaison Unit) consisted of special emissaries from ULTRA who distributed the results of encryptions to major commanders on a strict need-to-know basis. Aware of the importance of what they were working on, the more than ten thousand people involved in ULTRA carefully kept it secret, afraid that even a misplaced whisper might jeopardize the one weapon guaranteed to win the war. (They maintained their silence until 1974, when the British finally made public the existence of ULTRA.)

Second, the men of the *Oberkommandos der Wehrmacht Chiffrierabteilung* (*OKW/chi* cipher bureau), the organization responsible for Enigma and its security, could not bring themselves to believe that such an incredible machine could be compromised. The men who had developed Enigma were the arbiters of its vulnerability, and every improvement convinced them Enigma was absolutely invulnerable. It never occurred to them that the impossible could happen, that even better minds than their own could defeat what they had created.

This conviction persisted in the face of evidence close at hand. Germany's modest communications establishment, the *Forschungsamt,* had managed, with meager resources, to perform impressive decryption feats against some equally impressive Allied codes. It had managed to break into the main U.S. Army Air Force code and so learned of the impending attack in 1943 on the Ploesti oil fields in Romania. The Germans laid a trap of antiaircraft guns that slaughtered the American bombers. The *Forschungsamt* also managed to crack the highest-grade American diplomatic cipher, a break that enabled the Germans to learn of plans for a conference of the Allied leaders in Casablanca, North

Africa. The German SD planned to assassinate Churchill, Roosevelt, and Stalin, but a *Forschungsamt* translator assumed Casablanca ("white house" in Spanish) in the decrypted messages meant the meeting was to be held in Washington, D.C., beyond the German reach.

The *Forschungsamt* also broke high-level OSS (Office of Strategic Services) codes, ciphers used to conceal locations of shipping convoys, and many of the messages sent by U.S. military attachés abroad.

These successes should have alerted the guardians of Enigma that no cipher system could be considered absolutely immune to a determined assault. Yet right up to the day Germany surrendered, the experts of *OKW/chi,* as they preferred to call their organization, persisted in believing Enigma was safe. Whenever someone like Admiral Karl Doenitz, commander of the U-boats, would worriedly ask if the 43 submarines he lost in one month during 1943 might be due to the enemy reading his Enigma communications to the submarine fleet, the *OKW/chi* was reassuring: a special six-rotor Enigma developed specifically for U-boat communications could generate *one sextillion* possible initial settings. No one could solve such a complex machine "by any known method."

Those men of *OKW/chi* who survived the war and lived until 1974 would learn, to their complete shock, the impossible had been achieved decades before: Enigma had been solved. They would learn that an obscure Cambridge mathematician named Alan Turing was most responsible for the achievement. They did not know, however, that despite this triumph, Turing's life would end in tragedy.

In 1945 Turing had returned to his first love, pure mathematics, and worked on a machine he called a "computer," a revolutionary concept that featured a program stored inside the machine to do the work, along with a "subroute" concept that would allow the machine to perform a subsidiary task, then return to the program. But he did not live to see the eventual culmination of his idea in today's computer world. In 1952 he was arrested for "unnatural relations" with a nineteen-year-old unemployed factory worker. He was given a choice of prison or experimental hormone treatments. He decided on the treatments, but they caused his breasts greatly to enlarge and put him in agony. Further treatments caused only more agony. Unable to bear the pain and humiliation any further, one morning in 1953 he prepared a cyanide concoction in his home laboratory and drank it. His body was cremated and the ashes scattered. No memorial was erected to the man who contributed so much to achieve victory in World War II.

Almost four years to the day after his death, homosexuality was decriminalized in Great Britain.

7

"By Guess and by God"

Operation MAGIC
1936–1945

Tokyo laid bare

For a supposedly supersecret spy agency, the place struck Frank B. Rowlett as distinctly low-key. It was a drab office tucked away in a corner of the old Munitions Building in Washington, D.C., without the usual paraphernalia that attends such high-security operations: armed guards, identification badges, sign-in/sign-out registers. The wall decorations consisted of a single large sign that read THINK.

It was difficult to picture the office as headquarters of the U.S. Army's Signal Intelligence Service (SIS), a newly formed agency so secret in the small American intelligence establishment of 1929 that only a few people were even aware of its existence. Even fewer were aware of its mandate: intercept and read the communications of foreign nations.

Rowlett had been summoned to SIS by the thin, balding man seated behind a desk, William F. Friedman, its chief. A brilliant mathematician, Rowlett was being recruited by Friedman for what was vaguely described as an "exciting adventure." That adventure, Friedman revealed, was the challenge of cracking the world's top codes and ciphers. Rowlett was puzzled: he knew nothing of cryptology, so why was Friedman so avidly seeking his services? What possible use could a mathematician be in the esoteric world of such things as polyalphabetic substitution?

The answer would become clear, Friedman told him. Suddenly, he asked Rowlett, "What do you think of cryptanalysis?"

"I never heard of it," Rowlett replied.

"No wonder," Friedman said, smiling. "I just made it up."

On that curious note, Rowlett agreed to sign on as one of the first recruits to SIS. In time, there would be a dozen more, and they would go on to achieve one of the more astonishing feats in the history of cryptology, a feat whose effects were felt from the coast of France to Tokyo. In the process, they would create a troubling legacy.

The conversation between the young mathematician and the dapper, precise man in bow tie marked a significant way point in the history of American communications intelligence.

Only 12 years before, when America entered World War I, it had a grand total of three men in the entire military who knew anything about ciphers and how to solve them. While European nations were embarked on a furious race to develop advanced cryptosystems and sprawling intelligence organizations to crack the communications of their enemies, the new U.S. War Department telegraph codebook was just being distributed—after being printed by a local Washington commercial printer. It contained no security classification whatsoever. Appalled, British communications intelligence experts pointed out that a codebook run off by the little print shop down the street was hardly the way to protect sensitive communications. Puzzled, the Americans seemed not to understand when the British told them their new code was absolutely useless.

There was a dramatic change in June of that year, when a young State Department code clerk named Herbert O. Yardley, who had steeped himself in the arcana of cryptology, was recruited by the Army to set up America's first communications intelligence organization, a unit of Army Intelligence called MI8. In short order, Yardley created a first-class organization that scored many successes against German ciphers on the western front.

Among Yardley's early recruits was William F. Friedman, who had come to cryptology through an odd set of circumstances. The son of Jewish immigrants who had fled anti-Semitic pogroms in their native Romania, Friedman was a trained geneticist. In 1915 he got a job with an eccentric millionaire to research plant genetics, but in a development that was to alter Friedman's life, his patron became obsessed with proving that Francis Bacon was the author of many of Shakespeare's plays. The basis for this belief, shared by a number of people steeped in Elizabethan literature, was a series of ciphers left in some of Bacon's writings. Friedman, asked to examine these never-solved ciphers, found a childhood interest in cryptology reawakened. He taught himself everything there was to know on the subject and plunged into the Bacon ciphers.

He was not able to make much progress by 1917, when war intervened. Yardley, aware of Friedman's work on the Bacon ciphers, recruited him to run a crash training program for Army codebreakers. That assignment completed (the class picture of 80 graduates was arranged in a code that spelled out Bacon's famous dictum, "Knowledge is power"), Friedman was assigned to attack German military codes. Joined by his wife, Elizabeth, who also had become hooked on cryptology, he cracked the main German army field code. Meanwhile, Elizabeth Friedman, in a feat that greatly impressed the British, managed to break the code used by Hindu nationalists in communications between their Indian headquarters and various revolutionary activists around the world.

After the end of the war Friedman thought about getting back into genetics, but the lure of cryptology was too strong. Aware of his reputation, the American Telephone and Telegraph Company (AT&T) approached him with an interesting offer. The company had just perfected a state-of-the-art cipher machine. Before the company put it on the world market, would Friedman attempt to break what AT&T considered an "unbreakable" machine?

Unable to resist the challenge, Friedman worked 12 hours a day, seven days a week, for the next four months. Then he announced to crestfallen AT&T engineers that he had solved every message the machine produced. Word of this remarkable accomplishment quickly spread among America's nascent communications intelligence establishment, and the Army—eager to create a topflight codebreaking organization—approached Friedman. Appealing to their intense patriotism and love of cryptology, the Army hired Friedman and his wife as civilian employees to create and run a new organization called Signal Intelligence Service. Friedman was given carte blanche to run

The legendary William Friedman, the greatest cryptanalyst in American
history, analyzes a U.S. Army cipher device shortly after taking command of a
new Army cryptanalytical unit in 1931. Friedman and his handpicked
cryptanalysts, known as the Magicians, later broke the Japanese PURPLE
cipher machine. (*United States Army Signal Corps*)

the place however he wanted and to hire whomever he needed.
The Friedmans were to be paid $4,500 in annual salaries. It would
turn out to be one of the greatest bargains in the history of communications intelligence.

At that point American communications intelligence was
split among three agencies. In addition to Friedman's SIS, the
Navy had a flourishing operation known as OP-20-G, and the
State Department was running what would become the most famous such group—the so-called Black Chamber under America's
pioneer cryptologist, Herbert O. Yardley.

But in 1929 the Black Chamber was closed down by Secretary of State Henry Stimson, who curiously decided that "Gentlemen do not read each other's mail." The statement betrayed a
terrible ignorance about the reality of foreign affairs in the early
twentieth century, when *all* major powers were busy at work trying
to peek into each other's communications. And no wonder: as

World War I had taught everyone, there was no better source of intelligence on a nation's intentions. In a dangerous world, such intelligence was indispensable.

The Black Chamber handled diplomatic ciphers, a job now transferred to Friedman's organization. He had recruited seven of the most brilliant mathematicians he could find and set about training them in the cryptological arts. It was then that they understood why Friedman had so actively recruited them.

For many hundreds of years, Friedman lectured, cryptology (which he defined as the science of devising and breaking ciphers) was the province of humans with the kind of minds capable of seeing the hidden patterns that revealed a code or cipher. They operated by a sort of intuition, and their approach to solving secret messages relied on that instinct. Such "peculiarly constituted minds," he said, operated strictly "by guess and by God."

But like the Poles, Friedman realized such approaches would no longer work in the new world of incredibly complex enciphered communications, most especially those generated by the rapidly improving cipher machines. The answer was mathematics; only science would unravel what science had built.

Friedman formed his mathematicians into a tight little band who would come to develop a deep, affectionate respect for their chief, despite his stiff formality (no one ever addressed him other than "Mr. Friedman," even people who worked with him for years). He was devoted to them, and in their secret world he assumed the status of demigod; all his original recruits were to stay with him for the next forty years.

It was a world whose every waking hour was devoted to cryptography. Christmas cards among the SIS employees were always in cipher, with each sender vying to see who could draw up the most difficult cryptogram. The Friedmans liked to host dinner parties at their home for SIS people, but guests had to be alert. After the first course the Friedmans would present them with a cipher that announced at which restaurant the second course would be served. Anyone hungry enough for the second course had to solve the cipher, which also revealed the restaurant's address.

Such mind games were essential training for the challenge SIS faced. Its mandate was to attack the high-level codes and ciphers of major powers presumed to be the potential enemies of the United States in a future war. In 1930 top priority was assigned to Japan, with Germany second.

Each day, intercepts flowed in from a network of radio intercept stations the United States had secretly constructed around the Pacific and Atlantic peripheries. The raw signals of top-grade diplomatic and military ciphers—rows and rows of five-digit groups of numbers—were given to Friedman and his band. Hour after hour, they would sit at their desks trying to detect the system that had produced those numbers: was it a "hand" system using onetime pads, a transposition cipher, a "superencipherment" that used a cipher to encipher still another cipher, an ordinary book code, a codebook system using random additives, or a machine-produced cipher?

Friedman decided that he and Rowlett, his most apt pupil, would concentrate on the toughest nut of all, Japan. The problem was twofold: not only were the Japanese making rapid progress in developing cipher machines to hide their top-level diplomatic and military communications, the Japanese language itself was a complex maze that had to be overcome. Japanese use syllabic script and 5,000-plus characters in their language, of no use in modern ciphers, since the characters can't be transmitted. So the Japanese developed a special Latin alphabet for use in communications, but there were many linguistic subtleties and vagaries.

To make things even more difficult, Herbert Yardley inadvertently spurred the Japanese into making their communications still more impenetrable. Following the closing of the Black Chamber, Yardley was not only out of a job, he was broke as well, having lost his fortune in the stock market crash. Desperate for money, he put his experiences into a best-selling book about the Black Chamber. Among the more attentive readers of his fascinating foray into the world of cryptography were the Japanese, who learned that Yardley's Black Chamber had routinely read all of Tokyo's diplomatic traffic in the 1920s. The Japanese resolved no such penetration would occur again. To achieve that, they decided to develop a cipher machine so complex and advanced, no one would ever break it.

The result was something that was to dominate Friedman's life for the next ten years. He code-named it PURPLE.

Armed with Yardley's revelations, the Japanese first looked to Germany for a solution. The Germans provided an Enigma machine to their allies, but the Japanese weren't satisfied. As the Japanese technicians who examined the machine pointed out, its system, although complex, was vulnerable to attack. The technicians predicted, accurately, that Enigma eventually would be overcome by cryptanalysts who would build a replica of the machine by deducing its construction from its signals.

The answer, the Japanese decided, was to build a machine similar to Enigma, but make it much larger, with a second level of encipherment—meaning that the original enciphered message would be enciphered again through a spaghettilike maze of electrical wiring that would generate so many possibilities each time a key on the keyboard was struck, they would be beyond mathematical comprehension.

With typical ingenuity and industriousness, the Japanese finally produced what was then the world's greatest cipher machine, to be used for the most important diplomatic traffic. It was called *97-shiki-O-bun In-ji-ki* (alphabetical typewriter 97), a prosaic name for a stunning piece of technology. It featured a battery of six-level, 25-point stepping switches, a plugboard, and an intricate wiring system. The operator decided which key was to be used, then plugged in the plugboard and turned the machine's rotors to the indicated position. (The key was changed daily.) The operator then tapped out the message, which was enciphered through the complex electrical system and re-enciphered for extra security. Another machine at the receiving end using the same key would reverse the process and produce a deciphered message.

The first messages from the new machine convinced Friedman he was looking at a formidable challenge, for early attempts to break the cipher got nowhere by all known methods. Obviously, Friedman concluded, he was looking at an Enigma-like machine that was much more complex, with the ability to "super-encipher." He then decided on a daring approach: the messages would be mathematically analyzed, from which SIS would figure out the permutations and wiring diagrams that could produce those kinds of messages. At that point, SIS would actually build its own version of the machine, through which it would feed intercepted messages. Such an approach had never been tried before.

But early attempts using this approach also failed, and a sense of gloom settled over Friedman's staff, now expanded to 11 people. Their earlier successes against a variety of ciphers had led Friedman to call them magicians, but repeated pep talks about their abilities failed to inspire any breaks in the great Japanese machine. By 1938 SIS had been assaulting PURPLE for over two years, but their supreme efforts hadn't produced the slightest dent. The Munich Crisis and the Japanese invasion of China convinced Friedman that war was imminent, so there was greater urgency than ever to get an insight into Japanese communications.

In February 1939, Friedman ordered his staff to drop everything they were doing and concentrate on PURPLE, hoping such a focused assault might lead to a breakthrough. Nearly around the clock, Friedman and his magicians attacked PURPLE from every angle they could think of; armed with pencil and paper, the mathematicians worked out their calculations while several Japanese language experts Friedman had hired pored through the PURPLE messages, looking for language patterns that might unveil the cipher.

Finally, like the first small leaks in a dike that signal the oncoming collapse, the magicians began to penetrate PURPLE. First, aware that the exquisitely polite Japanese had the habit of using typically florid diplomatic greetings in their messages ("The Imperial Japanese government has the honor to inform you . . ."), the magicians looked for repeated patterns at the beginning and end of diplomatic messages. Then the mathematicians slowly began to unlock the linguistic patterns in the cipher letters. One of them, Genevieve Grotjan, made the crucial breakthrough: a mathematical reconstruction of the language patterns that revealed how the cipher worked. Typically, the magicians celebrated by sending out for Cokes.

By the summer of 1940, Friedman had enough to begin construction of a PURPLE machine. When it was finished, he had achieved the technological equivalent of cloning a human being without ever seeing the twin. The American PURPLE was cranked up, and to Friedman's delight, it almost immediately decrypted more than 90 percent of the intercepted Japanese messages. Japan was now an open book, at least in terms of its highest-level diplomatic messages.

But the strain of this feat, including 18-hour days of intense concentration, had taken its toll on Friedman. That December he collapsed with a nervous breakdown. He was hospitalized for three months, but while he was gone, the magicians of SIS began to gather the treasures of their victory over PURPLE.

Code-named MAGIC (chosen personally by Friedman in tribute to his magicians), the operation began producing decrypts, allowing the Americans to look over Japan's shoulder. They learned of Japan's growing alliance with Nazi Germany, negotiations over the Tripartite Pact (the Axis alliance), and above all, the growing estrangement from the United States. Quite unexpectedly, the Americans also got an insight into Nazi Germany.

The insight was provided by Oshima Hiroshi, the rabidly pro-Nazi Japanese military attaché in Berlin. Eager to convince the Japanese government to enter the war on the side of Hitler, Hiroshi was sending Tokyo lengthy reports about German military strengths and plans—all via PURPLE. Early in 1941, the MAGIC team received a blockbuster: a full report from Hiroshi concerning Hitler's plan to invade the Soviet Union, including such details as the numbers of planes and identities of which divisions would be involved in the attack. President Roosevelt ordered this priceless intelligence rushed to Winston Churchill, who in turn notified Stalin, without revealing the source. Stalin refused to believe it.

Closer to home, MAGIC detected the Japanese plans to strike southward, but since the Japanese Foreign Ministry had not been told of the plan to attack Pearl Harbor as the opening move in that offensive, nothing in the decrypts pointed to it. The closest MAGIC ever came was a decrypt in early December 1941, ordering Japanese diplomats in the United States to burn their codes—a certain indicator that the Japanese were about to strike.

After Pearl Harbor, MAGIC gushed priceless insights about the Japanese war machine. It provided a highly accurate picture of the Japanese order of battle and dispositions of forces, revealed that Japan had decided not to help Hitler by attacking the Soviet Union, and finally revealed that the Japanese would not surrender even in the face of a threat of American invasion of the home islands (intelligence that led to the decision to drop the atomic bomb). Additionally, MAGIC continued to read the messages of Hiroshi, the Japanese attaché in Berlin. One message gave exact details of German fortifications at Normandy, sufficient to allow bombers and navy guns to knock out, with great precision, the German big-caliber guns that threatened to destroy the landing craft during D-Day.

As in the case of the German Enigma, the question arises why the Japanese never suspected that PURPLE might be compromised. Like the Germans, the Japanese who created the wonder of PURPLE could not believe that so cunning a machine could ever be solved by the human mind. But there was an extra element in the case of Japan: a hubris that permeated the Japanese communications establishment. The Japanese were convinced that Western minds were not capable of breaking the PURPLE ciphers, for such minds could never hope to master the complex Japanese language.* Friedman's Japanese-speaking magicians proved them wrong. (After the surrender of Japan, SIS teams went looking for any surviving PURPLE machines. The Japanese had destroyed them all, except for a machine in their Berlin embassy that had been broken into eight parts awaiting final destruction. There was enough to show that Friedman had succeeded, five years before, in replicating the machine precisely.)

By war's end, the SIS staff had swollen to 9,000, a resource that soon was put to use in the Cold War as the United States created the National Security Agency (NSA), a vast, centralized communications intelligence monolith. Friedman, hired by the NSA as a special consultant to organize it and create a worldwide network that worked in conjunction with several other nations, was to become estranged from what he regarded as the Frankenstein he had created. Increasingly unhappy about the NSA's vast power, which sucked up virtually every electronic signal in the world, its routine decrypting of the messages of close allies, and its forays into domestic espionage against American political dissidents, the doyen of American cryptology would hold his head in his hands and moan, "How on Earth did I ever get into this?"

Displeased, the NSA finally decided to revoke Friedman's security clearance—only to discover, to its horror, that Friedman had never gotten one. Finally, NSA and Friedman parted company. In 1969 Friedman died and was buried at Arlington with full military honors.

Some of his friends marked his passing by inserting a newspaper death notice entirely in cipher. Reputedly, it has never been solved.

---

* In a tribute to the occasional superiority of belief over facts, in 1984 Kamaga Kazui, one of the last survivors of Japan's World War II army signal establishment, wrote a magazine article in which he declared that the Americans never could have broken Japanese codes, which he claimed were "safe" during the war.

8

The Key to Rebecca

Operation KONDOR
1942

The blinding of the Desert Fox

Covered with dust and burnished by the hot sun, the two men materialized out of the Western Desert one May morning in 1942 at a British army camp near Assiut, Egypt. They were surprised to see that their sudden appearance did not appear to alarm the soldiers patrolling the perimeter, despite the fact that several hundred miles to the west Field Marshal Erwin Rommel's *Afrika Korps* had invaded Egypt and was driving for the Suez Canal.

At the camp, the two men—one an American, the other an Egyptian—told soldiers about driving their jeep in the desert on an exploration trip, getting lost, and finally abandoning their vehicle. Could the soldiers give them some water and tell them how to get back to Cairo?

The soldiers could not have been more helpful. They brewed a pot of tea, the magic English elixir, and told the two men how to get to the railway station at Assiut, where they could catch a train for Cairo. They lingered for more pleasantries, and went on their way. Once they were out of sight, the radio at the army camp came alive with a message to British intelligence headquarters in Cairo: TWO PACKAGES ARRIVED.

And so the first act unfolded in what would become one of the more curious spy dramas of World War II, a strange saga that would involve the fate of the *Afrika Korps,* the future of Egypt, and the death of British imperialism in the Middle East. These consequences would flow from an almost unbelievably inept operation by German intelligence, one that was almost prototypical of the kind of espionage ineptitude it consistently demonstrated. In this case, it would prove very costly.

According to papers carried by the two men as they boarded a train at Assiut, one was a fair-skinned Egyptian named Hussein Ghafer, the other an American named Peter Monkaster. Actually, Ghafer's real name was Johann Eppler, and Monkaster was really Hans Gerd. They were *Abwehr* agents assigned the job of establishing a German intelligence presence in Egypt and paving the way for Rommel's conquest of that country. A rather formidable task for even the greatest of spies, and the two men were anything but.

Eppler, born of wealthy German parents in Alexandria, had spent most of his twenty-eight years as a playboy, occupying his time gambling and hanging around coffeehouses in Cairo. In 1938 Paula Koch, a top *Abwehr* recruiter based in Turkey who specialized in enlisting Middle East assets, appeared in Cairo. She fastened on Eppler, whose dual fluency in Arabic and German fit a profile very few potential assets could match. In the context of the *Abwehr*'s plan to build a large intelligence capability in the Middle East as a means of undermining British influence, Eppler was a prime recruiting target. Appealing to his German patriotism, Koch succeeded in enrolling Eppler for the *Abwehr,* with studiously vague hints on just what he was supposed to do for German intelligence. For the moment, Koch instructed, he was to act as a sleeper. He heard nothing more until July 1939, a few months before World War II broke out, when Koch switched him on. He was dispatched to Germany, worked for a while as an Arabic translator for Hitler's meetings with anti-British Arab leaders, and then delivered Arabic language propaganda broadcasts for German radio. Bored, Eppler wondered when he was going to be assigned some real spying.

The moment came in March 1942, when the *Abwehr* ran him through a brief training course in espionage tradecraft, then flew him to Rommel's headquarters in Libya. There, he was matched up with a typical *Abwehr* recruit, Hans Gerd. Born in what had been German East Africa before it passed to British control after World War I, Gerd was fanatically anti-British. An itinerant knock-about for most of his twenty-six years, Gerd was recruited by the *Abwehr* because of his fluency in English and trained as a radio operator.

Eppler and Gerd were now briefed on what was described as Germany's most ambitious intelligence operation in the Middle East. It struck Eppler like something out of a spy novel: he and Gerd would be infiltrated into Egypt via the Western Desert, a feat to be accomplished under the guidance of the famed Hungarian desert explorer Laszlo von Almasy. They would make their way to Cairo, where Eppler—under the name Ghafer, conveniently adopted from the name of the Egyptian who had married his widowed mother—would reestablish his persona as an idle playboy. Gerd, equipped with a forged U.S. passport as Peter Monkaster, would pose as a rich American friend of Eppler's. He would set up his radio somewhere in Cairo and broadcast the intelligence Eppler was to collect.

Actually, Eppler had a dual assignment. One, he was to gather details on the British military dispositions in Egypt, with emphasis on forces moving west to combat Rommel's invasion of Egypt. Second, he was to establish a liaison with a group of dissident Egyptian army officers who had made contact with the Germans to seek help in overthrowing the British occupation of Egypt. The group, led by a young officer named Anwar Sadat, was willing to provide intelligence on British forces in exchange for direct German help for its plan to stage an uprising.

All this amounted to a very ambitious intelligence enterprise, and even under the best of circumstances there were not many agents capable of carrying it out. The task was even further beyond Eppler's capabilities; barely trained, he didn't have the vaguest idea of how he was supposed to collect intelligence on the British military in the face of a very tight British security system, nor did he have any grasp of how he was supposed to aid the dissident Egyptian army officers.

To make things worse, the *Abwehr* also had very little concept of how Eppler and Gerd were to achieve their ambitious assignment. To Eppler's unease, it provided him with the name of the only other active asset recruited in Cairo: Hekmet Fathmy, the most famous belly dancer in Egypt. Virulently anti-British (a sentiment she carefully concealed), she had offered her services to the Germans.

Perhaps sensing Eppler's disquiet, his *Abwehr* controllers let him in on their greatest secret, which amounted to Rommel's secret weapon. Operating far ahead of Rommel's forward units, Eppler was told, the Germans had an elite commando unit that had been specially trained in radio intercept operations. They infiltrated deep into the British rear, tapped into telephone lines, and intercepted every radio signal they could reach. Whatever they intercepted was sent back to Rommel's headquarters; coded or enciphered material was forwarded to Germany for cracking by communications intelligence.

In early 1942, the commandos struck oil. They intercepted transmissions from Colonel Bonner Fuller, the U.S. military attaché in Cairo. Eager to get the Americans into the war, the British were telling Fuller everything about their military plans for North Africa, down to their most detailed dispositions, which Fuller was radioing back to Washington, along with his own expert evaluations on whether the British would be able to save Egypt from the *Afrika Korps*. The Germans discovered Fuller's transmissions were coded in a relatively low-grade U.S. diplomatic code known as BLACK. They cracked it without too much trouble and gave Rommel a priceless window into British military thinking. It had helped him outmaneuver the British in a number of big armored battles in the desert, given him advance word on some major seaborne convoys the Germans were able to defeat, pinpointed important targets on the island of Malta, and provided advance word on a large-scale British commando raid the Germans defeated with heavy casualties.

But as the *Abwehr* realized, there was no guarantee this intelligence fountain would keep spouting (as indeed it didn't, for in the summer of 1942 ULTRA detected the leak and shut it off). So Eppler would serve, initially at least, as the backstop for the BLACK intelligence, and later, if it were shut off, the replacement. He would broadcast his intelligence to the commando teams lurking somewhere in the desert, using a book code based on the popular Daphne du Maurier novel *Rebecca*.

Equipped with false papers, a radio, and $80,000 worth of British pound notes, Eppler and Gerd began their desert trek. Led by Almasy, they spent several weeks crossing the forbidden wastes until the Hungarian expertly dropped them off near Assiut.

All seemed to be going well so far, but in fact the British were onto them. After succeeding in his mission of crossing the desert, Almasy reported that success to the *Abwehr* in Libya, which in turn informed Berlin via Enigma. ULTRA immediately deciphered the message, and the British knew that two agents had been infiltrated into Egypt. Almasy's message did not reveal their identities, but the British immediately alerted their frontier posts to be on the lookout for two men without convincing explanations of why they were in the area. Further, the men were not to be detained; the British wanted to play out the string to see what might develop. The Assiut post made its report, along with the news the two men were apparently headed for Cairo.

Unaware they had already been detected, Eppler and Gerd reached Cairo. Eppler made contact with Fathmy the belly dancer, who searched for a suitable living place for the two men. Her first choice, an apartment, didn't work, because surrounding tall buildings blocked radio transmissions. She then found them a houseboat moored in the Nile. The two men outfitted the place in lavish style, including a fancy radio console in which Gerd hid his transmitter.

With that, Operation KONDOR, as the *Abwehr* called it, was ready for action. Gerd tapped out the first coded message to Rommel's commandos reporting their safe arrival. The commandos in turn relayed the message to headquarters, and a subsequent report to Berlin alerted the British, via ULTRA, that not only was there an *Abwehr* operation that had just come into play in Cairo, but it was transmitting to an unidentified radio somewhere in the desert. British radio direction-finders went to work and tracked down that radio. A raid captured two of Rommel's commandos. They refused to say anything, but among the material captured with them was a distinct oddity: a copy of the novel *Rebecca*. British counterintelligence took a careful look at the book, noticing a smudge in the upper inside right corner of the jacket. Under a microscope, the words "50 escudos" could be made out. That was Portuguese currency, and a check in Lisbon revealed that the book seized in the desert was one of six that had been purchased in a Lisbon bookstore several months earlier by the wife of the German military attaché at the German embassy. Another *Abwehr* operational mistake: having sloppily failed to hide the origin of the book, the Germans alerted the British that it was being used for a book code.

From there, it was elementary for the British to deduce that the two assets somewhere in Cairo would be using *Rebecca* as the book code to transmit messages. For skilled codebreakers, especially if they have the book in question, a book code is fairly easy to break. So the codebreakers waited for the first transmissions to work on. But there weren't any; Gerd began to experience serious problems with his transmitter, which he couldn't get to work.

While he was trying to fix it, Eppler set about establishing his cover. He played the part of playboy at Cairo's nightclubs, lavishly spending some of the $80,000 worth of pound notes he had been given. But Eppler's largesse exposed still another *Abwehr* operational error. The British had instituted strict currency controls to trace their money;* soon, they discovered that the pound notes were all issued by banks in Lisbon in exchange for German currency—a tip-off that the money was being spent by a German espionage agent.

Via Fathmy, Eppler arranged a secret rendezvous with Anwar Sadat, but the Egyptian was very skittish. The British had been tightening surveillance on the dissident army officers, and Sadat feared it was just a matter of time before they would be all rounded up and arrested. Besides, Sadat was not impressed with Eppler, who apparently had no idea of how the *Abwehr* was supposed to aid the planned uprising by army officers. Sadat provided a few items of intelligence but was not optimistic that his relationship with the Germans would flower any further.

What Eppler had gotten wasn't much, but he rushed back to the houseboat to transmit the few crumbs to Rommel. However, he discovered that Gerd still couldn't get his transmitter to work. Finally, he decided there was something fundamentally defective with it, and he set about getting a replacement. Eppler at the outset of his mission had been given the name of an *Abwehr* contact, a German national working at the Swedish embassy in Cairo. He was to be used for any help he might render only in the event of an emergency. This was certainly an emergency, Eppler decided, so he and Gerd went to the Swedish embassy.

They succeeded only in drawing the noose around their necks that much tighter. The British had the embassy under sur-

---

* The controls were in response to a huge German SD counterfeiting operation, which combed the concentration camps for expert engravers, then drafted them for forging pound notes, in exchange for their lives. Headquartered at the Sachsenhausen concentration camp, the SD's Operation BERNHARD turned out some $600 million worth of money so expertly forged it was virtually undetectable. About $36 million worth of forged notes was actually put into circulation. It took the British nearly a decade to track down and destroy the counterfeits.

veillance, and they spotted the two strangers in earnest conversation with a low-ranking employee who just happened to be German.

British counterintelligence began closing in, puzzled by the fact that their radio direction-finder teams could detect no transmissions from Cairo—or anywhere else, for that matter. Pinpointing their radio would have made finding the two agents that much easier, but the hunters already had plenty of clues to their quarry. They knew one of the two men had spent money in nightclubs; a check of their patrons turned up, fortuitously enough, a woman who worked for the Zionist underground's intelligence service who recalled meeting a free-spending Egyptian patron who struck her as someone "with something European in his background." (In those days, the Zionists were eagerly helping British intelligence in the hope that London would look with favor on the idea of a Jewish homeland in the Palestine Mandate.)

What happened next was pure police work. British teams, armed with Eppler's description, combed Cairo and gradually found merchants who recalled dealing with such a man. The hunt was narrowed to a section of the Cairo riverfront where a number of expensive houseboats were anchored. A surveillance operation, spotting Eppler, trailed him and Gerd to a nightclub, where they met Fathmy the belly dancer.

When the net closed, Eppler and Gerd were arrested, along with Fathmy and Sadat. The British concentrated their attentions on the two Germans, but both men refused to say a word. Jailed together in a small cell, they were circumspect in their conversations, suspecting (correctly) their cell was bugged. When the bugging didn't work, the British suddenly moved them out of their cell, saying they needed it for some incoming Italian POWs. The two Germans were moved into a tent on prison grounds. Assuming the British couldn't bug a tent, they spoke freely just outside the tent flap under the pole—where the British had located a microphone.

Taken to a new round of interrogations, Eppler and Gerd were shocked when their questioners demonstrated a complete knowledge of their mission. Gerd then tried to commit suicide, but he was revived. He reluctantly agreed to cooperate. Eppler was much more enthusiastic about cooperating with what the British had been planning for some time: doubling Operation KONDOR to feed disinformation. Armed with the book code and

Field Marshal Erwin Rommel, the famed Desert Fox, confers with his staff
shortly before the battle of El Alamein in 1942—a battle Rommel would lose
when British intelligence penetrated his greatest secret and blinded him.
(*United States Army*)

Gerd's transmitter—which the British got to work—a steady
stream of cooked intelligence began flowing to the Germans.

For Rommel, it was a poisoned apple. Shorn of the vital
intelligence he was getting from the compromised BLACK code,
he was desperate for intelligence on the forces gathering to stop
him in Egypt. The intelligence from KONDOR came just in time,
but as the Desert Fox was to discover, it was incomplete. KON-
DOR provided misleading figures on the size of the British forces
and somehow forgot to mention that the British were planning
a major counterstrike near a small town called El Alamein. When
the blow fell that autumn, Rommel was decisively defeated, beginning a retreat that did not end until his fabled army surrendered in Tunisia a year later.

The British worked an extra twist to the game, sending messages to the *Abwehr* emphasizing the tremendous success of KON-
DOR and its growing need for more help. As anticipated, the
Abwehr began sending more agents—all of whom were picked up
as they arrived. By this time, Eppler had become a virtual full-

fledged British counterintelligence agent; so enthusiastically did he throw himself into his double role, his warders let him out on the streets of Cairo, where he spent much of his time in nightclubs and gambling halls busily spending the largesse provided by the *Abwehr*. (After the war, he settled down to a quiet existence as a bookseller in Germany. Gerd went to Germany and disappeared.)

Eppler's belly dancer friend, Hekmet Fathmy, did not enjoy so pleasant an existence. She was arrested and jailed; released after a year because of illness, she retired from dancing to get married and become a homemaker.

If the consequences of KONDOR were severe for Rommel and German intelligence, they would also prove significant for the British. They arrested Sadat, but he escaped from a prison camp and hid out with the Egyptian underground until the end of the war. The British were unable to defeat that underground movement, and Sadat—along with his friend, another young officer named Gamal Abdel Nasser—survived to lead the revolt that overthrew British-supported King Farouk in 1953. Three years later, the Egyptians nationalized the Suez Canal, the act that marked the end of British domination of the Middle East.

Sadat went on to become president of Egypt and the hero of the Camp David accords. Before his assassination in 1981, Sadat in private loved to reminisce about the war years, wondering aloud whatever happened to "that strange German fellow."

THE ENEMY WITHIN

As John Dryden once reminded us, we "hate traitors and the treason love," which is another way of saying that treason is very much a matter of perspective. In the American pantheon of villains, Julius and Ethel Rosenberg rank high as despicable traitors, but the gallery would not include Oleg Penkovsky—the Soviet colonel who revealed secrets of his country's nuclear rockets to the United States—because he is regarded as a "hero for peace," a man whose conscience compelled him to betray his nation's deepest secrets because he was convinced the Soviet Union planned to start World War III.

But isn't that precisely the same argument that the Rosenbergs and others used to justify their betrayal of American atomic bomb secrets to the Soviet Union? Didn't they claim they were "heroes for peace," working to make sure the fearsome weapon did not remain the exclusive domain of an "imperialist power"? Yes, and that is why all nations still go through semantic gyrations to justify the treason of the people they have managed to recruit among their enemies, while at the same time condemning (usually by death) the very same crime among their own citizens.

Treason is a vital component of espionage. No better intelligence exists than the secrets spilling directly from sources on the other side who are in a position to know. These traitors are willing to reveal secrets because they feel politically or morally compelled to do so, or because they have no conscience and are willing to sell their country. Soviet intelligence likes to call it *razvedka* (roughly, "true intelligence"), meaning intelligence that, to cite Stalin's injunction to his intelligence services, "comes right out of the enemy's safe."

Intelligence agencies spend a great deal of time growing and nurturing traitors among their enemies. Huge chunks of intelligence training schools' curricula are devoted to the techniques of betrayal: how to spot potential traitors, how to cultivate them, how to exploit human weaknesses (sex, liquor, drugs), and how, when necessary, to create betrayal with such techniques as a "honeypot" operation (sexual blackmail).

The four case studies that follow underscore the principle that treason has always been, and remains, very much a question of which side is doing the judging. Two of the studies involve this century's greatest secret, the atomic bomb. The first concerns a righteous German who felt a moral imperative to betray a Nazi regime in whose hands, he decided, a nuclear weapon would represent the ultimate threat to civilization. The second study, something of a mirror image, concerns several men and women whose political convictions compelled them to betray America's greatest secret in the name of "world peace."

A third study addresses still another dimension of treason, the conviction by a group of people that betraying and then attempting to destroy their adopted country was justified because of that country's affiliation with the oppressors of their homeland.

The fourth study involves a very modern story of betrayal, with all the elements that have made treason so integral a part of human politics since the beginning of recorded history. It is the story of how the paths of two traitors crossed—one an idealistic man convinced his country's regime was evil, the other a man who betrayed that traitor purely for profit.

As these studies unfold we shall see how the labels of "patriot" and "traitor" can be quite tricky to apply. The cynical old political aphorism may put it best: "Treason is a matter of dates."

9

The Hollow Tennis Racket

Operation GRIFFIN
1937–1945

Germany's secrets betrayed

O n the evening of November 9, 1939, the defeat of Nazi Germany began on a quiet street in a fashionable section of Oslo, Norway. At Drammensvien 79, a young man hurried to the front door of the mansion housing the British embassy and asked to see Francis Foley, the passport control officer.

Told that Foley was not there, the man thrust a package wrapped in plain brown paper at one of the diplomats and said, "Mr. Foley must get this as soon as he returns." He left the embassy as quickly as he had arrived.

The diplomat who received the package was the naval attaché. He opened it and found a stack of technical reports written in German, along with several diagrams and a glass tube, which he deduced to be some sort of radio valve. He was particularly struck by one diagram that to his trained eye appeared to be a new type of advanced torpedo for German U-boats, an acoustic homing weapon far in advance of anything in the world at that point.

Impressed, the attaché put the material aside. Later, when Foley returned, he was given the package. He did not need to ask who delivered it, for he knew that the promise of the man he called GRIFFIN was now reaching full potential.

And it was GRIFFIN who for the next six years was to single-handedly reveal to the British every important development in Hitler's arsenal. He would betray the secrets of German science, the one great weapon that could have reversed the fortunes of war for Germany. GRIFFIN would neutralize that weapon, in the process saving countless lives and making a significant contribution to the defeat of Hitler. Seldom has one man been able so thoroughly to betray a nation's technical and scientific capability. Not the least of GRIFFIN's achievements was the revelation of German science's most ominous weapon, the atomic bomb.

GRIFFIN was the code name for Paul Rosbaud. Few people have ever heard of him, and still fewer know of his role as one of the great spies of modern espionage. That perfectly suited Rosbaud, a self-effacing and modest man who was content with obscurity. But his quiet personality concealed an inner storm set off by a terrible conflict between patriotism and evil. It was a conflict he resolved with an extraordinary betrayal.

Paul Rosbaud was a small, thin boy, a serious and studious child seemingly destined for an academic career. He was also a sad child: his mother, a German, had emigrated to Austria, where a love affair with an Austrian resulted in Rosbaud's birth in 1897 in the city of Graz. But Rosbaud's father deserted as soon as his son was born, and the boy spent a childhood without a father. Envious of other children who had fathers, he spent much of his time buried in books, mainly science textbooks.

At the outbreak of World War I, Rosbaud enlisted in the army and fought on the Italian front. He was captured by the British in 1917, and although he didn't realize it at the time, the experience would prove to be a seminal event in his life. He was treated kindly by the British, whom he came to like and admire.

After the war, determined to become a scientist, he studied chemistry at the Darmstadt Technical University and won a fellowship at the famed Kaiser Wilhelm Institute in Berlin, where he did pioneering work on X-ray cinematography. His work earned him a doctorate from Berlin Technical University.

His impressive credentials gave him entrée into the elite world of German science, at that time the pinnacle of world science. There was not a single scientific or technical field that was not dominated by the Germans, ranging from composite materials to nuclear physics. To the Kaiser Wilhelm Institute, the University of Goettingen, and the University of Heidelberg—the nerve centers of German scientific preeminence—came all the world's best scientists to study at the cutting edge. (Among them was a young American nuclear physicist named Robert Oppenheimer.)

For the physicists, especially, their arrival came at a momentous time in the history of science. Such titans of German science as Albert Einstein, Max Born, Otto Hahn, Lise Meitner, and Werner Heisenberg were turning classic physics upside down with a breathtaking series of discoveries. Few ordinary mortals fully grasped such things as the theory of relativity or the quantum theory, but everybody seemed to know that mankind's understanding of how the material world worked was being revolutionized.

There were so many discoveries and developments seemingly occurring almost daily that Rosbaud decided his best contribution to science would be disseminating them to the world at large. To that end he went to work for one of Germany's prestigious publishers to create a number of scientific journals and a line of books that would bring news of the scientific revolution to the literate world. His plan was to solicit papers from the leading scientists, edit them, and then publish their findings as rapidly as possible.

In the process, Rosbaud began to build a wide range of valuable contacts in the German scientific world. By 1933 he was on a first-name basis with the full complement of German scientific and technical genius, ranging from Einstein to the more obscure aeronautical scientists who were already hard at work in experiments to prove the feasibility of supersonic jet aircraft. Rosbaud was their vital link with the outside world, for his publications provided the essential airing of their work, the resulting feedback from other scientists, and the stimulation of further thought. In the collegial world of science, this was the process that led to further discoveries.

But in 1933 Rosbaud became progressively more disturbed as the Nazis threatened to destroy this collegial world. The Nazification of Germany was accompanied by the Nazification of science; to Rosbaud's shock, the theory of relativity was now derided as "Jewish science." The same kind of barbarity that had driven Einstein, Meitner, Born, and other great scientists out of Germany tossed some of the pearls of scientific literature onto bonfires—the literature Rosbaud had worked so hard to get published for the enlightenment of the world.

Slowly, a resolve began to build within Rosbaud: he would somehow find a way to destroy this cancer. His resolve was further hardened in early 1935, when the exiled Max Born returned to Germany to retrieve some of his personal effects and his library. Rosbaud accompanied Born to his house—already taken by the Nazi government as "reparations" for "Jewish crimes"—and encountered a gang of jeering Nazi thugs who called the titan of twentieth-century science a "Jew swine," threw his scientific notebooks into a bonfire, and spat on him. Born just managed to escape with his life. Rosbaud was outraged but felt helpless; he was in no position to take on a gang of thugs.

There now occurred a fateful encounter in his life. Increasingly concerned about his wife, who was Jewish, Rosbaud decided to send her to live in England until the Nazi tide in Germany had passed. He would stay in Germany to battle the Nazis—how, he didn't yet know. Rosbaud went to the British embassy in Berlin to secure a visa for his wife and met a remarkable man named Francis Foley.

A World War I infantry veteran who was reassigned to intelligence after being wounded in 1918, Foley was recruited into MI6 after the war, largely on the strength of his talent as a linguist (his German was so perfect, he could pose as a native speaker). Assigned to the Berlin embassy in 1931 under the then-standard MI6 cover of passport control officer, Foley monitored the rise of the Nazis. Morally outraged by Hitler and his henchmen, Foley bent the regulations (and sometimes broke them altogether) to write up large numbers of "tourist" visas for Jews trying to flee Germany, especially scientists and their families. As Foley was perfectly aware, these "tourists" had no intention of ever coming back.

By the time Rosbaud met him in late 1937, Foley was running a virtual smuggling operation to get Jews out of Germany. Foley happily obliged Mrs. Rosbaud with a visa to "visit" England, then suggested her husband might want to flee, too. Rosbaud declined. He and Foley had hit it off immediately, and as Rosbaud spoke frankly of his hatred for the Nazis, his determination to avenge their outrages against his scientist friends, and his dilemma of trying to reconcile his German patriotism with his intention to hurt the regime (and thereby also damage the country he loved), Foley proposed an idea.

Since Rosbaud visited Great Britain periodically to arrange English translations of his publisher's works, Foley suggested he could take the opportunity to have "discussions" with some prominent British scientists whom Foley just happened to know. It was a deliberately low-key recruitment; aware of Rosbaud's intense German patriotism, Foley moved very carefully. He was aware that the last thing Rosbaud wanted was to be considered a British spy, a traitor against his country.

And yet, that is precisely what Rosbaud became. On Foley's instructions, the encounters with scientists whom Rosbaud met during subsequent trips to Britain were low-key. Without seeming to push, they questioned him about the growing militarization of German science and some of the specific areas where the Germans appeared to have strong development interest. In an atmosphere of collegial scientific chat, Rosbaud freely discussed everything he knew about current scientific developments in Germany.

This low-key relationship suddenly changed on the night of December 22, 1938, when one of Rosbaud's scientist friends, the Nobel Prize-winning chemist Otto Hahn, called him with electrifying news. He and Fritz Strassman, conducting laboratory experiments involving the bombardment of uranium atoms with slow neutrons, had managed to achieve fission—in the process discovering that when the nucleus of the uranium atom fissions, a tremendous amount of energy is released.

Rosbaud suggested they bend every effort to get their results published in a scientific journal as soon as possible. Rosbaud ascribed this urge for haste to the necessity of sharing the details of this momentous development with the scientific world, but in fact he had other motives in mind. Rosbaud's background in nuclear physics allowed him to grasp the implications of the Hahn-Strassman development instantly: the two men had split the atom. And, as he further understood, if such a fission process could be controlled on a large scale, a weapon of incredible destructive power could be developed. Above all, he had to get word of this development out to the scientific world, where other nuclear physicists would draw the obvious conclusion.

Rosbaud managed to get a paper published by Hahn and Strassman on their experiment. There was no attempt by German authorities to halt publication; they had not yet grasped the implications of what had happened in Hahn's laboratory. Rosbaud acted just in time, for only a few months after the paper was published, the Nazi government ordered German nuclear physicists to begin work on a "fission bomb." All further discussions of such matters in the scientific literature were barred, and a tight lid of security settled over nuclear physics in Germany. Meanwhile, Rosbaud's rush to print had the desired effect: in New York the exiled Italian physicist Enrico Fermi read the Hahn-Strassman paper and held his hands in a grapefruit-sized ball. A bomb that size, Fermi told fellow physicists, could make the entire city of New York disappear.

The approach of war in 1939 badly complicated Rosbaud's secret life. Business trips to Britain would soon end, and the alternative—contacting Foley at the British embassy in Berlin—was out of the question, given the certitude that the embassy would be closed down at the outbreak of war. When war was declared that September, Rosbaud was cut off from trips to Britain and found himself without means of conveying information.

Foley, who had fled to the British embassy in Oslo just as the war erupted, devised an ingenious solution. He recruited a number of Norwegian exchange students who were studying in Germany and convinced them to serve as couriers. Presumed Nazi sympathizers by the Germans, the students were actually anti-Nazis who were only too glad to contribute to the downfall of Hitler. (They maintained their pro-Nazi pose even after the German occupation of Norway and right up to 1945.)

One morning that September, a Norwegian exchange student showed up at Rosbaud's Berlin home bearing "greetings from Mr. Foley" and announced he would serve as messenger for any "news" Rosbaud wanted to deliver to his old friend.

At this point Rosbaud became a full-fledged asset of British intelligence. He may have been too busy to consider the implications: the German scientific establishment, gearing up for war, had given Rosbaud much to consider. Among other things, he learned of a secret conference convened at a Baltic resort and presided over by an unknown Army rocket scientist named Wehrner von Braun. There the development of long-range military rockets was discussed. The news caused Rosbaud grave concern, for the possible mating of such rockets with atom bombs was a truly frightening prospect.

He began providing a growing stream of other important intelligence, including the news that the Germans were developing a rocket-propelled glider launched by aircraft that controlled the weapon by electronic signals. (Intended as an antishipping weapon, it went into action in 1943 but was defeated by Allied countermeasures devised as a result of Rosbaud's information.) He also revealed that German rocket scientists were developing the *Wasserfall* (waterfall), the world's first antiaircraft missile (never deployed), and a special proximity fuse for antiaircraft shells (also defeated by Allied countermeasures).

Rosbaud not only provided the information, he also began to forward technical plans, diagrams, blueprints, and, occasionally, samples of the actual military technology involved. Some of the papers were smuggled to Norway inside the Norwegian diplomatic bag, thanks to Foley's recruitment of Norwegian diplomats. After the German invasion of Norway, more ingenious methods of transmittal had to be found. One involved a Norwegian student who was a fanatic tennis player. Having received permission from German authorities to send his rackets home for occasional restringing, he agreed to have some of them hollowed out and filled with blueprints and diagrams.

As Foley and MI6 realized, the identity of their valuable source in Germany had to be protected at all costs. Under the code name GRIFFIN, which represented both Rosbaud and the operation, the case was run under very tight restrictions, with only a few officials aware of Rosbaud's real identity. Any intelligence from GRIFFIN had limited circulation and was given to allies only in highly sanitized form to remove all clues connecting it to Rosbaud. Foley decided that any form of radio would be too dangerous for Rosbaud to use, so a simple arrangement was worked out: GRIFFIN would regularly send written reports via the Norwegian students, subsequently conveyed to London by the Norwegian underground. After the report was received, BBC radio would broadcast the announcement, "The house is on the hill," followed by the number of doors and windows—references to specific paragraphs in Rosbaud's report for which MI6 needed further information.

Rosbaud had good cover, but it was by no means perfect. Since he was a long-established fixture on the German scientific scene, knowing just about everybody on a first-name basis, no scientist hesitated in freely discussing the latest developments in his presence. Rosbaud was always careful never to seem as though he were probing. As a publisher who had a virtual monopoly on all scientific literature in Germany, he was able to contact many scientists in the course of his work. Moreover, authorities consulted Rosbaud on what scientific material needed to be kept out of the open literature for security reasons.

Rosbaud focused his attention on the German atomic bomb program, the one scientific development, he realized, that could instantly turn the war in Germany's favor. By 1942, he discovered, the program was falling behind. One reason was the lack of resources; Germany did not have sufficient industrial resources to produce the large amounts of processed uranium necessary for an actual bomb. More important, the German "Uranium Club," as the German nuclear scientists liked to call themselves, was making some critical scientific mistakes. The chief one was thinking that a controlled nuclear reaction was the guts of any bomb; in fact, it was the reaction that produced the material for the bomb.

By early 1943, Rosbaud's information was enough to convince British intelligence that the Germans would not succeed in building a bomb. However, wary of what he called an "unanticipated breakthrough," Rosbaud continued to monitor the program closely. And to make certain that breakthrough would never occur, he moved to cripple the German program. He found out that a key component in the reaction process—so-called heavy water used to slow down the flow of neutrons in a nuclear reaction—was produced at a plant in Norway. The Germans in 1939 secretly had bought up controlling interest in the plant, and by 1943 they were generating several tons of the chemically produced water. Thanks to information from Rosbaud, a raid by Norwegian resistance commandos and a subsequent British bombing raid put the plant out of action; a shipment of heavy water on its way to Germany by ship was sunk before reaching its destination.

Meanwhile, Rosbaud was busy conveying Germany's other important technical and scientific secrets. For example, he discovered the Germans had developed an advanced ceramic material named *Cermet,* essential for such high-temperature applications as jet engines. (In addition to an actual *Cermet* sample he shipped to Foley, he also procured complete plans for the ME-262, the world's first operational jet fighter.) To the delight of the British Admiralty, Rosbaud provided details of the *schnorkel,* an advanced breathing-tube apparatus for U-boats that significantly increased their range.

Aside from his concern about the German atomic bomb program, Rosbaud was most worried about the development of long-range rockets. He had first discovered the Germans' interest in these rockets in 1939, and he later learned that the resort town of Peenemünde, where that first conference had been held, was being developed into a huge testing and launching facility.

This odd-looking contraption, found by U.S. intelligence agents in 1945 when they rounded up German nuclear scientists, represents the furthest edge of the German atomic bomb program: uranium cubes and a reactor vessel used to create a chain reaction. The Germans had failed to realize their system was too small to achieve a reaction of sufficient scale. (*United States Atomic Energy Commission*)

Armed with that intelligence, British bombers leveled Peenemünde in 1943, severely setting back the rocket program. The Germans succeeded in moving the program into an underground facility, but they lost time they could never make up. They managed to develop the rockets sufficiently for attacking London in 1944, but by then it was too late to have any major effect.

With the end of the war, Rosbaud suddenly faced a new menace: Soviet intelligence. Somehow, the Russians had found out about GRIFFIN (probably through one of their British assets), and they began trying to track him down. When Rosbaud detected this hunt, MI6 moved in and smuggled him to London. There, he performed one last service. He wrote an extensive report for the British and Americans, listing all the important German scientists he thought ought to be evacuated westward to keep them out of the hands of the Russians.

And with that, the espionage career of GRIFFIN was over. He resumed his career in scientific publishing and worked quietly until his death in 1963. He died virtually forgotten; no award or honor was ever given him, nor did he ever seek any recognition. He never accepted a cent for his invaluable work in World War II, nor did he ever discuss the crisis of conscience that led him to betray his country in the name of saving it. His entire estate amounted to less than $1,000; only three people attended his private funeral service, following which he was buried at sea.

Frank Foley, the MI6 agent whose own conscience led him to save several thousand Jews from Hitler, died in 1958 in the kind of obscurity British intelligence prefers for its operatives. There was no mention of his own great contribution to the winning of the war, and Great Britain gave him no awards or honors. But the Israelis awarded him an honor he probably would have regarded much more highly than anything the British government could have given him. In 1959, a year after his death, the Israeli government planted a grove of trees in his memory and declared him a "righteous Gentile."

10

The Biggest Secret

Operation CANDY
1941–1945

The Russians steal the atomic bomb

It was, she thought, something very much like a high-wire act: one small slip and she would fall to her death. At all costs, she could not arouse the suspicion of any of the dozens of FBI and Army security agents that seemed to be lurking everywhere. Even the tiniest mistake might focus their attention on her, and a search of her pocketbook would quickly uncover those four long strips of microfilm.

And that, as she well knew, would bring to an end Operation CANDY. With it would go the very future of the Soviet Union.

As she stood on the platform of the train station at Albuquerque, New Mexico, that crisp January day in 1945, she tried not to look at any of the men who squinted suspiciously at the waiting passengers. She also tried to ignore the random stopping of several passengers, who had to show their papers and endure searches of their briefcases or pocketbooks.

Lona Cohen, dedicated Communist and agent for the *Komit Gosudarstvennoy Bezopasnosi* (KGB), was acutely aware that she was standing in a virtual lion's den. Not too far away, at an obscure desert town called Los Alamos, one of the greatest secrets in history busily hummed around the clock: the Manhattan Project, the building of the atomic bomb. To protect this most secret of all secrets, a huge security force had been deployed. Every suspicious movement, every remotely suspicious person, and every hint, however faint, that the secret might be in jeopardy was scrutinized under wartime security regulations that dwarfed anything ever seen before. At places like Albuquerque, the Army liked to boast, not even a cockroach could move without someone checking it out.

But Lona Cohen knew the great secret had been penetrated from the inside, betrayed by a number of assets the KGB had recruited. Among the most important was a source known to her only by his code name, PERSEUS. Cohen, who along with her husband, Morris (also a fervent American Communist), had been recruited by the KGB some ten years before for espionage operations in the United States, was assigned the task of picking up material from PERSEUS that had been left at an Albuquerque dead drop, then getting it back to her KGB control in New York. It was not a perfect arrangement, but PERSEUS had sent word that the material he had was vitally important—sufficient to risk Cohen running the gauntlet of the tight physical security in the area.

Cohen's cover was thin. She had a driver's license and Social Security card in the identity of a Mary K. Johnson, along with papers certifying why she had traveled all the way to New Mexico. According to those papers, she was a tuberculosis patient who periodically visited a New Mexico sanatorium for treatment. But as she well knew, even a cursory check would reveal no such person as Mary K. Johnson existed, she didn't have tuberculosis, and the sanatorium in fact was a glorified doctor's office run by an American Communist willing to help in the deception.

With the train for New York about to arrive, Cohen decided she had to do something about that microfilm in her pocketbook. She bought a small box of Kleenex and in the station ladies' room removed the microfilm and inserted it among the tissues. Then, as the train arrived at the station, she pressed a tissue to her mouth, occasionally coughing in what she hoped was a good imitation of a tuberculosis sufferer.

As she prepared to board, she handed the box of tissues to a conductor on the platform who was helping passengers enter the train. "Could you help me, please?" she asked in her best helpless female voice. She could see several security agents staring at her intently.

The conductor helped her up the steps, at which point she made her move. She turned to enter the car, deliberately overlooking the tissues. As she had hoped, the conductor suddenly realized she had forgotten them. He bounded up the steps. "You forgot your tissues, ma'am," he said, handing the box to her, as she noticed the security agents were no longer staring at her. With a genuine sigh of relief, she gushed her thanks.

And so the most closely guarded secret of all time began its journey to Moscow. A few days later, a radio at the Soviet consulate in New York began beaming an hours-long transmission. The pages of five-figure code groups concealed an extraordinary message: a translation of top secret technical reports detailing the progress the Manhattan Project had made in overcoming the scientific and technical hurdles to building the world's first nuclear weapon. A short while later, given to a group of Russian scientists, those reports were regarded as the scientific equivalent of the Rosetta stone. All uncertainties and barriers were cleared away; they were sure, the scientists told Stalin, they could now build a Soviet atomic bomb in about four years, far less than the twenty or thirty years they once believed necessary. The Soviet Union would have its own wonder weapon that would make it a superpower.

Seldom in history has an espionage operation had so dramatic an impact on the course of world politics. Operation CANDY, Soviet intelligence's code name for the atomic espionage operation, proved to be a glittering success, one rarely matched before or since. The success owed everything to the operational brilliance of Soviet intelligence's professionals, most notably their ability to induce betrayal. As the Soviets are the first to admit, Operation CANDY could not have succeeded without a long list of traitors willing to betray their country in the name of what they believed was a higher political ideal.

They would pay a very high price for that ideal.

Operation CANDY began in 1938, when two German scientists experimentally split the atom and changed twentieth-century science forever. "We have known sin," the American physicist Robert Oppenheimer said later, by way of explaining how the worlds of nuclear physics and politics suddenly intersected—with significant results for both.

Like their colleagues around the world, Russian scientists understood that the German experiment had a momentous im-

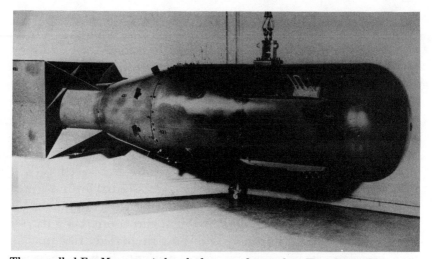

The so-called Fat Man atomic bomb that was dropped on Hiroshima. The
secrets of the bomb, although closely guarded, were penetrated by Soviet
intelligence's large-scale Operation CANDY. (*National Archives*)

plication: a nuclear weapon of unprecedented power—a true
"wonder weapon" capable of flattening a city in one blow—was
theoretically possible. The world of politics understood the im-
plication as well, and atomic weapons research was secretly begun
in a number of countries, including the Soviet Union. The first
efforts were relatively low-scale, for the scientists in Japan, Italy,
Great Britain, and the Soviet Union were aware of the immense
problems they confronted. It was one thing to split an atom in a
laboratory, it was quite another to do so on a large scale, somehow
control it, then harness that tremendous power to a weapon that
could be dropped on a target. There were many scientists who
doubted such a feat could be achieved in their lifetimes.

Both the GRU (*Glavnoye Razevedyaltelnoye*) and the KGB, the
main Soviet intelligence agencies, understood the scientific problems involved with developing nuclear weapons, but they also understood that good intelligence agencies don't take things for
granted. They resolved to find out if any of their enemies in the
West were capable of overcoming the formidable barriers.

Their chief concern was Germany, for the idea of a nuclear
weapon in the hands of Hitler, their sworn enemy who had vowed
to eradicate communism from Europe, was a truly frightening
prospect. Judged strictly by scientific standards, the development
of the atomic bomb would most likely be achieved by Germany.
Germany was preeminent in science, had made the first scientific

breakthrough in discovering atomic energy, had significant uranium deposits in the eastern part of the country, and had considerable technical resources that could be enlisted in a development program. Moreover, Germany had controlling interest in the world's only heavy water (deuterium, or "heavy hydrogen") plant. Located in Norway, the plant could produce plenty of the deuterium essential for slowing down neutrons in a controlled fission operation; its huge electrical turbines produced the power necessary to transform 100,000 gallons of regular water into a gallon of heavy water.

Above all, the Germans had the one essential ingredient for a successful scientific research program: brains. Although many of its greatest scientific minds had fled the country, Germany's scientific *wunderkind,* Werner Heisenberg, had decided to remain in Germany. "Germany needs me," Heisenberg had said in explaining his decision to stay. Needed him for what? A nuclear weapons program, obviously, since he was one of the world's greatest nuclear physicists, the man who at the age of twenty-three in 1925 had turned physics on its head, winning the Nobel Prize in the process. He had disproved the traditional model of the atom, in which particles move around the nucleus like planets around the sun. Actually, Heisenberg discovered, electrons jump from one orbit to another in quanta (packets of energy). It was not difficult to imagine that Heisenberg's brain, which had grasped the world of atoms, was also perfectly capable of finding a way to make them blow up.

There were other disturbing clues to worry the Russians. Coincidental with a speech Hitler made in Danzig in 1939 after it fell to Germany during the invasion of Poland, in which he talked about a mysterious weapon "with which we could not be attacked," the KGB learned that the leading German nuclear physicists had been gathered at the Kaiser Wilhelm Institute to begin nuclear weapons research. At the same time, all mention of nuclear physics research disappeared from German scientific publications. German newspapers hinted of a "death ray" under development, and an Istanbul newspaper, without citing any source, hinted that the Germans would soon build a "superweapon" that was "based on atomic energy."

Everything pointed to a German atomic bomb under development. The German invasion of the Soviet Union in June 1941 made the task of Soviet intelligence more urgent than ever: Stalin ordered an all-out effort to discover whether Hitler was about to be armed with a weapon for which the Russians had no defense. Stalin's intelligence establishment was able to give him the answer, although it would arrive from an unanticipated source: Great Britain.

Like the Russians, the British and their American allies were gravely concerned about the possibility of a German atomic bomb. The British had begun their own program, code-named Tube Alloys Project, which was inspired by the warnings of emigré German scientists that their colleagues who remained in Germany were preparing to develop an atomic bomb. A similar program in the United States, code-named Manhattan Project, was also at work. The Manhattan Project had been set up after Albert Einstein had written a letter to President Roosevelt warning of a German atomic bomb. (Eventually, the British and American development programs were merged to concentrate resources in a project that produced a working bomb in 1945.)

The British-American atomic bomb project had high priority, despite the fact that British intelligence concluded fairly early in the game that the Germans would not develop a bomb. The Americans found the British surprisingly well informed about the details of the German nuclear program, but the British refused to enlighten their allies when pressed on the source for this certitude. Intent on protecting their "most valuable source" in Germany (Paul Rosbaud, GRIFFIN), British intelligence did not want to reveal how they were learning all the details. For that reason, when the British confidently told their allies that the Germans had taken a "wrong turn," and there was no possibility of a German bomb before war's end, the Americans were skeptical.

Among the more skeptical was General Leslie Groves, head of the Manhattan Project and simultaneously chief of its intelligence arm, whose sole function was to divine the extent of the German nuclear program. Without sources like GRIFFIN in Germany, Groves's intelligence people sifted indirect clues to the German program, emerging with the conviction that the program was well along and would produce a nuclear weapon momentarily. The OSS, also without German sources, came to the same conclusion.

Both judgments were wrong. In fact, GRIFFIN (along with the British) was right: the Germans were hopelessly muddled. They had not only missed the idea that plutonium, the product of processed uranium, was the essential ingredient in bombmaking, they also failed to make their controlled nuclear reaction experiment of sufficient size so it would work. (Enrico Fermi, who didn't commit that mistake, made the world's first controlled nuclear chain reaction in 1942, the critical first step toward making a bomb form of such a reaction.)

The British challenged Groves to cite even the slightest bit of hard evidence to support his conviction of an imminent German atomic bomb. Groves admitted he didn't have any but went on to propound an interesting conclusion: since there was no evidence, that meant the German bomb was a certitude. The very paucity of evidence suggested watertight security to prevent any leakage of the secret.*

When the British argued with him, Groves would simply repeat, "Well, you can't be *sure.*" Actually, thanks to GRIFFIN, the British were, but just to be absolutely positive, they assigned one of the young, bright physicists attached to the Tube Alloys Project to assess the GRIFFIN material scientifically and decide if it was absolutely reliable. The scientist chosen for this task was named Alan Nunn May, and he just happened to be a KGB asset already providing details of Tube Alloys to Moscow. Now he began paying extra dividends. Not only did the Russians discover that the Germans had no hope of making a bomb, they also learned that the Americans, convinced of the threat of a German bomb, were dead set on making their own.

At this point, Soviet intelligence made a dramatic decision. Since the German bomb would not come to pass, the only real potential for one was in the British-American project. Only the two allies, clearly, had the kind of resources necessary to build atomic weapons. Therefore, Soviet intelligence would ignore the German program and concentrate all efforts on the British-American project. Put simply, the threat of an American atomic bomb—and the kind of postwar leverage it would provide for the "main enemy"—represented something much more serious

---

* Groves came up with the idea of kidnapping Werner Heisenberg as a means of crippling the German bomb. The OSS, which was supposed to carry out the operation during a Heisenberg scientific lecture in Switzerland, abandoned the idea but sent one of its agents, the former Red Sox catcher-turned-spy Moe Berg, to infiltrate the lecture. Berg, a learned man who reputedly spoke nine languages ("And couldn't hit in any of them," a teammate once sourly remarked), was armed with a gun, with which he was to assassinate Heisenberg if the physicist began discussing "significant developments" in nuclear weapons physics. Since Berg knew nothing of physics, how he was supposed to understand what Heisenberg was talking about remains unclear. In any event, he decided not to shoot him.

than the thin possibility of a German bomb. A maximum effort was ordered: uncover the secrets of the Allied bomb so that the Soviet Union could keep pace. It was code-named Operation CANDY.

Like a huge machine clanking into operation, the Soviet foreign intelligence establishment got down to work. In Britain, the KGB's star mole, Donald Maclean, was ordered to produce anything he could find on British-American discussions about the bomb (he produced a gem: a 60-page top secret report on what the British and Americans had jointly decided). The KGB also recruited Bruno Pontecorvo, an emigré Italian Communist physicist whose great value was a close friendship with fellow emigré scientist Enrico Fermi, a connection that provided the Russians with the critically important intelligence about Fermi's successful nuclear reaction experiment in 1942.

Meanwhile, KGB and GRU agents based in Canada, where much subsidiary work on the bomb was going on, quickly cranked up a dozen Canadian Communists who ferreted out details on such vital technical secrets as the gaseous diffusion process used to produce weapons-grade plutonium. The Russians got a bonus when Alan Nunn May was assigned to the Canadian end of the bomb program, from which position he provided the Russians with an actual sample of processed uranium.

But it was in the United States that Operation CANDY reached full fruition, largely because of the efforts of five highly talented intelligence officers:

GREGORY KHEIFETZ: *Rezident* in San Francisco, Kheifetz had been a student at the Massachusetts Institute of Technology (MIT) in 1939, giving him a sound grasp of nuclear physics. He had carefully cultivated a wide range of contacts with Communist sympathizers in the American scientific community. Those contacts now paid off: Kheifetz was able to infiltrate the Radiation Laboratory at Berkeley, center of U.S. research on atomic energy and prime recruiting ground for the Manhattan Project (its director, Robert Oppenheimer, became head of the project). Thanks to three assets working at the lab, Kheifetz in late 1941 was able to inform Moscow of the scope of the American bomb project, noting that the commitment of resources was so great, the Americans obviously were certain they could succeed.

VASSILI and ELIZABETH ZARUBIN: *Rezident* in Washington, D.C., under diplomatic cover, Vassili Zarubin was in overall charge of Operation CANDY in the United States. His wife, Elizabeth, a topflight KGB agent fluent in five languages with extensive contacts among American Communists, recruited scientists sympathetic to her argument that the Soviet Union, an ally, deserved to share the atomic bomb. She recruited PERSEUS, a leading scientist involved in the project (his identity has never been revealed by the KGB), and handled Klaus Fuchs, an emigré German scientist and Communist who had been working for the KGB in Britain when he was assigned to Tube Alloys. He was shifted to work at Los Alamos, where he provided the Zarubins with detailed technical intelligence on the bomb's construction—intelligence that proved crucial in helping build the Soviet Union's first atomic bomb.

GAIK OVAKIMIAN: A top KGB operative working under cover as the AMTORG (Soviet trade organization) representative in New York, Ovakimian was considered a recruiting genius. He had enlisted a long roster of American Communists during the 1930s to steal American technology. He shifted them into atomic espionage and discovered that two of his assets, Julius and Ethel Rosenberg, had a relative who worked at Los Alamos. The relative, Ethel's brother David Greenglass, had a low-ranking technical job, but it was a critical one: he made molds for the bomb's unique implosion design, one of the project's most closely guarded secrets.

ANATOLI YATSKOV: Another top KGB agent based in New York, Yatskov also had extensive numbers of recruits among American Communists, especially several with U.S. government jobs. He was able to provide the KGB with important insights on the scope of the Manhattan Project, including production facilities for its uranium requirements (which allowed the Russians to estimate how many bombs the Americans were capable of producing).

By 1944 the Manhattan Project had been so thoroughly penetrated by Operation CANDY, there was virtually nothing the Russians didn't know. Moscow had received 286 top secret documents stolen directly from the project's nerve center; combined with the intelligence provided by nearly two hundred assets, Operation CANDY's coverage was complete.

But at the very moment of triumph, disaster struck. It came from a direction the Russians never anticipated—their radios. As they now discovered, the burden of radioing that vast pile of material to Moscow had overtaxed the cipher clerks. In the urgent press of sending vital intelligence, the clerks had made mistakes. On some occasions, they committed the sin of using the same onetime pad twice, on other occasions they had resorted to simple ciphers to transmit material more quickly, and on still other occasions they had sloppily included too much detail about various agents and assets. The American and British communications intelligence establishments, retargeted in 1945 against the Russians, began to break into that vast pile of wartime Soviet intelligence communications.

Soon, the dimensions of Operation CANDY were exposed. Fuchs was caught, as was one of Zarubin's key couriers, Harry Gold. The KGB sought to evacuate as many assets as possible; it succeeded in getting Lona Cohen and her husband out, but the Rosenbergs were caught before they could get their fake passports. Bruno Pontecorvo was able to flee, but Fuchs (who confessed) and Alan Nunn May were arrested.

To make matters worse, a GRU cipher clerk named Igor Gouzenko defected in Ottawa, Canada, with 110 ciphered telegrams that provided further breaks into the Operation CANDY traffic. The entire Canadian end of the operation was exposed, along with other assets in the United States.

Thanks to diplomatic immunity, the Zarubins and the other top Soviet intelligence agents were able to return to Moscow as Operation CANDY crashed around them. They were greeted with some coolness at KGB headquarters, known as Moscow Center, which blamed their poor cipher security for the disaster. As senior KGB and GRU officials never tired of reminding them, the vast network Soviet intelligence had created to steal the atomic bomb would have come in handy for future operations, but it now lay in ruins. It would take Moscow many years to reconstruct a similar network (although they never succeeded in doing so).

The real burden of Operation CANDY's demise, however, was borne by the Communists who had so enthusiastically thrown themselves into the service of Soviet intelligence at its hour of greatest need. Their treason, now exposed, removed any political credibility they had. They would be shattered in the fury of the Cold War witch-hunts that destroyed American communism forever and, to a lesser extent, its British and Canadian counterparts.

In the end, there was a curious, though significant, footnote to Operation CANDY. It came at an English estate where Heisenberg and other German nuclear scientists were interned in the spring of 1945. The Germans assumed they were there to have their brains picked by the Americans, British, and Russians. To their shock, however, nobody made any attempt to find out what they knew. There was an even greater shock to come: on August 7 they heard a radio report of the atomic bomb that dropped on Hiroshima.

At that moment, the Germans realized they were bit players, not stars, in the century's greatest scientific drama. As Heisenberg noted, history had passed them by. The power of science, now the arbiter of national destinies, had moved into other hands. "And God help us all," he said.

11

Black Tom

The German Sabotage Operation
1915–1917

Blowing up America

It was an unseasonably cool 74 degrees in New York City during the predawn hours of Saturday, July 29, 1916, climaxing a week of uncharacteristically beautiful weather. Delightedly surprised by the interruption in the city's usual steamy summers, many New Yorkers planned to spend the next day outside—visiting the playground of Coney Island or watching baseball games involving one of the city's three professional teams.

The newspapers coming off the presses early that morning were full of news about the war raging in Europe, but most readers would focus their attention on accounts of the most exciting baseball season in years. There would be stories about an outfielder named Casey Stengel of the Brooklyn Robins (later the Dodgers), who the previous day had hit an eighth-inning triple at Ebbets Field to defeat the St. Louis Cardinals, and the big Saturday game at the Polo Grounds between the Giants and the Pittsburgh Pirates, featuring the great Pirates shortstop Honus Wagner.

At Black Tom, a huge storage area on a promontory jutting out into upper New York Bay from the New Jersey side near the Statue of Liberty, several night watchmen of the National Dock and Storage Company made their rounds. They checked the large piles of artillery shells, rifle ammunition, and boxes of gunpowder stored there, awaiting shipment the next day to the battlefields of Europe. There were millions of tons of explosives covering every inch of Black Tom's 45 acres, the output of American arms factories turning a tidy profit supplying Great Britain, France, and Russia with the tools of war.

There was no public outcry about this vast tinderbox only five miles from one of the most densely populated areas on earth. Arms factories working around the clock were keeping a lot of men employed, and the Port of New York was enjoying a land-office business. The war meant prosperity to the arsenal of America, and nobody was about to criticize prosperity. To be sure, most Americans, like President Woodrow Wilson, thought the war an abomination, but since the United States was firmly neutral, there was no possibility of Americans becoming involved. Safe behind a 3,000-mile-wide ocean, there was no harm in turning a profit while Europeans were killing each other.

But at 2:08 A.M., the war came to America.

A tremendous blast suddenly erupted at Black Tom, turning night into day. Shock waves from the blast shattered windows in Manhattan, shrapnel struck the Statue of Liberty, and large holes were blown in the sides of buildings at Ellis Island, the immigrant gateway. The Brooklyn Bridge swayed. People as far south as Maryland were awakened by the sound of the blast.

In Manhattan, people thought the end of the world had come. Thrown out of their beds amid the sound of breaking glass, they rushed into the streets, trying to understand what had happened. They saw what appeared to be a huge fire to the south, on the New Jersey shore. As they watched, they heard several, much more subdued, explosions, but twenty minutes later there was another huge blast. Tall buildings shivered like saplings in the wind. Then it was quiet. To the south, huge fires were raging, sending up mile-wide columns of smoke.

At dawn, authorities began to get some sense of what had happened. Black Tom's piles of ammunition had blown up in a stupendous blast, reducing the vast storage facility to piles of ashes and pieces of twisted steel. Miraculously, only two people—both night watchmen at Black Tom—had been killed; another 38 persons had been injured, most of them Manhattan residents cut by flying glass.

It took more than a day to put out the fires. By then the fire marshals, industrial explosives experts, and others who had come to look at the blast site deduced that some sort of errant spark, or perhaps a stray bolt of lightning, had ignited the ammunition. Angry New York City officials were assured that in view of the explosion, perhaps it was not such a good idea to store ammunition in the open at a place like Black Tom. New, safer storage facilities would be constructed, the officials were told, and something like Black Tom would never happen again.

Gradually, Black Tom faded from public consciousness, replaced by other diversions in that glorious summer of 1916. But the executives of the Lehigh Valley Railroad were not about to forget so easily; having lost millions when their freight cars, tracks, and switching facilities were vaporized at Black Tom, they were determined to find out the cause of the explosion. If they could prove that the National Dock and Storage Company had been negligent in some way, that would allow a civil court suit to recover the railroad's losses.

A team of private detectives hired by the railroad went to work and within days heard reports that the watchmen at Black Tom had the habit of lighting fires at night to drive away the clouds of mosquitos that plagued them. But eyewitnesses in New Jersey who lived near Black Tom said they saw no such fires the night of the explosion; they saw only a small fire in a boxcar resting on a track in the middle of Black Tom. That made no sense. The detectives tracked down every watchman who had ever worked at Black Tom. Some admitted the practice of lighting fires in barrels along the shore to combat mosquitos, but all of them were puzzled about the report of a boxcar fire. They were very careful to keep the antimosquito fires away from explosives, lighting them in big steel barrels as close to the water as possible. Nobody would light a fire in a boxcar with all those shells piled around.

The detectives got a break—and an answer they weren't expecting—when they tracked down a man who had worked as a night watchman at Black Tom but quit several months before the explosion. An Irish immigrant, he at first claimed to know nothing about the event, but the detectives quickly perceived that he was a drunk. They took him out to a bar, and after plying him with a few straight whiskies, they found he was much more talkative. He began boasting of all the money he had made from the explosion, claiming he was part of what he began to call "the plot," and then he told the detectives, "It was the *Jairmans* what did it." He went on to outline a fantastic plot involving a group of German spies, their plan to blow up Black Tom as a means of intimidating U.S. arms manufacturers from supplying the Allied powers in the war, secret meetings at a Manhattan brownstone, lavish spending to recruit anti-British Irish immigrants, bribery of watchmen to find out Black Tom's security arrangements, and, finally, a team of crack German saboteurs who had planted bombs at Black Tom, almost blowing themselves up in the process.

It sounded like lurid spy fiction, but the detectives did some more digging, sufficient to convince them that the drunken watchman was probably telling the truth: Black Tom had been sabotaged. The railroad was not entirely thrilled by the news, although there was still hope of using the revelations to make a case for lax security by the storage company. But when the detectives returned to the watchman to get an affidavit from him, he was gone. Neighbors reported that he had left with some "German men." Subsequently, he disappeared.

It would take another 63 years before final confirmation of the truth the railroad detectives first suspected. And it would require almost that much time for the full meaning of the Black Tom explosion to become clear.

Black Tom represented a high-water mark of sorts for German intelligence in the United States during World War I. But the spectacular sabotage operation, conceived and carried out by Germany's best agents, was also an unmitigated disaster for the Germans. In one spectacular fireworks display, German intelligence self-immolated and guaranteed it could not succeed in the mission to which it originally had been assigned. There were any number of serious consequences for the Germans from Black Tom, not the least of which was a corrosive effect on American public opinion; Black Tom began a reversal of American popular attitudes that was to culminate, finally, in an American declaration of war—the one event in World War I that ensured Germany's defeat.

For the immigrant Americans recruited to aid the Germans in this disaster, the consequences were also severe: a renewed native distrust of "hyphenated Americans" and a hardening of the political divisions of their homeland. There were also consequences for American society: the creation of America's first internal security apparatus, accompanied by one of the most serious threats to civil liberties in the nation's history.

All this stemmed from the actions of a small band of men whose background and outlook made what happened inevitable.

Nine days after the outbreak of World War I, Count Johann von Bernstoff, German ambassador to the United States, was summoned to a secret conference in Berlin at the Foreign Ministry. Von Bernstoff was informed that *Dienst III-B,* the intelligence section of the German General Staff, had decided on a major intelligence operation in the United States. It would have four main objectives: (1) keep the Americans neutral, (2) run extensive propaganda operations to counter the anticipated British propaganda offensive, (3) collect intelligence on arms shipments to the Allied nations from American ports, and (4) sabotage those shipments whenever possible through recruited assets whose connection to Germany would be disguised.

Von Bernstoff would be in overall charge of this operation, but he would spend most of his time working the corridors of power to keep the Americans out of the European war. For the remaining tasks, *III-B* would send some of its best operatives to America. They would be paid out of a $15 million budget—an incredible sum in those days—under von Bernstoff's control.

The agents who subsequently showed up in America represented a variegated lot that gave von Bernstoff pause. Among them was Karl Boy-Ed, a naval officer who had drifted into intelligence work—mainly, von Bernstoff discovered, because as a fanatic German patriot, he thought espionage would be of greater help to the Fatherland. Boy-Ed's definition of espionage seemed to center on blowing things up.

A similar outlook dominated the leading agent among the group, a Prussian cavalry officer named Franz von Papen. Like his naval colleague, von Papen seemed obsessed with sabotage, despite von Bernstoff's warnings that such operations in the United States were a bad idea, since they would adversely affect American public opinion. Von Papen hardly seemed to be listening.

Horst von der Goltz, another member of the group, made von Papen look like a Sunday school teacher. Fairly seething with fury against the hated British, von der Goltz immediately announced a plan to recruit large numbers of Irish immigrants and carry out an invasion of Canada. Von Bernstoff firmly quashed the idea, but he had the sense there would be further trouble with von der Goltz.

While the ambassador had fewer qualms about two other members of the group, he wondered how such people had been recruited by German intelligence. One, Heinrich Albert, was sent to America under cover as commercial attaché at the German embassy, with instructions to serve as paymaster. Von Bernstoff discovered that Albert was an absentminded bumbler who could barely dress himself each morning. Similarly, he was not impressed with Martha Held, a beautiful, buxom opera singer who was to occupy an expensive Manhattan brownstone secretly purchased by German intelligence. The plan was for her to live in the brownstone, which would serve as a safe house for intelligence operations in New York, particularly those directed against British shipping. Von Bernstoff wondered about this arrangment: Held, with her booming German voice and her habit of practicing Wagnerian choruses each night, would certainly stand out in the neighborhood, not to mention the fact she spoke not a word of English.

Nevertheless, the German spies initially scored some successes. Von Papen set up an operation that recruited waterfront dregs to apply for passports, which he then altered for use by several thousand German military reservists who had been trapped in the United States by the outbreak of war because they could not return through the British naval blockade. With passports certifying their status as neutral Americans, they were free to travel.

Boy-Ed ran an operation that smuggled deadly cultures of glanders, a contagious horse disease; they were used to infect horses and mules scheduled for shipment to Britain and France. Meanwhile, the energetic von der Goltz rounded up chemists who developed explosives in the shape of cigars and lumps of coal. Equipped with hidden timers, they were dropped into the holds of ships bound for Britain; far out at sea, the bombs would explode, setting off fires. A number of ships disappeared on the high seas this way.

However impressive these first results, *Dienst III-B* decreed in 1915 that much greater efforts were needed to cut off the Allied arms pipeline from American factories. Over von Bernstoff's objections, a full-scale sabotage operation was ordered.

Von Papen, the old Prussian cavalry officer, led the charge. Spending lavishly, he and the other Germans went recruiting among America's large Irish immigrant population, promising them the opportunity of defeating the hated oppressor of their

Franz von Papen, the infamous intriguer for German intelligence, in U.S. custody in 1945 following the collapse of Nazi Germany. Von Papen organized large-scale operations in the United States during World War I, including the spectacular Black Tom explosion. (*United States Army*)

Irish homeland. The Germans dangled before them an even more enticing reward, a promise of a free and independent Ireland following the British defeat.

Seduced by such promises, hundreds of Irish-Americans, joined by similar numbers of German-Americans convinced they were duty-bound to aid the Fatherland, enlisted in the crusade to choke off Allied supplies. First, they targeted the Welland Canal, intending to blow up the waterway that linked Lakes Ontario and Erie and was used to move shiploads of iron ore and other vital raw materials for the arms factories. They weren't able to penetrate the military security that guarded Welland, though, so they shifted their attention to an even more lucrative target: Black Tom.

Thanks to the many Irish immigrant workers at Black Tom, the Germans learned the place had virtually no security, save for a few watchmen. Relatively little would be needed to blow it up, since Black Tom included huge assembly areas where gunpowder and explosives were mixed before shipment to Europe; with all that gunpowder lying around, even a small bomb would set off a conflagration.

Two veteran saboteurs in the German ring, Lothar Witzke and Kurt Jahnke, posed as workers and carried out a reconnaissance of Black Tom, a mission that convinced them the lack of security would make blowing up the place that much easier. They collected a cache of explosives, which they hid inside the brownstone where Held lived. The same brownstone was used for nightly strategy meetings, at which the Germans would meet with several Irish-Americans they had recruited to help them in the actual sabotage operation. The Irish dreaded these meetings, for they were forced to endure the night's entertainment—Martha Held singing Wagnerian opera while accompanying herself on the piano.

The actual operation went off without a hitch. In the dark, early morning hours of July 29, 1916, Witzke and Jahnke, with two Irish assets, rowed a boat loaded with time bombs and incendiary devices to Black Tom. Easily evading the watchmen, they planted the bombs and then began furiously rowing away. But the resulting explosion was greater than anticipated, and the saboteurs were almost drowned when the shock wave sent water crashing over their boat. Reaching shore, they stopped to watch the results of their handiwork.

That spectacular was followed by another, at the Canadian Car and Foundry Company plant in Kingsland, New Jersey. The plant, which was turning out 3 million artillery shells a month for the British, had a number of Irish immigrant workers. They were recruited by the Germans to plant bombs at the factory. One night, 500,000 shells and the entire factory went up in a mighty blast. There were no casualties.

Berlin was delighted by these sabotage feats, but the American network's luck was about to run out. For one thing, word that the Black Tom blast was sabotage had leaked out; combined with the sabotage at the Kingsland plant, the news filled American newspapers with scare stories about armies of German saboteurs prowling the land. No citizen was safe.

That was bad enough, but then the Germans committed an unbelievably stupid error. It was made by Heinrich Albert, who traveled to New York with a briefcase full of money to pay the assets of the saboteurs, along with detailed lists of names and plans for future sabotage operations. Traveling on the elevated subway line one morning, Albert fell asleep. When he awoke near his stop he hurriedly left the train without his briefcase. It was found and turned over to police, who then gave it to the Department of Justice.

British propaganda had a field day, for there was no denying the evidence in Albert's briefcase. Infuriated, President Wilson ordered Albert out of the country, along with von Papen and Boy-Ed. Other members of the ring fled to Mexico, including Martha Held, who abandoned the Manhattan brownstone but helpfully left the keys on the dining room table for the next tenant.

Ambassador von Bernstoff, having worked so long and so hard to convince the Americans of his country's peaceful intentions, now watched all that work go up in smoke. He frantically tried to repair the damage, but there was little he could do in the face of massive publicity about German nefariousness in the United States. Worse, he could see the hardening of U.S. public opinion toward Germany and the growing use of the word "Huns" in America's newspapers to describe his countrymen.

Berlin seemed to have learned nothing from the disaster, for the shattered American network was reformed in Mexico in 1917 and ordered to foment a revolution and create a government that would invade the United States. This crackpot idea found favor at the highest levels of the German government, and Foreign Minister Arthur Zimmermann actually put it in a message to the Mexican government. Zimmermann offered German military help for Mexico to "recover lost territory," defined as California, New Mexico, Arizona, and much of Texas. British cryptanalysts intercepted and cracked the message, then released it publicly. Two weeks after the notorious Zimmermann telegram was released, President Wilson asked Congress for a declaration of war against Germany.

There was another, more subtle, effect of the German intelligence disaster. It set off an obsession within the American government about the "enemy within," the German-Americans and Irish-Americans who had lent aid and comfort to the Germans. In quick order the Espionage Act was passed, mandating death for those aiding a foreign power in event of war, and a whole new internal security machinery came into being. Among its components was an obscure Justice Department agency called the Bureau of Investigation. Expanded and reinvigorated under the new leadership of a department bureaucrat named J. Edgar Hoover, it was renamed the Federal Bureau of Investigation and began to enforce new laws against so-called internal enemies. That category was expanded to include Bolsheviks, anarchists, and Socialists, and by the end of the war, American civil liberties had virtually disappeared. The courts later redressed the balance, but the problem of civil rights and internal security would remain a difficult one for decades to come.

For Irish-Americans, the legacy of the German sabotage operation was even more troubling. Discredited by the involvement of some of their compatriots with the Germans, they lost any influence to affect "the troubles" that afflicted their homeland and led to its division. The problem persists to this day.

What happened that Saturday morning at Black Tom also lingered for a long time in the form of a legal knot that took more than sixty years to untangle. After the war, the U.S. and German governments set up a mixed claims commission to pay out claims for damage arising from the war. Germany paid $2.5 million to relatives of those Americans killed in the sinking of the *Lusitania,* but it balked when confronted by some $23 million in claims from corporations over losses in the Black Tom explosion. To the anger of American delegates, the Germans denied they had sabotaged Black Tom and refused to pay a cent.

The Americans produced overwhelming evidence that the Germans had blown up Black Tom, but the Germans still wouldn't budge, arguing that since their own intelligence records had been destroyed, they had no way to verify the American records. The case dragged on until 1936, when a compromise was struck: Germany would pay 50 percent of the claims. But a year later the Nazi government repudiated the settlement.

In 1941 some of the Black Tom claims were paid out of German funds seized in U.S. banks. The rest was not paid until 1979, when the West German government quietly settled the case. Since all the original claimants were long dead, the money was paid to their estates.

In the process, the West Germans admitted "with regret" that Germany was responsible for the Black Tom explosion. It remains unclear what the West Germans meant by "regret." Perhaps they had in mind Franz von Papen, who returned to Germany after Black Tom, went into politics, and in 1932 engineered the deal that made Adolf Hitler chancellor of Germany. No more regrettable development can be imagined.

12

A Bullet for General Polyakov

Operation TOP HAT
1959–1985

The CIA penetrates Moscow

Like an eighteenth-century minuet, the dance of the spies was slow and highly ritualized. FBI counterintelligence liked to call it "dropping the handkerchief," the process of indicating interest to a Soviet intelligence agent. The signals were deliberately subtle: we know you're a spy, and if you're unhappy with your lot in life, we're ready to help out. Either the spy "picked up the handkerchief" or let it lie in the path, pretending he or she hadn't noticed.

The dance involving the man the FBI called TOP HAT began in October 1959 at the United Nations (UN) headquarters in New York. The Soviet mission was crawling with KGB and GRU agents, mostly young up-and-comers cutting their teeth on their first major overseas assignment. There wasn't much in the way of hot intelligence to be found around the UN, but it served as good training ground for agents destined later to handle much more intricate and dangerous assignments.

TOP HAT was Dmitri F. Polyakov, and in targeting him, the FBI was seeking to hook a very big fish. Clearly, he was a rising star. In 1951 a thirty-year-old GRU operative, he was first posted to New York at the Soviet UN Mission under cover as a diplomat assigned to the UN staff. His relative youth in an important overseas assignment, along with heavy responsibilities (obtaining U.S. technological secrets), marked him as a man being groomed by the GRU for bigger and greater things. By 1956, when Polyakov finished his tour of duty at the UN and returned to Moscow, the pervasive FBI surveillance of the Soviet intelligence station at the UN listed him as one of the GRU stars who bore special watching.

Three years later, when Polyakov returned to the UN for another tour of duty, intense FBI surveillance of him turned up something interesting: he was becoming disillusioned with the Soviet system. Mostly, the FBI discovered, Polyakov's disillusionment centered on money. Despite his elevation to colonel, climaxing a series of promotions that indicated a meteoric career rise in the GRU, Polyakov was paid a paltry salary of $10,000 a year, most of which he had to return to Soviet authorities. This was standard practice in the Soviet system, but it left Polyakov to live like a pauper, unable even to buy presents for his wife and three children living in Moscow.

At the same time, Polyakov was increasingly struck by the disparity he could see every day on the streets of New York. While Americans earning even modest salaries could afford to feed their families and enjoy some of America's consumer cornucopia, Polyakov's wife each morning had to stand on a long line to buy bread. But the Soviet Communist party and government bigwigs didn't stand on line; they had special state stores where they could buy anything with the special "gold rubles" (as distinct from ordinary Russians' worthless paper rubles) paid to them as a mark of their membership in the elite.

Operatives like Polyakov were expected to endure a penurious existence until they were able to work their way into the upper ranks of the elite, there to enjoy the luxuries of life on the gold ruble. But Polyakov had no intention of following the standard career track. Instead, he resolved that this system, which he became convinced was ruining Russia, would have to be destroyed. And he was a man in a position to wreak a lot of damage.

Polyakov made his intentions known early in 1960 when two FBI counterintelligence agents deliberately made themselves known to him. Nothing was said about espionage during this encounter, which occurred one morning on a city street while the Russian was out for a stroll. As if they were two old college friends meeting a classmate after many years, the agents simply exchanged pleasantries, chatted about their respective families, and then told Polyakov to meet them again if he had any "problem" he wanted to discuss. Polyakov answered noncommittally, but significantly enough, he did not spurn the approach; or, as Soviet intelligence regulations required, under pain of death, report it to his superiors.

In other words, the FBI had dropped the handkerchief, and Polyakov had picked it up. A short while later Polyakov made his move. At a diplomatic reception he approached an American diplomat and told him he wanted to talk to the FBI.

There now began one of the more significant chapters in Cold War espionage, a saga that would go on for another twenty-five years. It would become the centerpiece of a great subterranean war between Soviet and American intelligence. Fundamentally, it was a war of traitors, as each side sought to induce treason on the other side. At no time in recorded history had treason been raised to so pervasive an operational art form, with traitors betraying other traitors, false traitors deployed to entrap real traitors, and a supreme political cynicism reigning, which dictated that the word "treason" applied only to people the other side recruited; the ones your side recruited were "patriots."

The war would finally end in the collapse of the Soviet Union, but there were many casualties along the way. Among the losses was TOP HAT—betrayed, ironically enough, by another traitor.

Polyakov looked almost pained. No, he informed his FBI listeners coldly, he didn't want any money. "I am not doing this for you," he said. "I am doing this for my country."

Apparently concerned about offending his hosts, Polyakov hastily added that there was one material indication of the FBI's gratitude he would be happy to accept. He was a passionate collector of antique and custom-made guns. One day he had seen a beautiful custom-made shotgun in the window of a fancy Fifth Avenue store. The price was far beyond his modest means, but he often returned to that store window to stare longingly at the masterpiece of the gunsmith's art. He would be delighted if the FBI would secure it as a gift for him.

Some $6,000 of the taxpayers' money was subsequently spent for this token of American appreciation. As a grateful Polyakov was to prove almost immediately, that money would turn out to be one of the wiser investments in espionage history.

During the meetings with TOP HAT in safe houses around New York City, the FBI learned it had recruited an asset of pure gold. Polyakov's biography told the story: the son of a Ukrainian bookkeeper, he served as an artillery officer during World War II, when his bravery and leadership won him a postwar appointment to the prestigious Frunze Military Academy, the Soviet Union's West Point. A star pupil, he was recruited by the GRU, which plucked the cream of the academy's students for intelligence careers. After his first overseas posting at the UN in 1951, he subsequently was assigned to Berlin, one of Soviet intelligence's most important stations. There, he ran illegals into West Germany, operations so successful he was a full colonel by 1959, on a short list to become one of the GRU's future leaders.

When Polyakov got down to business, he had very disturbing news for his FBI handlers. "We have penetrated your military," he said. "Everything is an open book to us. There are traitors who are helping us." He then blew the GRU's prime assets in the American military.

JACK E. DUNLAP: A drunken Army sergeant recruited strictly for money, Dunlap had become a chauffeur-courier for the supersecret National Security Agency (NSA). He provided NSA documents to the GRU, which photographed the papers with special high-speed cameras and returned them without any delay in Dunlap's courier schedule. Completely unsuspected, Dunlap had been letting the Russians peek into the NSA for years, in return for lavish payments that allowed him a lifestyle of fancy powerboats, fast cars, and an expensive mistress.

WILLIAM H. WHALEN: One of Soviet intelligence's most valuable recruitments in the United States, Whalen was an Army lieutenant colonel who in 1959 served as an adviser to the Joint Chiefs of Staff, a priceless vantage point from which to provide intelligence. Like Dunlap, Whalen betrayed his country strictly for money; in return for nearly $400,000, he gave the GRU details on American nuclear weapons, operational plans for U.S. forces in the event of war, and American intelligence estimates of Soviet military capabilities, along with anything else of interest that came across his desk.

NELSON DRUMMOND: As in the case of Dunlap, Drummond had a lowly military rank that belied his importance. A Navy yeoman, he nevertheless was involved in his service's top secret communications systems. Based at a naval communications center in London, Drummond had access to a wide range of top secret cables on Navy deployments and technical details of weapons systems and cipher systems. He betrayed them all for money. After Polyakov exposed him, the Pentagon had to invest several hundred million dollars to replace everything he had given away.

HERBERT W. BOECKENHAUPT: Still another low-ranking soldier with precious access, Boeckenhaupt was an Air Force staff sergeant who handled top secret communications. A mercenary traitor, he sold details of the Air Force's code and signaling systems and, most damaging of all, special cryptographic systems for the Strategic Air Command that were to be used in the event of world war.

As Polyakov hardly needed to point out, it was fortunate that the United States had not gone to war with the Soviet Union anytime during the late 1950s, because they would have lost it. The intelligence from Whalen and Boeckenhaupt alone meant that U.S. military plans amounted to an open book. The British wouldn't have done much better, Polyakov noted, for the GRU had recruited a man named Frank Bossard, researcher in the British guided missile industry, who for lavish payments revealed the details of all British missiles.

Any doubts that Polyakov might have been a GRU plant were removed when the FBI started investigating his revelations about GRU assets in the United States. He turned out to be absolutely right, and the FBI began knocking the assets off, one by one. They were to suffer varying fates for their treason: Dunlap committed suicide as agents began to close in, Whalen was murdered in prison after receiving a 40-year sentence, and Drummond and Boeckenhaupt were sentenced to long prison terms by a federal judiciary that traditionally regards treason as the most heinous of crimes. (Bossard was nailed by British counterintelligence and sentenced to a lengthy prison term.)

The FBI moved very carefully in these cases, for at all costs it had to conceal the role of TOP HAT in uncovering them. Through an elaborate set of ruses and false clues, the FBI succeeded in convincing the GRU that causes other than a traitor somewhere high in the ranks of the GRU were responsible for the loss of precious assets.

Such subterfuge was important not only to protect TOP HAT, but to prepare the ground for the next phase. In late 1962

A Soviet MIG-23 fighter on combat patrol, with air-to-air missiles beneath the wings. TOP HAT, among the CIA's best sources on the Soviet military, revealed how KGB thefts of U.S. technology enabled the Russians to develop this advanced fighter in a short period of time. (*Department of Defense*)

Polyakov, his tour of duty over, was to be transferred to new overseas postings. By law, the FBI cannot work in overseas intelligence operations, so control for Polyakov passed to the Central Intelligence Agency (CIA). Despite skepticism from CIA counterintelligence, which tended to regard all Soviet assets suspiciously, Polyakov quickly proved he was the genuine article.

First assigned to Rangoon, Polyakov—known to the CIA by his code names of BOURBON and GT/ACCORD—gushed top-grade intelligence. He provided everything the GRU knew from its unsurpassed data bank on Chinese and Vietnamese armed forces, details on the GRU's technology theft operations (revealing how advanced Soviet warplanes had incorporated stolen American technology), and his most sensational coup, inside details on the Sino-Soviet split. Polyakov's intelligence was so detailed, it played an essential role in the Nixon administration's decision to exploit the rift and forge the "opening" to China: the singular event that would lead to the ending of the Vietnam War.

By 1974 Polyakov was promoted to general, a career rise aided in no small part by the bits of intelligence the CIA fed him to bolster his bona fides. It was all part of a careful management plan to deflect any suspicion away from him while at the same time nurturing his career. Security precautions were extremely tight; when Polyakov was reassigned to Moscow in 1978, the CIA decided that dead drops or any other kind of direct contact with him would be too risky. Instead, they formulated an advanced piece of technology for their star asset. It was a special communications device, about the size of a medium-sized calculator, into which Polyakov could type up to 50 pages of intelligence. The device would automatically encrypt it, then transmit the intelligence in a 2.6-second burst. The procedure was highly secure: when Polyakov had something to send, he entered the information into the device, then simply took a bus headed for downtown Moscow. As the bus passed the U.S. embassy, Polyakov pressed a button on the device, which then transmitted to a special receiver at the embassy.

Such precaution was well worth the effort, for by 1980 Polyakov was the crown jewel in the CIA's roster of 11 assets in the Soviet Union. His reports already filled 25 filing cabinets at CIA headquarters, and there was more coming. Polyakov had access to internal military studies by the Soviet General Staff, which he was funneling to the CIA. Among other things, the CIA learned that the Russians finally had concluded there was no possibility of the Soviet Union achieving victory in a nuclear war.

By 1985 Polyakov had been a prime American asset for nearly twenty-five years, an unusually long period. Yet, despite the hemhorraging of Moscow's secrets and the destruction of its important assets in the West, not a hint of suspicion wafted anywhere near Polyakov. But on a January morning that year, an American traitor sat in a KGB safe house in Bogotá, Colombia, and uttered the words that were to destroy Polyakov: "They're cleaning your clock."

Even the most charitable evaluation would not hold Aldrich Ames in high regard. Plodding, unimaginative, lazy, and plagued with a bad drinking problem, Ames was not the kind of man any organization would be proud to have. Yet, despite these very real defects, Ames was a senior CIA officer.

There remains no plausible explanation of why such a man was to be promoted routinely in the course of a 32-year career to senior management positions. One explanation may lie in his antecedents: the son of Carleton Ames, himself an undistinguished CIA official, the man most often called Rick Ames joined the CIA in 1962, apparently relying on his father's coattails to find him a job when he revealed an unsuitability to do anything else with his life.

That old-boy network probably also explains why superiors—many of them friends of the elder Ames—routinely gave him good job performance evaluations, despite his lackluster achievements. Somehow, these evaluations overlooked such incidents as the time when, assigned to the Rome station, Ames was found passed out dead drunk in a gutter.

Fellow CIA agents regarded Ames as an inept clown, a verdict that persisted through a variety of foreign postings. Aware of the contempt, Ames became embittered; it took the form of a smoldering resentment, accompanied by a growing arrogance that he was smarter than any fellow agent. As things turned out, this state of mind was to prove very dangerous.

In 1983 Ames underwent an experience that was to change his life. Assigned to Mexico City, he recruited Maria del Rosario Casas, a cultural attaché at the Colombian embassy. Rosario also happened to be an asset of the Cuban DGI, and Ames had been assigned the task of doubling her on the presumption that she had become disillusioned with Castro communism. In one of his rare successes, he managed to win her over, but in the process he committed the unpardonable case officer's sin of becoming romantically involved with his asset. Ames was married at the time, and the affair soon wrecked his marriage. The divorce was bitter, and Ames found himself with a new wife to support (he and Rosario married in 1985) and alimony payments on a $54,000 annual salary.

Whether it was the pressure of money or a recruitment by his new wife that pushed him over the edge will never be known, but in 1985 Ames approached the KGB and offered to betray whatever he knew. At first glance, despite the fact that he was a CIA agent, Ames's offer did not promise great benefits to the KGB. After all, he did not have access to much the Russians would want to know. But it had long been KGB practice to be patient, so the Russians began lavishing large amounts of cash on Ames on the theory that such largesse might eventually pay off if he were to achieve some kind of position.

Only a year later the KGB was rewarded for its patience far beyond anything it could have hoped for: Ames, incredibly, was named as chief of the counterintelligence division of the CIA's Soviet Division. Immediately, given the very nature of his job, Ames had access to every secret about CIA operations in the Soviet Union, most importantly, the names of assets.

Accustomed to a long string of uninterrupted success in recruiting Soviet assets, the CIA was all the more shocked in 1985 when everything seemed to go wrong at once. One after the other, the assets were disappearing, the unmistakable sign they had been blown and were being ground up in a KGB counter-intelligence process that almost invariably resulted in a bullet in their heads. Among the victims was Dmitri Polyakov.

Simultaneously, the successful FBI recruitment efforts were also failing. The Bureau was most disturbed about two diplomats it had managed to recruit at the Soviet embassy in Washington, Valeri Martynov and Sergei Motorin. No sooner had the FBI routinely notified the CIA of their recruitment than they were suddenly recalled to Moscow and executed. The FBI began to think the unthinkable: was there a KGB mole at the highest levels of the CIA?

The very same thought occurred to the CIA, but just as suspicion deepened, what appeared to be the answer arrived in the person of KGB agent Vitali Yurchenko, who defected in Rome. Yurchenko, a high official in KGB counterintelligence, blew a number of important KGB assets in the United States, most importantly Edward Lee Howard. A former CIA agent who had been assigned a posting at the Moscow station, Howard found his assignment withdrawn when a CIA polygraph test uncovered drug use and other character defects. Howard, who was fired, then approached the KGB and sold them everything he knew.

Howard fled to the Soviet Union before he could be arrested, but everything now made sense: obviously, he had been responsible for all those CIA and FBI failures. But as the failures continued, it was clear there had to be another KGB source somewhere in the CIA. For one thing, the CIA learned that one of its prime assets, a senior official in KGB counterintelligence, had been arrested and executed. Howard did not know about that source. Nor did he know about Oleg Gordievski, a KGB agent who had been recruited by MI6 while he was serving as *rezident* in London. Gordievski, recalled to Moscow, managed to escape. When he reached safety, he warned MI6 and the CIA that the KGB apparently had a high-level CIA source.

Now began the dreary task of drawing up lists of all agents with access to such highly compartmentalized intelligence as the existence of Polyakov and Gordievski. Ames was on the list, but he made no move to deflect suspicion away from himself. In fact, he did everything but put up a neon sign advertising his treason. With the nearly $1.5 million provided by a grateful KGB for the betrayal of all 11 of the CIA's prime assets in the Soviet Union, Ames bought a $540,000 house, a Jaguar, and an entire catalog worth of consumer goodies. The conspicuous spending, normally a suspicious sign for a man earning $60,000 a year, bespoke an arrogance that he would never be caught. It might also explain how he was able to pass two polygraph tests.

But, inevitably, it would be only a matter of time before someone on the other side who knew about Ames would put his neck in the noose. Ames's moment came in 1989, when a KGB defector who worked in the agency's cipher section provided clues that pointed to a KGB source in the CIA, with the additional information that the source had met several times with his KGB control in a Bogotá, Colombia, safe house. A comparison of those dates with CIA vacation schedules turned up a match: those meetings coincided with Ames's vacations—when he traveled to Bogotá.

By 1991 an FBI surveillance began turning up prosecutable evidence that Ames was their man. Astonishingly, Ames was very careless, keeping incriminating documents around his house, along with computer disks containing copies of reports he had typed for the KGB. An FBI search of his house turned up documents showing he had received $2.7 million from the KGB, along with the promise of a beautiful riverside *dacha* when he finally retired from the CIA and settled in the Soviet Union.

Ames was finally arrested in 1993, along with his wife, who aided his treachery (he was sentenced to life in prison). Asked why he had never considered fleeing eastward when the big mole-hunt in the CIA began, he replied simply, "I'm an American, and I'll always be one." It was an eerie echo of what Polyakov had once said when he was urged to flee westward if the KGB began to close in on him. "No," he said. "I'm a Russian. I'll die a Russian."

A WILDERNESS
OF MIRRORS

"We've got a mole, Jim," says the old spymaster in John Le Carré's *Tinker, Tailor, Soldier, Spy,* and no word is more calculated to send a chill through an intelligence agency. Its meaning, involving a carefully calculated deep penetration into an opponent's innards, is unique to the espionage business.

Penetration operations are the staples of espionage fiction because they involve the savory elements of detective story and suspense drama, along with the timeless themes of trust, betrayal, and suspicion. In the real espionage world, penetration operations involve much more ambiguity than the plot lines of fiction, for such operations are rarely resolved to the certitude of absolute truth.

Typically, a penetration operation has a dual purpose. First, it is designed to get inside an enemy's inner councils to find out what he is thinking and planning. The second purpose, and the point at which things start to get complicated, is to mislead an enemy, either by causing him to misdirect his strength or by concealing the opponent's real purpose. Like an expanding maze, however, that goal can involve multiple layers of deception within other deceptions until the ambiguity becomes a thick fog.

Counterintelligence organizations can easily get lost in this maze, most evocatively described by James Angleton, former head of CIA counterintelligence, as a "wilderness of mirrors." Take, for example, the case of agent X who defects from the other side. She claims to be politically disillusioned and goes on to tell her new protectors that her country's leadership has decided its vast military might will be used for defensive purposes only. That could be true, but it might also be a deliberate lie, designed to conceal that country's hostile intentions and lull its opponents. But proving the case one way or the other leads into a dark thicket: intentions are difficult to discern, so there may be no final answer as to whether the defector was telling the truth—unless war breaks out. Absent a war, adherents of cutting a nation's military establishment will cite the defector's revelations as proof of their contention that the establishment is too large, while opponents will argue that the defector is a fake who is spreading disinformation.

Or take the case of agent Y. He is in charge of his intelligence agency's evaluations of another nation's equivalent, and he concludes that agency is weak and ineffectual and poses no threat to his country; they have no important sources. But a defector from the second country's intelligence service says that agent Y in fact is working for the other side, and his evaluations are deliberate distortions to conceal the existence of major assets. Agent Y denies it and says that the defector is actually a penetration agent assigned to sow discord in the intelligence agency and tie it up in knots. Like the famous logical paradox that begins, "All Thebans are liars," the knot will prove very difficult to unravel, if ever.

This kind of ambiguity is a recurrent theme in the four case studies that follow. The first concerns the most complex maze in espionage history, the 12-year-long "war of the moles" between the KGB and the CIA in the 1960s and 1970s, an event that inspired an entire library of espionage fiction. The other three studies concern, in turn, a famous humanitarian mission that became caught up in the complexities of Cold War espionage; a multilayered CIA penetration operation that ultimately involved four intelligence services and enough ambiguity to make it almost opaque; and a penetration by German intelligence of the highest levels of the U.S. government that was used by British intelligence to discredit the father of a future president of the United States.

13

The Mole War

The CIA-KGB Struggle
1961–1974

A death in Dallas

If Yuri Nosenko had any last-minute doubts about his decision to defect to the CIA that February of 1964, they were removed the moment he arrived at his new home. Mansion would be more like it: it was a huge CIA safe house on a sprawling Virginia estate, complete with indoor swimming pool and fully equipped gym.

From the harshness and deprivations of Soviet life, Nosenko had emerged into a world he had only been able to dream about. His every want attended to by a staff of servants, Nosenko spent part of his time each day in friendly debriefings with CIA officials. The atmosphere was collegial as Nosenko told them everything he knew about the operations of his former employer, the Second Chief Directorate of the KGB's First Department (foreign intelligence).

The CIA apparently had thought of everything to make its defector comfortable. He was provided with his favorite Cuban cigars and taken on regular trips to Baltimore and Washington, D.C., where he would spend a night with prostitutes provided by the CIA.

But a month later, just as Nosenko was becoming very fond of this existence, it suddenly ended one night, as though he had awakened from a pleasant dream. He was asleep just before dawn when he was roughly shaken awake by a man dressed in a black uniform who pressed a gun to his head. "Get up and get dressed," the man said. As he did so, Nosenko noticed three other men, also dressed in black uniforms, standing in the room.

They seized him, clapped handcuffs on his wrists, and dragged him outside, where he was pushed into the back of a truck. For five hours the truck drove in what seemed to be a circuitous route. Finally, it stopped in front of a nondescript house in a densely wooded area that to Nosenko appeared to be a world away from the mansion he had just left. (He didn't know he was now only 50 miles from that luxurious safe house.)

Taken inside, Nosenko was shoved into his new living quarters: a 12-foot by 12-foot makeshift cell, lit by a single lightbulb. The only furnishings were a stool, a metal cot, and a slop bucket. He was locked inside and left alone to figure out what had happened. Nosenko frantically paced his cell, trying to understand. Who were those men? Why was he being imprisoned?

Nosenko would not learn the answers for another three years. For all that time he would be a prisoner, enduring a nightmare of psychological torture, constant interrogations, and the terrifying realization that this horror might last for many years. He knew he was alone and forgotten; no one would come to his aid. He would die in that cell.

What happened to Nosenko would become one of the most shameful incidents in the history of American intelligence. A Soviet KGB defector was illegally imprisoned for three years, subjected to the kind of abuse forbidden by U.S. law, and deprived of even his most minimal rights as an immigrant.

The Nosenko episode was the low point in one of the darkest periods of Cold War espionage, a no-quarter underground war between the CIA and the KGB as they jockeyed for dominance. For 12 years a battle of double agents, triple agents, moles, and defectors raged. In the end, it was difficult to determine which side "won," a word that must be used advisedly in this context. Both sides were torn apart by the struggle, and both were to suffer lasting damage.

The war began when James Jesus Angleton discovered he had been suckered by Harold Adrian Russell Philby.

It was said that nobody loved the intricacies of the intelligence game more than Angleton, a man of considerable intellectual gifts who had decided to turn his mental powers to the arcane art of counterintelligence. Recruited into the OSS during World War II from Yale, where he ran a literary magazine and served as the campus's reigning student aesthete, Angleton found his life's mission in the OSS X-2 (counterintelligence) branch. By war's end, only twenty-eight years old, he had established a brilliant record rolling up German intelligence operations. Inevitably, he joined the CIA at its birth in 1947, and he quickly became the most noted of its charter members. As chief of CI (the new CIA's counterintelligence division), Angleton wielded great power thanks to his mandate to ensure the agency was not penetrated by the KGB. He reviewed all operations for their counterintelligence implications (vulnerability to penetration by the Soviets), saw all messages, oversaw all hiring and appointments, evaluated all incoming intelligence for possible deception material, and monitored CIA relations with other intelligence services, alert for any clues that a liaison officer from one of those services was attempting to obtain more intelligence from the CIA than he or she was entitled to.

It was this last function of Angleton's that in 1949 brought him into contact with the newly assigned MI6 station chief in Washington, Philby. As most often happens in such situations, both men began a subtle ritual, each one seeking to find out what the other side was *really* up to. British and American intelligence agencies had formed close bonds during the war, but as everybody involved understood, intelligence is a cynical business. The British were not about to tell their American cousins everything, and the Americans were not prepared to show all their cards, either.

Angleton and Philby, in addition to a close working relationship, also became social friends. Several times a week, they would have lunch together in a quiet Georgetown restaurant, there to ply each other with liquor (both were prodigious drinkers), hoping enough alcohol would induce a slip of the tongue. As experienced intelligence officers, they were each aware of the game the other was playing and occasionally would laugh uproariously at the sheer silliness of it all.

Angleton came to respect Philby's abilities and never doubted for a moment his loyalty to the Crown. In 1951, following the defection of Guy Burgess and Donald Maclean, some CIA officials began to suspect that Philby was the "third man" who had warned Maclean of his impending arrest and was himself a

KGB mole. Angleton vigorously defended Philby, mainly on what his colleagues perceived was an abiding faith in his own intuitive abilities: his sixth sense deduced that Philby was loyal, so therefor. he was.

The shock was consequently all the greater in 1955, when accumulating evidence showed that Philby was indeed a KGB mole. Those who knew Angleton well would say later that he was shattered by the news, and that he began to see himself as the chief target of the entire Philby deception. Whatever the reason, Angleton now began to formulate a theory of a massive and cunning plot by the KGB to fool the West—an unprecedented deception operation whose goal was nothing less than weakening the West in preparation for the final Communist takeover. For those who doubted the existence of such a monster plot, Angleton would always cite the case of Philby. Here was a man, Angleton argued, who had come within a hairsbreadth of being the head of MI6—the result, obviously, of a brilliantly conceived operation by the KGB to take over that agency. And how many other KGB moles had aided the operation, moles still at work? Further, Angleton noted, since the KGB considered the CIA "the main enemy," it was safe to assume the Russians had conceived a similar operation to destroy the CIA from within. And there was no doubt in his mind that Philby had been providing the Russians with advice on how to do it.

Judged strictly by the kind of paranoid logic that tended to dominate counterintelligence, the theory made sense, although Angleton conceded he didn't have any proof. He would get that proof someday, Angleton vowed, in what his listeners took to be an obsessive compulsion to avenge the betrayal of Philby. They assumed that like the Bermuda Triangle and alien abductions, no solid proof would ever be found by Angleton for this theory.

But in 1961 the proof arrived—or so Angleton believed.

That December a squat, bullnecked KGB officer named Anatoli Golitsin defected to the CIA in Helsinki. Thanks to his job at KGB headquarters involving Western Europe operations, Golitsin had a detailed overview of the lengthy roster of assets the KGB had recruited. He blew dozens of them, most importantly a ring codenamed SAPPHIRE operating at the upper levels of the French government. For good measure, he provided the final proof that Philby had been a KGB mole since 1934, a revelation that compelled Philby to flee to Moscow.

However valuable, these revelations were regarded by Angleton as secondary to Golitsin's real value: his knowledge of the KGB master plot to destroy Western intelligence. With the air of a man revealing the location of the Holy Grail, Golitsin told Angleton of attending a special KGB conference in Moscow in 1959 during which senior KGB officers were briefed about a plan to "affect the fundamental reasoning power of the enemy." According to Golitsin, this plan involved sending waves of false defectors westward to feed out disinformation, misleading the West about the Soviet Union's real intentions, and creating several huge deception operations to lull the West into reducing their military preparedness.

Golitsin claimed that the Stalin-Tito split and the Sino-Soviet rift were elaborate deceptions, an assertion that most CIA officials found laughable. Nevertheless, given Angleton's influence in the agency, a special committee was formed to examine Golitsin's assertions. Sardonically calling themselves the "Flat Earth Society," the committee members unsurprisingly concluded that a mountain of evidence proved Tito had in fact split from the Soviet Union, and that the Sino-Soviet rift was very real.

Golitsin was unfazed by this rejection, now claiming it only proved the success of the KGB's disinformation campaign. More ominously, he convinced Angleton that the main reason why the CIA establishment failed to recognize such deceptions was because like all Western intelligence agencies, it had been penetrated by KGB moles. There was a "supermole" high in the CIA's Soviet Division, Golitsin asserted, a cunning KGB asset whose main function was to protect other KGB assets and ensure that the CIA would accept Moscow's disinformation. Golitsin didn't know the supermole's identity but claimed to know his code name: SASHA.

Convinced he was now entering the heart of the great conspiracy he had already decided existed, Angleton set up Golitsin as a virtual one-man counterintelligence agency. In great secrecy he moved Golitsin into a New York apartment, to which couriers brought him the CIA's top secret personnel files. Golitsin was to peruse the files, searching for clues that would point to SASHA.

This appalling breach of CIA security was bad enough, but Golitsin now compounded it with still another venture into molethink. Since he was so dangerous to the KGB, Golitsin told Angleton, Moscow would undoubtedly send a false defector, a clever double agent whose mission would be to discredit everything Golitsin was claiming. With Golitsin discredited, the great mole inside the CIA and his lesser minions would have a clear path to destroy the agency.

Again, Angleton found this incredible scenario perfectly in accord with his own notion of the KGB master plan. And just as Golitsin predicted, in early 1964 a KGB officer decided to defect. His name was Yuri Nosenko.

Like a number of KGB officers who joined the agency after the death in 1953 of its chief, Laventri Beria, Nosenko owed his KGB career to important family connections in the Soviet hierarchy. His father, a friend of Nikita Khrushchev (a connection that earned him a job as minister of shipbuilding), had important behind-the-scenes power, which he used to get his son a commission in the Navy. Yuri, not especially enamored of the naval career his father wanted for him, then drifted into naval intelligence. After three years on the job, he got a transfer to the KGB through his father's connections.

At the time, the KGB was regarded as a very good career choice. Given its special role in the Soviet system, the KGB could offer its members privileges, including pay, far beyond what ordinary Russians could obtain. A flash of the KGB identification, with its distinctive red shield, was sufficient for any KGB employee to be waved to the head of a theater or movie line, or to get the best seat in a restaurant.

Nosenko, considered by his father an aimless dreamer, demonstrated an unexpected aptitude for counterintelligence work. By 1955 he was a leading agent in one of the KGB's most secret sections, the Seventh Department, which operated blackmail and entrapment operations against American tourists, visiting academics, and businessmen. The standard technique was to set up an American with a female prostitute (known as a "raven" in Soviet intelligence slang) or a male hustler ("swallow"), secretly photograph the result, then threaten to show the pictures to the target's spouse or employer—unless the victim wanted to "cooperate."

But by 1962, disillusioned with the Soviet system, Nosenko decided to contact the CIA. Assigned to Geneva to accompany a Soviet disarmament delegation (his job was to keep a watch on them for the KGB), Nosenko spotted the CIA man attached to the U.S. delegation and indicated he wanted to talk. Later, at a CIA safe house, Nosenko announced he would remain an agent in place, with the understanding he would never meet CIA agents in the Soviet Union. Asked to explain why, Nosenko said the KGB had developed a special chemically treated powder that Russian workers at the U.S. embassy in Moscow (all of whom worked for the KGB) dusted on the soles of shoes belonging to known CIA agents. Special KGB chemical detectors were used to keep tabs on the CIA agents, no matter where they went.

After blowing a few low-scale KGB assets to demonstrate his bona fides, Nosenko returned to his delegation, telling the CIA he would contact them when he had further intelligence to impart. Nothing more was heard from Nosenko, but meanwhile his fate was being sealed at Anatoli Golitsin's New York hideout. Shown the transcripts of the first CIA conversations with Nosenko, Golitsin immediately branded him a "deception." Golitsin derided Nosenko's spy dust story, saying it was only an elaborate fairy tale designed to conceal the KGB supermole in the CIA who was betraying the identities of CIA agents operating under diplomatic cover in Moscow. He went on to predict that Nosenko at some point would defect, with the specific assignment of discrediting him.

Sure enough, just as Golitsin predicted, in early 1964 Nosenko reappeared in Geneva and contacted the CIA. He said he had just received a recall telegram to return to Moscow—a certain sign, he said, that he had come under suspicion. He announced his intention of defecting immediately. Just to ensure that the CIA understood his value, he then dropped a bombshell. Some years before, he said, when a disaffected American named Lee Harvey Oswald lived in the Soviet Union, the KGB assigned him to keep watch on the young ex-Marine to determine if he were a plant by the CIA. Nosenko concluded he wasn't. Then the KGB considered the idea of recruiting him but finally decided that Oswald was a "loon." Thereafter, they let him alone and even allowed him to return to the United States with his Russian-born wife when he grew tired of Soviet life.

The Nosenko case now entered a very dark morass. If, as Golitsin claimed, Nosenko was part of a KGB deception operation, that could only mean that everything he said about Oswald was a lie. In Angleton's reasoning, the KGB was sending Nosenko out into the cold as a false defector to achieve several objectives, one of which was to convince the CIA that it had nothing to do with Oswald. Thus, the opposite was true: that the KGB *did* have an involvement with Oswald, raising the specter of a presidential assassination arranged by the KGB.

As the plane bearing Nosenko to the United States touched down in Washington, he had no idea of the terrible storm brewing on the ground far below. His early kind treatment was deliberate, designed to soften him up and render him unprepared for the shock to come. In his imprisonment he underwent a series of psychological tortures designed to break him and get him to confess to what Angleton had already decided was fact: Yuri Nosenko was a KGB plant whose mission included misleading the CIA about KGB involvement with the assassination of President Kennedy.

But none of these tactics worked. His jailers alternated his cell temperature between very hot and very cold, dragged him out for interrogations at odd hours, made him live on starvation rations for weeks at a time, refused him tobacco, subjected his cell to bright lights that kept him awake, and pounded him with hostile interrogations by teams of questioners who told him they could kill him at any time without anyone ever knowing.

To be sure, Nosenko had provided his interrogators with some ammunition. That "recall telegram," for instance. A check of the records of the National Security Agency—which was monitoring Soviet communications during the disarmament talks in Geneva—showed that no such telegram had been sent from Moscow. And his claim of being a colonel in the KGB was also proven false; actually, he was a major. Nosenko admitted both lies but said he only wanted to enhance his importance in order to ensure the CIA would bring him to the United States. And no matter what further horrors his jailers abused him with, Nosenko held firm to his story: he was a genuine defector, and Lee Harvey Oswald was a nutcase the KGB decided not to recruit. As for Golitsin, Nosenko said the KGB was glad to be rid of him; an insufferable egomaniac, he had once actually proposed an entirely new Soviet intelligence structure, with himself as chief.

Nosenko did not realize he was only putting his neck closer to the guillotine blade. His stubborn refusal to crack was interpreted by Angleton as simply proof of his dedication to his KGB mission. For the moment, there was no resolution of the Nosenko matter, so Angleton and Golitsin occupied their time deciding how many probable KGB moles Golitsin had unearthed from the CIA personnel files. They came up with the astounding total of

120 "suspects," narrowed, finally, to 50 "serious suspects," and then a final list of 16 "espionage cases."

The sole basis for suspecting 16 CIA officers of the serious crime of espionage was Golitsin's perusal of the CIA personnel files. In an arcane deductive process that only Angleton seemed to comprehend, Golitsin made his conclusions about who was a probable KGB mole by spotting what he called "unmistakable clues" in someone's personal history, meaning personality traits that fit his conception of what a KGB mole was supposed to be. For good measure, Golitsin convinced Angleton that Averell Harriman and British Prime Minister Harold Wilson were "probably" working for the KGB.

Despite the sheer lunacy of this kind of thinking, Angleton unleashed a molehunt that was to destroy a dozen careers of CIA officials now under suspicion of working secretly for Moscow. (Among them was the head of the Soviet Division, suspected of being the supermole SASHA.)

But as time went on and the CIA was torn apart in Angleton's mad search, it was clear that no KGB moles, super or otherwise, were about to be turned up. Nosenko, still secretly imprisoned, was sticking to his story, and Angleton's CI staff could not find even a scintilla of evidence against the suspected moles. The CIA's upper echelons began to get jumpy, and Angleton was ordered to resolve the Nosenko matter once and for all. A final round of intense interrogation got nowhere, and Nosenko was ordered released. Concerned about any public revelation of Nosenko's treatment, the CIA gave him a cash payment of $30,000 and (to Angleton's fury) a consulting job at the agency while CIA Director Richard Helms ordered an in-house review of the case. The review concluded that Nosenko was probably genuine.

The decision to accept Nosenko was the beginning of the end for Angleton and his magic fountain of wisdom, Golitsin. There were growing complaints about Angleton, and in 1974 the new CIA director, William Colby, discovered that the CI chief had committed a number of felonies in the course of protecting the CIA from the fabled KGB moles, not least among them the illegal imprisonment of Nosenko. But Colby also discovered that Angleton had illegally bugged the homes of CIA officers he suspected and for years had been running an illegal mail-opening operation designed to see if the international mails were being used by the KGB to communicate with their agents. (They weren't.) Angleton was compelled to resign; Golitsin was informed his services were no longer needed.

The great molehunt was over. A year after Angleton's dismissal, his successor, George Kalaris, convened an extraordinary event at CIA headquarters. It was a lecture on Soviet counterintelligence techniques; the lecturer was Yuri Nosenko. When he had finished his lecture, Nosenko told the standing-room-only audience his own story; at the end, in tears, he said, "But I still love America." He was given a standing ovation.

Later, there would be compensation quietly paid to the victims of the molehunt, the CIA officers whose careers were blighted by suspicion. Angleton, until his death in 1987, continued to insist that he had been right all along, and it was only a naive CIA that refused to understand it had become a virtual KGB adjunct.

It very well may be that Angleton was the chief casualty of the great underground espionage war between the CIA and the KGB at the height of the Cold War, a time of ambiguity, doubt, and corrosive confusion—the very elements that had so attracted him to intelligence work in the first place. The KGB had plenty of its own, much less publicized, casualties in this war. Many KGB veterans recall with bitterness a time when the agency had become so enmeshed in its games of moles, countermoles, false defectors, and disinformation, nobody was trusted anymore—and nobody seemed to know what the truth was.

Were he still alive, Angleton might be bemused by one of the more interesting aftereffects of the KGB-CIA war. It is a lengthy report, prepared by an in-house CIA committee after his departure, to measure how badly the agency had been hurt by that war. Concluding that the agency had been severely damaged, the report then deduced that the damage had been caused by a deliberate KGB operation to disrupt the agency, an operation headed by a cunning "supermole" at a very high level.

The name of that KGB master mole, the report concluded, was James Jesus Angleton.

14

The Mystery of a "Righteous Gentile"

The Wallenberg Case 1944–1990

Poison in Lubyanka

Even in a world full of extraordinary events that winter of 1944, the men working at the German military headquarters in Budapest had never seen anything quite like it. One December day a thin, balding Swedish diplomat stormed into the headquarters building, barged his way into the office of General August Schmidhuber, and proceeded to threaten him.

Not many people would be so foolhardy as to threaten such a powerful man as Schmidhuber. Commander of nearly a half-million troops with supreme powers in a country forcibly occupied by Germany several months before, Schmidhuber with a snap of his fingers could have had this impertinent diplomat done away with in a second. But something about Raoul Wallenberg's forceful intensity made him listen quietly as the diplomat lit into him.

He had learned, Wallenberg said, that Schmidhuber had been ordered by Berlin to cooperate with local Fascists in destroying the Jewish ghetto in Budapest and hand over its 70,000 terrified inhabitants to the *Schutzstaffel* (SS) for shipment to Ausch-

149

witz. "If this happens," Wallenberg warned with a glare, "I personally will see to it that you are prosecuted for war crimes."

Schmidhuber said nothing for a moment. Then, to the astonishment of his staff, he picked up a telephone and barked out an order: the Jewish ghetto was to be inviolate, under German military protection; anyone seeking to harm any of the 70,000 Jews there would be summarily shot. Hanging up, he shook Wallenberg's hand and ordered him out of the building.

Raoul Wallenberg had won another victory in his crusade to save the Jews of Hungary, but he took scant comfort from it. There were too many defeats as the Nazis frantically worked around the clock to exterminate the Jews before the invading Russians could complete their conquest of Hungary. Hundreds of thousands of Jews would end up in extermination camps. Their fate tormented Wallenberg, who had risked his own life to defeat a murder machine.

In the end, Wallenberg managed to save somewhere around a hundred thousand Hungarian Jews. For that, he has been enshrined by history as one of the few, sadly, who did anything to save the Jews of Europe. For the Jewish people, he will be forever remembered, along with Oskar Schindler, as the greatest "righteous Gentile," the force of good combating evil.

The story of Raoul Wallenberg is both inspiring and tragic. It is also one of the great mysteries of modern history, for only a few weeks after achieving his greatest feat—saving the Jews of the Budapest ghetto—Wallenberg was seized by the Russians and never seen again. For the next fifty years his fate exuded a magnetic fascination for millions of people, a puzzle made all the more opaque by the Soviet Union's refusal even to discuss his case. In the deep shadow that became the case of the disappearing diplomat, there were recurring rumors. He was shot by the Russians, who thought he was a spy. He was imprisoned and died in 1947. He was still alive in a Siberian prison camp as late as 1965, driven mad by torture. He was all along a secret Russian agent who returned to his homeland and assumed a new identity. He was an American spy found out by the Russians, who turned him to become a KGB deep penetration agent under a whole new identity.

Now, nearly a half-century after his disappearance, the mystery has finally been cleared up. The real story of Raoul Wallenberg turns out to be a complex espionage puzzle, composed in equal parts of Stalinist paranoia, double-dealing, distrust among

The Swedish diplomat Raoul Wallenberg, the "righteous Gentile" who tried to rescue the Jews of Hungary from the Nazis and became caught up in international intrigue. His fate would precipitate a mystery that would take nearly fifty years to solve. (*Library of Congress*)

ostensible allies, and, above all, the distinct personality of a supremely moral man.

The most important fact to remember about Raoul Wallenberg was that his very birth guaranteed a life insulated from the tensions of pre–World War II Europe. Born into the fabulously wealthy Wallenberg banking dynasty in Sweden, he was groomed at an early age to become still another family banker, brokering the big international deals that had so enriched the Wallenberg banking empire. Marcus Wallenberg, Raoul's uncle, headed the Enshilda Bank, the largest in Sweden, which had extensive dealings with other big European banks, most notably the German Reichsbank. Jacob Wallenberg, another uncle, was also a prominent banker who had a huge network of important contacts throughout the world financial establishments, including the Soviet Union. These contacts would lead to political involvement by the Wallenbergs, with fateful consequences.

A brilliant linguist who had mastered a half-dozen languages, Raoul early in life began to think about a career other than banking. He studied architecture at the University of Michigan and returned to Sweden still not certain exactly what he wanted to do with his life. Marking time, he reluctantly agreed to work in the family bank. In 1938, then twenty-five years old, Wallenberg underwent an experience that was to change his life.

Sent to Palestine as the family bank's representative to negotiate some deals, Wallenberg encountered large numbers of Jewish refugees from Europe who told him horror stories about what the Nazis were doing to the world's largest Jewish community. Appalled, Wallenberg asked what the rest of the world was doing to stop it. The answer: nothing.

Returning to Stockholm, Wallenberg, largely because of his linguistic skills, was assigned the task of heading up an import-export firm the family bank owned. One of his partners was a Hungarian Jew who confided his deepening worries about the fate of Hungary's 700,000 Jews. Hungary's Fascist government, drawing closer to Nazi Germany, had sought to curry favor with Hitler by instituting so-called race laws, modeled on similar laws in Nazi Germany that barred Jews from a wide range of professions, prohibited contact with non-Jews, banned travel, and confined Jews to designated areas. It was but a prelude, the partner warned, to greater evils to come.

The partner was no longer able to travel to Hungary, so Wallenberg in 1941 made a business trip in his place. In Budapest, he found that the city had lost none of its legendary gayness, even though Hungary had joined Hitler in the war, dispatching forces to aid the German invasion of the Soviet Union. But, Wallenberg discovered, the Jews were extremely tense and fearful. And no wonder: the jackbooted soldiers of the Arrow Cross, Hungary's native Fascist movement, were everywhere. They threatened Jews on the streets, occasionally beat them up, and generally made life miserable. In the cafes, the traditional sources of information, there were whispers that Hitler was pressuring the Hungarian government to turn over its Jews for "resettlement." Thus far, the Hungarians had refused, hoping Hitler would be satisfied with the deprivation of Hungarian Jews' civil rights, but how long could the Hungarians hold out against the relentless pressure from Berlin?

Wallenberg was sickened by what he saw in Budapest. On his return to Sweden he began hectoring his family and their well-connected friends: couldn't anybody do anything to stop these terrible crimes? He was met with shrugs and intricate explanations of "political realities" that prevented any intervention. What they did not tell him was that the Wallenberg family had other things on its collective mind, mainly international intrigue.

The intricate story began in 1942, when Boris Rybkin, KGB *rezident* in Stockholm, worked out a secret deal with the Swedes. Desperate for high-tensile steel for their aviation industry (Soviet metallurgical plants had been seized by the Germans), the Russians were willing to trade their reserves of platinum for Swedish steel. The deal, a gross violation of Swedish neutrality, was brokered by the Enshilda Bank, with Jacob Wallenberg playing a key role. Wallenberg made a hefty profit for the bank on the deal, but it had brought him to the attention of the KGB, which began to calculate the ways in which Wallenberg could be of more help to the Soviet cause.

Marcus Wallenberg, meanwhile, was concerned about the bank's investments in Finland. These holdings were in grave danger as a result of Finland's decision to aid Hitler by invading the Soviet Union. In Wallenberg's calculation, if the Russians won the war, they would seize Finnish assets as war reparations. The Wallenbergs would suffer severe setbacks, since the Soviets were not noted for their eagerness to compensate capitalists for losses. And the Wallenbergs certainly were capitalists.

To forestall such a disaster, Marcus secretly approached the KGB via Rybkin with an offer: given his influence in Finland, he would try to work out a peace deal between Moscow and the Finns. With nothing to lose, the Russians gave him their blessing. In 1944 Marcus played a key behind-the-scenes role in a peace treaty between the Russians and the Finns under which the Wallenberg holdings were protected. As in the case of his brother Jacob, Marcus, whether he realized it or not, was now regarded as a virtual asset for the KGB. Both men, the Russians decided, might come in very handy someday.

But the Wallenbergs had also done much to fuel Stalin's paranoia. Marcus, the KGB discovered, had very close ties with the British establishment and had handled the secret negotiations to allow Swedish firms to sell vital raw materials to Great Britain in violation of Swedish neutrality—and without the Germans knowing about it. At the same time, Marcus maintained close relations with many officials high in the German government. Thanks to its sources in Great Britain, the KGB found out, much to its disquiet, that Marcus in 1940 had acted as middleman in an abortive peace feeler from Berlin to London. The feeler, which almost certainly came at the instigation of Hitler himself, was finally turned aside by the British, but a black mark was entered against Marcus Wallenberg's name in the KGB's roster of suspicion. Was it possible that Marcus was some kind of British intelligence asset?

The KGB would come to find even more suspicious aspects of Jacob Wallenberg. He was a close friend of the German Socialist politician Karl Goerdler, who by 1942 had helped organize an underground network of anti-Nazis in Germany that sought to depose Hitler and create a new government that would immediately sign a peace agreement with the West.* Several German diplomats who were part of the underground secretly had approached their British counterparts to sound out their willingness for such a deal. Apprised of this development by one of their top British moles, H. A. R. Philby, the KGB was alarmed; a separate peace deal—which presumably would allow the Germans to continue the war in the East—was Stalin's central, obsessive fear. Philby was able to sidetrack the German underground's feeler, but the KGB began to build an extensive dossier on Jacob Wallenberg. In the KGB's view, he was a man clearly playing both sides of the fence, helping the British while at the same time trying to broker a deal between the German underground and London. He could be an asset of the intelligence service of either side—or both.

Although he was unaware of all this international intrigue, Raoul Wallenberg was to discover that it would finally determine his fate as he became involved in the mission that would make him famous.

Wallenberg's mission was born in the predawn hours of March 19, 1944, when Hitler ordered German troops to seize the Hungarian government and occupy the country. Hitler moved when he learned that the Hungarians, weary of the war in which hundreds of thousands of their young men had died, had sought to sign a separate peace with the Russians.

Twelve days later the very embodiment of Nazi genocide, Adolf Eichmann, arrived in Budapest. Summoning the Hungar-

---

* In July 1944 the underground tried, but failed, to assassinate Hitler. Subsequently, a vengeful Hitler had the underground's members hunted down and exterminated. The main leaders, including Goerdler, were strangled with piano wire; their final agonies were filmed and shown to Hitler and his inner circle as post-dinner entertainment.

ian Jewish Council to a meeting, he announced, "Do you know who I am? I am a bloodhound!"

The Jews would learn quickly what he meant. Forced to register and wear yellow stars, they were rounded up by the thousands, jammed into cattle cars, and shipped to Auschwitz at the rate of 3,000 a day. By the early summer of 1944, over 250,000 Hungarian Jews had been gassed. It seemed only a matter of time before Eichmann succeeded in his announced goal of making Hungary *Judenrein* (Jew-free). He and his squads of killers, aided by Arrow Cross thugs, were working virtually around the clock, for the Russians had invaded Hungary from the east and were gradually gaining the upper hand. Eichmann was determined to finish his mission before the Russians took over the country.

The American ambassador Herschel Johnson, heartsick over the slaughter, begged President Roosevelt to do something. Roosevelt, working with the War Refugee Board and the World Jewish Council, decided on a plan to rescue as many Hungarian Jews as possible. A neutral representative would be assigned to Budapest, armed with extraordinary powers to cut through diplomatic red tape and get Jews exit visas to neutral countries. It was decided that a representative from Sweden, a neutral with ties to both sides in the war, would be ideal. The Swedes agreed to the plan and settled on Raoul Wallenberg—fluent in several languages, knowledgeable about both Hungary and Palestine—as the perfect man for the job.

Eichmann was not impressed when he first encountered Wallenberg in the fall of 1944 in Budapest. "A typical decadent diplomat," he told his assistants, adding that this unprepossessing man dressed in rumpled suits (Wallenberg was indifferent about such things) would prove no hindrance to their mission of genocide.

But Eichmann had badly underestimated Wallenberg. Within a few days of his arrival the indefatigable Swede was everywhere, bribing, cajoling, threatening, and doing everything he could to keep the Jews out of Eichmann's clutches. Infuriated, Eichmann threatened to have Wallenberg killed, but Berlin firmly ordered him to leave the Swedish diplomat alone; eager to maintain friendly relations with Sweden, Germany wanted no incidents to sour those relations. Eichmann was to carry on as best he could.

A terrible race was on: Eichmann was rounding up as many Jews as he could get his hands on, while Wallenberg was rescuing as many as he could. His favorite tactic was the issuance of thousands of Swedish visas certifying the holders were under Swedish protection because they were about to become Swedish citizens. (For diplomatic reasons, Berlin ordered the Germans to respect such documents.) Wallenberg also set up a thriving forgery operation that created false papers for Jews. On other occasions he talked his way into prison camps run by the Hungarians where Jews had been rounded up awaiting shipment to the ovens. He would either bribe the Hungarians to let the Jews go or, when that failed, threaten them with prosecution for war crimes unless they released all their prisoners.

By the winter of 1944 he had saved 20,000 Jews with Swedish papers, hidden another 13,000 in safe houses around Budapest after getting them released from Hungarian camps, and pressured the German military commander into saving another 70,000 Jews penned up in the Budapest ghetto.

Wallenberg did not dwell on these successes, for he was aware that nearly 400,000 Hungarian Jews had either perished already or were in the process of being shipped to death camps. The Russians were drawing nearer to Budapest every day, so Wallenberg worked harder than ever, convinced that if he could save as many Jews as possible, they would be safe when the Germans were finally driven out of Hungary.

He operated in an atmosphere of bloody terror. The Fascist Arrow Cross, unleashed by their Nazi masters, were seizing Jews at random. Some were shot and their bodies left on the streets, others were hacked to death in broad daylight, and still others were taken to the banks of the Danube, ordered to strip naked, and then thrown into the freezing water for what the Fascists liked to call "swimming lessons." Wallenberg, an upright man, had often wondered what pure evil was like. Now he had found it.

The nightmare ended in January 1945, when the Russians entered Budapest. But Wallenberg's real ordeal was just beginning. He was unaware that KGB agents in Budapest had been keeping a careful watch on him from the day he arrived. The KGB had been especially concerned about events in Hungary ever since the Hungarians had put out the first feelers to both sides about getting out of the war. As the Russians were aware, the Hungarians had approached Moscow, but unforgivably in Moscow's view, they had also approached the British and Americans. This move was bad enough in Stalin's eyes, but the Americans had compounded the Stalinist paranoia by sending a secret

OSS mission code-named SPARROW in early 1944 to negotiate a separate peace. To Stalin, the mission represented a willingness for double-dealing by his ostensible allies.

Further deepening Stalin's paranoia were the KGB dispatches from Budapest, reporting that the Swede Wallenberg had been seen in the company of German generals, Hungarian Fascists, and even the SS. Could it not be reasonably inferred that he was part of some sort of nefarious British-American plot to work out a deal with the Germans? Moreover, he was a member of the Wallenberg family, two of whose most prominent members had also participated in suspicious double-dealing. At this point, Stalin decided that Raoul Wallenberg was no ordinary diplomatic representative; his mission of saving Jews was some sort of cover for a deeper game. It was time to do something about the Wallenbergs.

On January 17, 1945, Raoul Wallenberg was summoned to a meeting with the Soviet military commander at his headquarters outside Budapest to discuss plans to provide food and shelter for the thousands of Jews Wallenberg had managed to save. He never returned from that meeting. When 24 hours passed, his worried assistants and the Jewish community leaders asked the Russians where Wallenberg was. The Russians blandly replied that he had never shown up for the scheduled meeting. Days, then a week went by. Still no sign of Wallenberg. He had disappeared off the face of the earth.

Nearly fifty years would pass before it was learned precisely what happened to Wallenberg that January morning in 1945. It is now known that when he arrived for the meeting he was taken into custody by KGB agents, along with his driver, the Hungarian Vilmos Langfelder.

At first, Wallenberg was treated like an honored guest. He was taken to Moscow aboard a luxury train and confined in a special section of the KGB's main prison reserved for VIP prisoners, with all the atmosphere and amenities of a modest hotel. He was taken for a tour of Moscow landmarks, including, oddly enough, the Moscow subway system. All the while, the KGB was busily trying to seduce him; the plan was to recruit Wallenberg as an asset whose main duty would be to provide a window into the powerful Wallenberg family and its extensive economic and political connections.

At the same time, the KGB was intent on finding out just what Wallenberg was up to in Budapest. Unable to believe that

this scion of a rich family would devote himself to saving Jews, the
Russians interrogated him gently but relentlessly on which intelligence service Wallenberg was working for. Wallenberg replied
over and over he wasn't working for any intelligence agency and
went on to make it clear he had no intention of working for the
Russians.

As it became obvious that the soft touch wouldn't work, Wallenberg's treatment changed abruptly. He was thrown into one
of the worst sections of the KGB's main prison and put into the
hands of Viktor S. Abakumov, among the KGB's most sinister
thugs. A Stalinist acolyte who was KGB leader Laventri Beria's
chief henchman, Abakumov had a reputation as a sadistic brute
whose forte was getting results where no one else could.

Wallenberg's supreme ordeal began: round-the-clock interrogations, starvation rations, constant beatings, and every refine-
ment of torment Abakumov could remember in a career devoted
to the art of breaking men. But to Abakumov's shock, Wallenberg
didn't break. Like Eichmann, Abakumov underestimated the
Swede; the small, thin man who looked like a bank clerk was made
of much sterner stuff than his appearance suggested.

Impatiently, Stalin waited for Abakumov to achieve the kind
of results he had never failed to deliver. But as the weeks dragged
by, Wallenberg showed no sign of giving in. Meanwhile, the Russians played for time: they sent a cryptic telegram to Wallenberg's
father that said only, "Your son is in Russia. All is okay."

There was no further word as diplomatic pressure from the
Swedes mounted. The Russians were maddeningly vague in re-
sponse to all requests for information on Wallenberg, while the
KGB was busily planting various rumors. Among them was a re-
port that Wallenberg had been murdered by die-hard Hungarian
Fascists, and another that he had decided to go to the Soviet
Union to "work for world peace."

As 1947 began, it was clear there was no hope of breaking
Wallenberg. But the Russians now faced a delicate problem: two
years of torment had broken Wallenberg's health. He was seriously ill and looked like an old man. There was no way they could
release him into a world that had become increasingly curious
about his fate. Stalin finally decided that the evidence would have
to disappear.

On July 17, 1947, Wallenberg was taken from his cell and
told he would be escorted to the infirmary to take medicine for
a worsening heart problem. At the infirmary he was handed a

vial of liquid that was actually a powerful poison. He died instantly. His body was immediately cremated and the ashes scattered. A year later Langfelder, his driver, underwent a similar fate. Abakumov then carefully weeded the records, destroying any paper trail of Wallenberg's imprisonment by the KGB.

A veil of silence settled over the Russian end of the Wallenberg mystery. To all inquiries and demands for information, the Russians insisted they knew nothing. That didn't change until 1956, three years after Stalin's death, when Moscow suddenly told Swedish diplomats that Wallenberg had been arrested in 1945 on charges of "spying for Germany" and had died of natural causes in prison in 1947. They blamed it all on Abakumov of the KGB, noting the notorious KGB bully had been arrested for "crimes against the state" in 1953 and executed a year later. Regrettably, the Soviets claimed, Abakumov took whatever Soviet knowledge existed about Wallenberg to the grave with him.

With that, another veil of silence fell, punctuated during the next three decades by KGB disinformation fairy tales, among them that Wallenberg was alive but in a mental hospital, that he was alive in the Gulag as late as 1977, that he had died in 1961 from heart failure, and that he had confessed his involvement with Western intelligence agencies and begged the Russians for mercy and forgiveness.

It was not until after the fall of the Soviet Union that the truth finally emerged. In response to pressure from Sweden, where the Wallenberg case had become a persistent public controversy, the Russians permitted a Swedish delegation unprecedented access to KGB officials known to have some involvement with the case. The results were contradictory; since the Russians had lied so many times, they no longer seemed to know what the truth was.

In 1990 the answer to the mystery arrived in the person of Oleg Gordievski, a senior KGB official who defected to the British. Gordievski, who had seen secret KGB reports to Stalin (and his successors) on the Wallenberg case, was able to give a comprehensive picture of precisely what had happened. He also provided Wallenberg's epitaph, calling him "a very great and very brave man."

15

The Lady at the Kiosk

The Berlin Spy Carousel
1966–1989

A triple agent

In the jargon of American espionage the practice of flaunting very attractive bait to the other side is sometimes called a "dangle" (the British prefer the more resonant "trailing one's coat"). As with fishing, from which the term is borrowed, the hope is that dangling attractive bait will lure a big fish to bite—and swallow the hook.

In the case of Hu Simeng Gasde, a very big fish took the bait and got caught. But, as things turned out, that was only one aspect of a case that wound up somewhere in the nether reaches of Cold War espionage. In the end, there were so many bewildering twists and turns, no one involved could quite grasp who was spying for whom. If ever there was a case that perfectly illustrated the "wilderness of mirrors" effect, it was the matter involving the Chinese lady of multiple loyalties, a news kiosk in West Berlin, the CIA agent who could barely speak German, some very busy East German spymasters, several confused KGB agents, a snookered Chinese intelligence service, and a husband-and-wife team who discovered that in a seller's market, espionage can be very profitable.

It all began with Hu Simeng. She was a thirty-year-old graduate student at the University of Beijing in 1966 when she met and fell

160

in love with Horst Gasde, an East German graduate student studying Chinese dialects. Their shared love of language quickly overcame the cultural and ethnic gulf that separated these two very different people. Hu Simeng, who was studying Western languages with the aim of eventually becoming a translator, could happily converse with Gasde in German, in which she was fluent, while Gasde, fluent in Chinese, could talk with her in that language. Often, as a form of mental gymnastics, they would alternate sentences in German and Chinese, delighting in their ability to switch in and out of different languages.

A year later they were married. Hu Simeng decided to accompany her husband when he finished his studies and returned to East Germany to take up a post as professor of languages at Humboldt University. It was at this point that their odyssey into espionage began.

First, Gasde was recruited as an informant for East German intelligence, mainly to report on foreign students (most of them Chinese) in his classes. He was instructed to pay special attention to any foreign students who might be susceptible to recruitment by the East Germans. Lurking in the background was the KGB, which had an acute interest in any Chinese students who might fulfill one of the KGB's pressing needs, native assets in China, where Russians were blocked from operating as illegals because they could not blend into a sea of oriental faces.

Among the first potential assets Gasde recommended to his East German control was his own wife. As he pointed out, she was working as a language tutor to Chinese diplomats and businessmen stationed in East Germany who were attempting to perfect their German. Subsequently, an approach was made to Hu Simeng, who agreed to spy on the Chinese community in East Germany, with particular attention to the diplomats. The East Germans congratulated themselves on a successful recruitment of an asset who could penetrate a very difficult target. They did not know that their new asset had been recruited by Chinese intelligence to spy on the East Germans. Her husband knew but did not object, for the development raised interesting possibilities. Things were beginning to get complicated.

While the East Germans were purring contentedly over their prime Chinese asset, the Chinese were equally pleased to have their own asset. To Hu Simeng's delight, she was being paid by both sides, a largesse that, combined with the money her husband was getting from the East Germans, allowed them a lifestyle their fellow citizens only rarely achieved. They had a new car, a nice house, a personal computer (an unheard-of luxury for East Germans), and upscale wardrobes enriched by periodic shopping binges in West Berlin.

The Gasdes were pure mercenary spies; having discovered that intelligence services will pay a lot of money for what they perceive as important intelligence, they became blank pages onto which anyone could write—for a fee. They quickly realized that there was a mother lode to be mined: the great intelligence void created by the Sino-Soviet split. The East Germans, the satraps of the Soviet Union, were desperate to get anything they could about the Chinese for Moscow. In turn, the Chinese were desperate for anything they could obtain on the Soviet Union; East Germany, they believed, was a convenient backdoor way to get it.

At root, the Gasdes were apolitical ciphers. Hu Simeng liked to tell the East Germans she was willing to betray her country because of the excesses of the Cultural Revolution. To the Chinese, she was a dedicated revolutionary who told them she betrayed the East Germans because they were insufficiently Communist and were in league with the hated Russians, to boot.

Neither side had the slightest doubt about her loyalties. Invited to visit China periodically for in-depth discussions on what she had learned about the East Germans (and, by extension, the Russians), she was treated like a queen: VIP hotel suites, lavish banquets, and plenty of time to visit her family. Her relatives were quite impressed with her obviously important status and wealth, although they wondered how she could have achieved so much on the money earned tutoring in the German language.

The East Germans were also prepared to show their gratitude. In addition to the $300-a-month stipend (an East German workingman's yearly salary those days), the Gasdes were granted that most treasured of all privileges, permission to travel to West Berlin as often as they wanted. There, they could stock up on the consumer goods unavailable in East Germany.

As the Gasdes were aware, this prosperous life could be jeopardized at any moment if either the East Germans or the Chinese caught onto their game. To prevent that from happening, Hu Simeng played a bold gambit: she informed both sides she had been approached for recruitment by the other. As she anticipated, each side was delighted at the news. She was encouraged to play along with the recruitments as a means of penetrating the opposition.

The game had now gotten extremely complex, but the Gasdes pulled it off with great skill. They revealed to the East Germans the identities of all the Chinese intelligence officers with whom Hu Simeng had come in contact, then turned around and blew the identities of East German intelligence officers to the Chinese. Even more delicious, from the Gasdes' standpoint, was the next move: each side began feeding them disinformation to introduce into the bloodstream of the other side. Of course, the Gasdes informed each one of their clients about the disinformation, spinning off still further plots to confuse the other side with ever more contrived intelligence.

By 1977 this bewildering intelligence carousel had been spinning for nearly ten years, and the only result was enrichment of the Gasdes, along with total confusion in the East German and Chinese intelligence services. There was also confusion in the KGB, which took a growing interest in what the East Germans had claimed was a double-edged penetration of the Chinese: not only were their assets collecting intelligence, but they had gone along with a Chinese recruitment. Thus, the Gasdes could not only tell the East Germans about the Chinese, they also knew the personnel and methods of Chinese intelligence. Meanwhile, the Chinese believed the precise mirror image.

How the Gasdes managed all this without ever slipping remains a tribute to their abilities to deceive. They even managed to lull the ever-suspicious minds of the KGB, whose officers confessed some confusion over just what the Gasdes were up to—and where their actual loyalties lay. Still, content to get some rare intelligence on the Chinese, the KGB was willing to let the East Germans run things and try to sort out all the complexities.

But the tangle was about to grow still more complex, because the East Germans in 1978 decided to introduce another player into the game: the CIA. This new layer of complexity was to present the Gasdes with their ultimate challenge.

For some time, the East Germans had been keeping careful tabs on the CIA station in Berlin. Based on those observations, the East Germans concluded that the station was not one of the more efficient in the CIA stable. The quality of its agents was generally poor (many did not even speak German), their tradecraft was inefficient, and their attention to security was somewhat lax. Although the CIA station for many years had devoted almost all its energies to the Russians and East Germans, the historic détente between the United States and China had caused the CIA to devote a larger chunk of its resources to China. Bereft of good sources in China, CIA stations around the world were ordered to concentrate on recruiting Chinese working abroad. Among the overseas stations ordered to focus on recruiting Chinese was the Berlin outpost.

As the East Germans noted, the CIA's recruitment efforts tended to be flatfooted. Most often, CIA agents simply approached Chinese directly and asked them if they'd like to work for the United States. It was not a very effective way of recruiting assets, but the CIA station obviously was under great pressure to come up with assets as quickly as possible.

In this fervid atmosphere the East Germans felt it was the perfect time to use a "dangle." The chosen bait was Hu Simeng.

Among the places the CIA liked to approach Chinese was a large kiosk in West Berlin that offered an extensive selection of foreign publications, including all the leading Chinese newspapers, magazines, and books. Beginning in the spring of 1978, Hu Simeng crossed over from East Berlin and went to the kiosk daily, spending hours browsing among the publications. And just as the East Germans had predicted, it was only a matter of time before the CIA took notice of the Chinese woman leaving East Germany each day to browse so assiduously among the kiosk's offerings. One day she was approached by an American who introduced himself as a "research assistant" in an institute that concentrated on East European politics. His German was so bad, Hu Simeng switched the conversation to English because she could hardly understand a word he said.

The American, who did everything but wear a nameplate advertising himself as a CIA man, tried to strike up a friendship, but he tipped his hand by pumping her about her background, where she worked, and what she thought of life in East Germany. Hu Simeng played along carefully with some cautious statements indicating she was not very happy about what was happening in China and even less enthused about life in East Germany. The CIA man nodded sympathetically, then told her he was seeking Chinese who could "write reports" for his institute's publications on political and other developments in China. Of course, he hastened to add, the authors of such "reports" would be well compensated for their work.

Hu Simeng feigned moderate interest in the proposal, then asked for time to think about it. She made arrangements to meet the CIA man a few days hence. Returning to East Berlin, she delivered the news: the bait had been taken.

Within a week, Hu Simeng became a full-fledged CIA asset. She would regularly cross into West Berlin via Checkpoint Charlie, then be picked up by car and taken to one of a number of safe houses throughout West Berlin. There, she would rattle off whatever intelligence she had collected about the Chinese diplomats and businessmen operating in East Germany. The CIA assessed this material as top-grade, well worth the $300 a month it was paying its new Chinese asset. They did not know that the intelligence had been cooked by the East Germans—which in turn based its disinformation on disinformation Hu Simeng provided from the Chinese.

Such were the dizzying distortions that had now involved four separate intelligence agencies. If all that weren't enough, Hu Simeng introduced still another twist in the game: she suggested to the CIA that her husband be recruited, claiming he was disenchanted with the East German regime but had access to high-level government officials.

Horst Gadse was subsequently signed up by the CIA (adding another $300 a month to the flourishing Gadse bank account), and the carousel was now complete. This intelligence free-for-all is not easy to summarize, but it looked something like this: Hu Simeng worked for the Chinese, who did not know she also worked for the East Germans, who did not know she was a Chinese asset, but who did know she worked for the CIA, which didn't know she also worked for both the Chinese and the East Germans. The material she provided the Chinese was in fact East German and KGB disinformation, but the Chinese knew that, so they provided disinformation for Hu Simeng to give to the East Germans, who in turn produced disinformation based on disinformation to give to the CIA, which had no idea that three other intelligence services had some role in cooking up the material she was providing. Meanwhile, Horst Gadse was an asset of the CIA, which didn't know he actually worked for the East Germans, who provided disinformation to be fed to the CIA, which was unaware that the Chinese knew about it because he told his wife, who in turn told the Chinese, but not before she told the East Germans.

The Gadses managed to keep this bewilderingly complex game going for another ten years, until they were finally exposed. As the East German regime collapsed, its intelligence files fell

Checkpoint Charlie in Berlin, the chief crossroads of East-West espionage during the Cold War. Through this window in divided Berlin moved such infamous agents as Hu Simeng Gasde. (*Library of Congress*)

into the hands of the West German government. Gradually, the West Germans came across the files dealing with the Gadses, which also revealed Hu Simeng's role with Chinese intelligence. The CIA was informed, and Langley quietly let the Chinese know that Hu Simeng had suckered them.

Her husband boldly showed up for his last meeting with his CIA contact and even more boldly demanded to be paid for the previous month's "work." Rebuffed, he made some vague threats.

"So sue me," the CIA agent said, in the classic gesture of American dismissiveness.

And with that, the Gasde multiple deception was at an end. In 1990 one of their former East German intelligence controllers showed up at their door and, unbelievably enough, tried to recruit the Gasdes for the KGB. He was turned down; at long last, the Gasdes had tired of the game.

16

Mr. Kent Comes to Tea

The Theft of American Secrets
1939–1941

The ambassador as target

On the morning of May 18, 1940, Guy Liddell, head of the British MI5's counterespionage section, called the office of U.S. Ambassador Joseph P. Kennedy and sought an appointment at three o'clock that afternoon for his assistant to meet with the ambassador and discuss a "delicate matter."

That was something of a typical British understatement. When Liddell's assistant, Maxwell Knight, arrived, he informed Kennedy that the ambassador's chief code clerk, Tyler Gatewood Kent, was a spy for the Germans. Knight showed a shocked Kennedy more than two thousand top secret diplomatic cables that had been seized from Kent's apartment just hours before. Among them were transcripts of highly sensitive private communications between President Roosevelt and Winston Churchill.

Kennedy's shock turned to anger as Knight outlined the dimensions of the case against Kent. With a tight little smile, Knight said that MI5 had been keeping a close watch on Kent since he arrived in London in October 1939 to take his post at the London embassy. At that time, Knight said, MI5 spotted Kent meeting with a known German SD agent. From that point on, he was under MI5 surveillance, which was able to detect his treachery.

"Are you telling me that Kent was under surveillance for *eight months* before I was informed of this matter?" an angry Kennedy asked. "This is unacceptable."

Knight apologized profusely but said MI5 was unable to confirm Kent's treachery "until only recently."

Kennedy was only partly mollified, for he began to suspect that Knight hadn't told him the whole truth. No fool, he also began to get the feeling that there was something very strange going on with this case. In that mood he vented his anger on Kent, whose diplomatic immunity was lifted. Arrested on espionage charges, Kent was tried in camera (both the British and Americans did not want those secret Roosevelt-Churchill conversations entered into public evidence), convicted, and sentenced to 12 years in prison.

And that would seem to be the end of what was apparently a relatively simple espionage case. According to the case prepared against him, Kent was a Nazi sympathizer of muddled motives. Virulently anti-Semitic, he was also an isolationist who believed that Roosevelt was deliberately leading the United States into the war. He provided diplomatic cables to the Germans as a means of warning them about the sub rosa arrangements between Roosevelt and Churchill to aid the British. He did not regard his actions as either treason or espionage.

But appearances were deceiving. In fact, Kent was a minor pawn in an intricate game by British intelligence, whose objective was nothing less than the removal of an American ambassador considered defeatist. It was part of a larger plan to draw the United States closer to Great Britain and, eventually, into the war. But there was another player in this intricate game, one the British did not know about: the KGB.

Kent, a bubblehead who didn't have the first inkling of what he was involved in, was not only an asset of German intelligence; he was also a KGB asset and, more important, an unwitting asset in a carefully planned British operation. In other words, he was a stooge. Given his persona, he was just about perfect for the role.

Born into a prominent family of the eastern WASP establishment, Tyler Gatewood Kent from an early age pictured himself as a prominent diplomat. However much he thought his prep school and Ivy League background provided an entrée into the Foreign Service, the State Department did not agree. It rejected his application on the grounds he was "neurotic." Possibly that referred to Kent's rabid anti-Semitism, which he liked to express publicly, loudly, and often.

But thanks to pressure from his well-connected parents, the State Department was moved to find a slot somewhere for him. In 1934, when Kent was twenty-three years old, he was offered a post in the new U.S. embassy in Moscow—although a lowly one as code/cipher clerk. Kent was angered that the State Department had failed to recognize his brilliant talents (or at least as he perceived them) and reluctantly took the job under pressure from his family. But he resolved to get his revenge.

The opportunity arose almost immediately after he arrived in Moscow, for he fell into a classic KGB "honeypot" operation. The honey in this particular operation was Tatiana Ilovaiskaya, a beautiful Bolshoi actress whom the KGB had recruited for the express purpose of seducing young American diplomats at the U.S. embassy. Ilovaiskaya succeeded in luring a half-dozen of them, including Kent, who spent their off-duty hours in her luxurious Moscow apartment or country *dacha* dipping into her apparently inexhaustible supply of liquor, drugs, and beautiful women.

The KGB recorded and filmed these goings-on and used the results to blackmail certain participants into cooperation. The assistant to the U.S. ambassador, for example, was filmed having sex with young boys and was subsequently pressured into becoming a KGB asset, a role that continued until his death some thirty years later.

Kent also was blackmailed, but the reason in his case had to do with money. He went into the black market business with Ilovaiskaya and soon was earning enough money to buy two cars and a long list of luxuries ordinarily out of reach of a code clerk's modest salary. Assuming such wealth came from his well-to-do family, embassy officials paid scant attention. They should have, for Kent had been ensnared in a KGB blackmail trap: work for us, or we charge you with illegal black market transactions, thus ruining your diplomatic career. He began providing copies of secret diplomatic cables that came across his desk.

Actually, there was not much in the way of vital intelligence of interest to the KGB at the U.S. embassy, but the recruitment of people like Kent promised future dividends. In 1938, his four-year tour of duty over in Moscow, Kent was ready for his next posting. At the suggestion of the KGB, he applied for Berlin, where diplomatic messages would be of much greater interest to the Russians. Instead, Kent was assigned to London. The KGB was disappointed, but as things turned out, Moscow got an unexpected bonus.

At first it appeared as though the KGB's new American asset had run dry. For reasons he did not explain, Kent broke off contact with the KGB after he left Moscow; even hints of diminishing subtlety about his black market involvement failed to stir a response. But then an odd incident occurred that changed everything.

Traveling westward toward his new assignment by train, Kent struck up a conversation with a German businessman one day. They hit it off immediately, largely because they shared a rampaging anti-Semitism. Finally, after Kent had expressed admiration for Hitler's anti-Jewish crusade, the German asked him to perform a favor. When he reached London, could he deliver a small package to a friend who was staying in a London hotel? Kent obligingly agreed.

Once in London, Kent sought out the recipient and handed over the package. He was unaware that the man was an SD agent. More significantly, he was unaware that the SD man was under MI5 surveillance. MI5 did not know quite what to make of the American (was he an SD courier?), so they resolved to keep a watch on him to see what developed.

This initial MI5 look at Kent was to prove significant later, for it provided the perfect foil in an operation with high stakes. The target was U.S. Ambassador Joseph P. Kennedy.

From the time Kennedy arrived at his post in 1938, the British were appalled. Patriarch of a Boston Irish clan noted for ruthlessness, Kennedy had amassed a large fortune and had bought political influence with lavish contributions to the Democratic party. Roosevelt, who disliked him, had given him the ambassadorship to Great Britain as his reward—although he was aware, as was just about everybody else, that Kennedy's mind was dominated by an ambition to become president of the United States. His other consuming ambition was making money.

To the dismay of the British, Kennedy seemed to spend most of his time either politicking or playing the stock market to enhance his $400 million fortune. Occasionally, he brought his two oldest sons, Joseph Jr. and John, to London to make the rounds of the British upper crust, but the British weren't impressed. Both

young men, clones of their father, seemed preoccupied with female flesh and demonstrated little grasp of world politics.

The elder Kennedy considered himself something of an expert on that subject, and that's where the real problem arose. He
became an appeaser and crypto-admirer of the Nazis, and his
reports to Washington had a consistent theme: Nazi Germany was
the wave of the future, and the British had no hope of ever prevailing. After the outbreak of World War II, Kennedy insisted that
the British would be defeated by the Germans, and therefore
there was no reason why the Americans should waste their time
aiding a country certain to go down to defeat. He urged an "understanding" between Washington and Berlin, presumably meaning an American acceptance of Hitler's territorial claims in
Europe.

Although Kennedy didn't know it, his enciphered messages
to Washington were being read by the British, whose communications intelligence establishment had managed to tap into the
Atlantic cable and break the cipher used by the State Department
for sensitive overseas cables. What they read was alarming, for the
idea that Kennedy's defeatism and outright anti-British bias
would have any effect on American official opinion was a dangerous prospect. It was for precisely that reason that Churchill
bypassed Kennedy and opened a secret, private communications
link with Roosevelt. Nevertheless, Kennedy remained a serious
problem. Something would have to be done to neutralize him—
or, even better, get rid of him. But how?

Tyler Kent provided the answer. Continued MI5 surveillance
on him turned up nothing, for Kent seemed to do his work dili-
gently and spent his evening hours in a passionate affair with a
married American woman. But early in 1940, watching MI5
agents saw him drift into the orbit of a strange organization called
the Right Club. Composed of anti-Semites and assorted right-
wing crackpots, some of whom were pro-Hitler, the organization's
social center was the Russian Tea Rooms in London. No relation
to the famous, similarly named New York landmark, the cafe was
run by an emigré Czarist Russian ex-admiral named Nicholas Wolkoff. Kent became friends with the admiral's daughter Anna, a
loud and virulent anti-Semite who, interestingly enough, was
working for British intelligence in a secret project that steamed
open and read mail to and from the Soviet Union.

MI5's Maxwell Knight, in charge of counterespionage operations involving German penetration of domestic political

Joseph Kennedy, left, arrives in London in 1938 to take up his duties as
American ambassador. A defeatist and apologist for the Nazis, Kennedy was
undermined by a British intelligence operation that thoroughly discredited him.
(*National Archives*)

groups, resolved to keep a close eye on this developing situation.
He enlisted three women to infiltrate the Wolkoff cafe, get close
to Anna Wolkoff, and find out what Kent was doing there. Additionally, they were to find out whether the right-wingers had established any contact with the Germans.

Knight's three female agents, posing as disaffected War Office employees who were bitter anti-Semites and admirers of Hitler, gradually infiltrated the Right Club circle. One of the agents,
Joan Miller, was able to win Anna Wolkoff's confidence. As they
grew closer, Wolkoff revealed that her friend Tyler Kent had told
her of seeing secret cables between Roosevelt and Churchill that
convinced him there was a conspiracy to get the United States
into the war on Great Britain's side. He wanted to expose this
plot but didn't know how.

At this point, Knight simply could have informed the U.S.
embassy that Kent was a security risk. Kent would have been recalled, and that would be the end of it. But Knight had more
important objectives in mind, and he set in motion a chess game.

His first move was to order Miller to advise Wolkoff that Kent should steal some of the more interesting cables and hand them over to her. Then she would pass them to the Germans. Wolkoff and Kent readily agreed.

Wolkoff didn't know how she would get Kent's material to the Germans, but she suddenly remembered she knew Antonio del Monte, an assistant military attaché at the Italian embassy. Apparently aware that del Monte was the chief representative of Italian military intelligence in London, she began to provide copies of Kent's stolen cables to him. Shortly, the cables found their way to the Germans, who were most interested in such details as Roosevelt's message to Churchill reporting that because of prevailing political conditions, he would be unable to give the British 50 overage U.S. destroyers.

Having set up the Kent operation, Knight now let it run for a few months while he moved to achieve two objectives. One was obtaining sufficient evidence to justify interning some members of the Right Club under wartime internal security statutes. Up to this point, the Right Club had been all talk and such childish stunts as clandestinely putting up posters at night that read, ENGLAND: LAND OF DOPE AND JEWRY. Now, with incontrovertible evidence that Anna Wolkoff, one of the group's leading members, was involved in espionage, MI5 had enough to cite a real internal security threat.

But the second objective, demolishing Ambassador Joseph P. Kennedy, turned out to be the most significant effect of Knight's game. When Knight walked into Kennedy's office that day in May 1940 to deliver the bad news about Kent, he was perfectly aware that the ambassador was now in big trouble. For one thing, news of the security breach in the London embassy would reflect badly on Kent's boss; the White House could only wonder what kind of sloppy security existed in Kennedy's office to allow such a grave leak of American diplomatic secrets. For another, the British, thanks to the trove of cables found in Kent's apartment, could quietly leak Kennedy's appeasement to the press without having to reveal their interception and cracking of U.S. diplomatic codes. Kennedy had assumed those reports, loaded with scornful comments about such British leaders as Churchill, would remain secret.

Obviously, Kennedy's diplomatic position was suddenly rendered untenable, all the more so because Roosevelt began to cast a suspicious eye on events in London. The idea that a low-ranking

code clerk could simply walk out of the embassy with an armload
of secret cables and turn them over to the Germans strained credulity. Was it possible that Kent was simply the chosen instrument
of someone higher up in the embassy, someone pro-German who
wanted Berlin to know about the Roosevelt-Churchill connection
and other interesting details the Germans might find helpful?

It was merely the whiff of a suspicion, but it was poisonous
in the context of relations between the president and his ambassador in London. In the wake of Kent's arrest, Kennedy detected
a deepening chill in the White House, confirmed when he
learned, to his mortification, that Roosevelt had kept him out
of the loop when he began negotiating with Churchill on a
destroyers-for-bases deal. Humiliated, Kennedy resigned, and
British-American relations immediately underwent a change for
the better, finally to blossom into the "special relationship" of
close allies.

The new British-American relationship tended to obscure
some nagging aspects of the Kent case, among them MI5's admission that it had Kent under surveillance for eight months—
all the while he was stealing cables. Why hadn't MI5 notified the
Americans immediately that one of their employees was jeopardizing the security of the most sensitive area of the American
embassy? And if MI5 was aware that Kent was giving these cables
to the Germans, why did it let that serious security breach go on?
To prove espionage, MI5 did not need Kent to steal some two
thousand cables; just a few would have been sufficient for a
charge of espionage.

The FBI began to wonder about these unanswered questions. Not satisfied with the answers he was getting from MI5, J.
Edgar Hoover ordered a full-scale investigation into the Kent
case. FBI agents started in Moscow, where they uncovered the
shocking security lapses in the American embassy, the Bolshoi
actress's seductions on behalf of the KGB, and the black market
operation that ensnared Kent. Convinced that Kent was a KGB
asset, the agents began to see his activities in London in a whole
new light.

Anna Wolkoff, at first thought to be a right-wing nut, now
assumed a somewhat different coloration. Sentenced to prison as
a co-conspirator with Kent (she would die there a few years later),
she was uncooperative when FBI agents came to ask about her
role in the case. But the agents found out about her intelligence
job secretly opening mail—an operation that had come to the

attention of the KGB. Suspicion grew that Wolkoff had betrayed it to the Russians, which meant she was a KGB asset all the time she was arranging for the transmission of Kent's cables to the Germans. Had she made extra copies for the KGB?

The FBI was never able to prove the matter one way or the other. As late as 1972 some agents were still pursuing leads, including an interview with Kent himself. By that time Kent, who had been released from prison in 1946, was merely a footnote in American history, long forgotten by most of his fellow citizens. The years had not changed him: as the FBI agents discovered, he was still a muddleheaded anti-Semite who continued to insist he had done nothing wrong. He knew nothing about any KGB role in the case and denied he had ever been blackmailed by the Russians, nor had he ever given diplomatic cables to the KGB. (The FBI knew better, but the statute of limitations had expired, making the question academic.)

The FBI found Kent in somewhat luxurious circumstances. Following his release from prison, he married the heiress to the Carter's Little Liver Pills fortune, which among other things allowed him to buy a small Florida newspaper that he used as a megaphone for his crackpot ideas on how the Jews were taking over the world.

But it was not to last. An inept businessman, he invested his wife's entire fortune in some speculative Mexican investments that failed. By 1982 they were living in near-poverty in a small trailer in Texas. He died six years later of cancer, his passing barely noticed.

With him died the real secret of his betrayal. We are left only with the enigmatic statement uttered by Maxwell Knight of MI5 after Kent had been arrested in 1940: "Sometimes it is necessary to catch a monkey in order to scare a tiger."

DISASTERS

As with all other areas of human endeavor, espionage is subject to Murphy's Law, which dictates that what can go wrong, will. CIA officials like to call it "flap," the distressing tendency of certain major intelligence operations to go badly awry, too often with the kind of spectacular explosion that tends to attract a lot of public (and unwelcome) attention.

The reason, of course, is that human beings devise and run such operations, with all that implies. Despite their position at the apex of the evolutionary scale, humans nevertheless have the habit of making mistakes. In fact, espionage may bring out the worst in that tendency, for it is an area of human activity rife with ambiguity, suspicion, uncertainty, prejudice, and, too often, sheer guesswork.

"When I make a mistake, it's a beauty," Harry Truman would confess occasionally, and that's as good a guidepost as any for the three case studies that follow. The first concerns the very metaphor for intelligence disaster, Pearl Harbor. Although it is commonly assumed that the failure was strictly American, in fact this enduring symbol of espionage bumbling was double-edged: the Japanese erred as badly as the Americans, and in the end they paid a terrible price for their mistakes.

Another case study, directly related to the first, discusses an American intelligence obsession during the pre–World War II era concerning the Japanese. A poorly conceived operation ended in spectacular failure, in the process consuming a brilliant Marine Corps officer and a famous aviatrix. Ironically, as things turned out, the operation was pointless.

The remaining study examines a historically crucial post–World War II event, when the world's new superpow-

ers, the United States and the Soviet Union, confronted
each other in Eastern Europe. An American intelligence
crusade to halt the Soviet tide failed, and the reverberations
were felt for years afterward.

17

East Wind, Rain

Operation Z
1932–1941

The Pearl Harbor catastrophe

On the evening of December 5, 1941, Ito Morimura, vice-consul at the Japanese consulate in Honolulu, received an urgent message from Tokyo. Without fail, he was ordered, he must make an absolutely accurate census of which warships were in Pearl Harbor and send that intelligence to Tokyo no later than 6:00 P.M. Hawaii time the next day.

The message did not explain the sudden urgency about Pearl Harbor, a place Morimura had been spying on for months, but he could put the clues together. Just 24 hours before, the consulate had received orders to begin burning its codebooks and other vital papers. Clearly, Japan was about to go to war against the United States, a war it would commence with an attack on Pearl Harbor.

With the weight of history on his shoulders, Morimura the next morning began his final espionage mission in Hawaii. No one could have guessed that this short, bespectacled man visiting the sights above the harbor waters had so momentous a responsibility. He looked like just another of the many Japanese tourists who visited this lush paradise and tried to see everything worth seeing while absorbing every possible detail.

Typically enough, Morimura was outfitted with a pair of binoculars, a camera, and a small notebook for recording his impressions. No one paid much attention to this relatively common sight, nor did anyone consider it suspicious when he stopped at a restaurant at lunchtime and asked for a table on the outdoor veranda overlooking the harbor. And there was still nothing that struck anyone as unusual when Morimura lingered over his lunch, periodically sweeping the harbor with his binoculars and making notations in his notebook. After all, there wasn't anything secret about Pearl Harbor; it was visible for miles around. Indeed, there were regular sightseeing tours of the harbor, where tourists were even allowed to take pictures of the warships at berth, the Navy dockyards, and the port facilities.

That night, Morimura sent an enciphered communication to Tokyo via the consulate's radio. It reported in detail on all the U.S. Navy ships in the harbor, including the news that three battleships had joined the five already at anchor. When the transmission was finished, Morimura and several other consular employees demolished the PURPLE cipher machine over which the message had been sent. Then they carted several filing cabinets' worth of documents outside. Using two large barrels, they methodically burned every scrap of paper.

Less than 24 hours later, when Pearl Harbor was still covered with a pall of smoke from wrecked ships and shattered planes, Morimura waited quietly as a grim-looking party of FBI and ONI (Office of Naval Intelligence) agents strode into the consulate. They formally announced that in view of the state of war that now existed between the Empire of Japan and the United States of America, Japanese diplomatic personnel were being interned, to be exchanged later for American diplomats being held in Japan.

At that moment, the espionage triumph that the surprise attack on Pearl Harbor represented would appear to be Morimura's. He had spied on the sprawling American naval base for almost a year, ably fulfilling all requests from Tokyo for detailed intelligence on U.S. Navy strength and the precise location of every ship. By contrast, the American failure could not have been more stark. The Americans had failed to discern the Japanese decision to go to war against the United States, had failed to learn of the preparations for an attack on Pearl Harbor, had failed to detect the Japanese naval task force that carried it out, and had failed to warn Pearl Harbor in time to prevent a crushing blow. No greater intelligence fiasco could be imagined.

And yet, the fact is there were two great intelligence failures at Pearl Harbor. One of them was American. The other was Japanese. The Japanese failure had everything to do with the very nature of Japanese intelligence and the methodology of one of its typical operatives, Ito Morimura—or, to use his real name, Ensign Takeo Yoshikawa of the Third Bureau of the Imperial Japanese Navy intelligence division.

Yoshikawa was a typical product of the prewar Japanese military culture. Destined from childhood for a military career, he was a schoolboy champion in traditional bamboo sword fencing and would swim eight miles in choppy seas to further harden him for the arduous tasks ahead. He joined the Japanese navy, but in 1936, when he was only twenty-three years old, the young officer was afflicted with a chronic abdominal disorder that blocked him from his dream, active duty aboard one of the warships in Japan's burgeoning navy.

Confined to desk duty, he applied himself with the same fervor and dedication he had demonstrated for sea duty. The young ensign was recruited into intelligence and assigned to the American desk. He studied English intensively for four years, and at the beginning of 1941 he was selected for the most important assignment in all of Japanese intelligence.

Taken as a whole, Yoshikawa's assignment was simple. He would be sent to Honolulu under diplomatic cover with the new identity of Ito Morimura. His mandate was to collect every possible scrap of information on Pearl Harbor: the number and type of ships, how many soldiers and sailors were stationed there, defensive preparations, and any vulnerabilities.

In early 1941 the new Japanese vice-consul arrived in Honolulu. Within hours of his arrival, he set about fulfilling his mission. Over the next several months the indefatigable, totally dedicated, and nerveless Yoshikawa was to provide Japanese intelligence with a small mountain of details about Pearl Harbor. The problem was that he found out everything except what Japan really needed to know.

Pearl Harbor had been a focus of Japanese naval attention ever since 1932, when Admiral Isoroku Yamamoto, commander of the Japanese navy, noticed something interesting. The U.S. Navy had conducted a large exercise called Fleet Problem XIV, which assumed an air raid on Pearl Harbor against the concentration of the U.S. Pacific Fleet. The exercise revealed that an air raid from aircraft carriers some two hundred miles from Hawaii invariably succeeded against the base's defenses.

Yamamoto, preparing his navy for what was assumed to be an inevitable showdown with the United States, now began to think of using an opening air strike against Pearl Harbor to cripple the Pacific Fleet. By 1940 he had worked out the details of Operation Z, a massive southward thrust of Japanese naval power, preceded by a decisive strike against the U.S. Pacific Fleet that would prevent the Americans from reinforcing such vital bastions as the Philippines.

The plan for the opening strike was daring and fraught with risk. A naval strike force would move all the way across the northern Pacific in strict radio silence and avoid all known shipping lanes. At a point some 250 miles from Pearl Harbor, it would launch an air strike. The planes would fly in air corridors known to be used by American air patrols; the Japanese hoped the delay the Americans would need to determine whether the planes were friendly or hostile would be enough to allow the Japanese squadrons time to get at the ships anchored in the harbor.

A believer in detailed planning, Yamamoto gathered his task force and put them to work rehearsing the actual attack in Kagoshima Bay in Japan, roughly approximate to the size and appearance of Pearl Harbor. In the fall of 1940, Japanese intelligence gave him an extra weapon.

All along, Yamamoto assumed that his pilots would need to develop the highest possible bombing accuracy, for the carrier-based planes had a limited bombload; each bomb would have to be dropped precisely on target. He assumed he could not use aerial torpedos, which were devastating ship killers, because Pearl Harbor's shallow depth (around 40 feet) was insufficient for an air-launched torpedo's requirement of roughly 70 feet of depth. But in September 1940, the British conducted a highly successful raid using torpedo planes in the Italian harbor of Taranto. The Italian fleet was crippled by the torpedos, for it had not bothered to put up antitorpedo nets, considered unnecessary in Taranto's shallow waters. Thanks to their contacts with German intelligence, the Japanese obtained access to Italian after-action reports, which noted the British had used torpedos modified for use in shallow waters.

With that intelligence, Yamamoto's engineers were able to reconfigure the Japanese torpedos, adding special wooden fins to allow them to operate in shallow depths. Tested against dummy targets in Kagoshima Bay, the new torpedos worked perfectly. Yamamoto now had a devastating weapon that could be launched by attack planes at relatively long distances against anchored ships. Even one torpedo, properly aimed, could break the back of a battleship if it hit a vital spot.

But to get maximum advantage from the torpedos, Yamamoto's pilots required precise information on the location of the targets so they could launch their weapons at just the right point. The same requirement applied to the planes that would drop bombs. Overall, the entire attack plan was a high-stakes gamble; as Yamamoto understood, given the limited weapons-carrying capacity of his carrier-based planes and their equally limited range, he had only one shot to knock out the Pacific Fleet. Anything less than a perfect strike would be a disaster.

The stage thus was set to place a heavy burden on Japanese intelligence: it had to provide extremely specific intelligence on the Pacific Fleet at Pearl Harbor, sufficient to allow Yamamoto's attacking force to carry out Operation Z with precision. For that reason, the mission of Takeo Yoshikawa was absolutely vital.

As Yoshikawa learned, Pearl Harbor had all the security of a public park. Surrounded by residential areas, it was a prime tourist attraction (private planes were permitted to overfly the base at will), and each day it admitted thousands of civilian workers without any security requirements whatsoever. From the hills overlooking the harbor, anyone could spot and photograph all the installations and ships at anchor.

But Yoshikawa was not satisfied with even these advantages. To gather more detailed intelligence, he disguised himself as a poor, barefoot Filipino garbage worker; with that cover, he carefully analyzed the contents of dumpsters at Pearl Harbor for clues as to how many sailors were stationed there, along with any classified documents that might have been carelessly thrown away. He swam the waters around the seaward side of the harbor, measuring the beach gradients and tides. At night he hung around bars and nightclubs where U.S. Navy personnel congregated, hoping to pick up any tidbits he could.

Yoshikawa was backed up by other forces Japanese intelligence deployed in and around Hawaii. Submarines periodically crept near the harbor, taking reconnaissance pictures through their periscopes. In Hawaii itself, the Japanese recruited a network of 12 Japanese-born residents of the islands to collect intelligence about Pearl Harbor. (They turned out to be useless; one of them, an ex-Japanese naval officer, liked to show his neighbors his collection of autographed pictures of fellow officers—including one of himself.)

Aware that Japanese operatives would have a difficult time blending in among white American faces, Yoshikawa's superiors hit upon the idea of recruiting a non-Japanese assistant for him. A request to German intelligence produced an itinerant knockabout named Bernard Kuehn. For $25,000 provided by the Japanese, Kuehn emigrated to Honolulu with his wife and daughter, bought a house, then announced to Yoshikawa his plan to penetrate Pearl Harbor. It consisted of his wife setting up a beauty shop near the base; Navy wives, Kuehn assured Yoshikawa, would be lured by cut-rate prices to the shop, there to gossip about their husbands while under the hair dryers. An amazing amount of intelligence would be obtained that way, Kuehn said.

Yoshikawa was not impressed, and he was even less taken with another Kuehn idea: when the Japanese actually struck Pearl Harbor, he and his wife would arrange a signal of house lights and patterns of washing hung on a clothesline to report progress of the raid that Japanese submarines could monitor. This was the stupidest idea that Yoshikawa had ever heard, but he politely said nothing and merely passed on to Tokyo details of Kuehn's plan. (To his surprise, Tokyo thought the plan was brilliant.)

By November, Yoshikawa had filed 24 lengthy reports with Tokyo that contained an amazing amount of detail on the Pacific Fleet, the Pearl Harbor installations, the American air patrols, and the specific locations of every ship in the harbor. He learned that the most vulnerable time for the fleet was Sunday morning, when reduced crews and patrols meant that the Pearl Harbor base was at a low state of alert. He also learned that torpedo nets were not normally deployed in the harbor because the Navy did not want to restrict an already narrow shipping channel to the sea. (Besides, U.S. Navy experts were certain that aerial torpedos were unable to operate in Pearl Harbor's shallow depths.)

But taken as a whole, Yoshikawa's diligent collection of information illustrated Japanese intelligence's worst fault: an obsession with bean-counting, collecting vast amounts of information, trivial and otherwise, to build a comprehensive picture of an enemy's capabilities. The Pearl Harbor operation illustrated the problem perfectly. Yoshikawa's reports could tell Tokyo everything it wanted to know about such esoterica as how the Amer-

ican battleships were aligned while at anchor, but the Japanese
had no insight into what the Americans intended to do with those
ships—or whether they were of any value as prime targets in the
first place.

More important, among Yoshikawa's major intelligence targets were the four aircraft carriers of the Pacific Fleet. Again,
Yoshikawa was limited in the intelligence he could provide; he
could tell his superiors if the carriers were in port at any given
time, but he had no insight into their sailing orders. As things
turned out, that proved to be a critical intelligence lapse. Yoshikawa was unaware that several days before the Japanese attack the
Lexington and the *Saratoga,* two of the four American carriers usually stationed at Pearl—the other two were on the West Coast—
received orders to deliver planes to Wake Island and Guam. On
December 5, Yoshikawa noticed they were missing. He could report the ships weren't in the harbor, but he had no idea where
they had gone or why they had sailed. For all the Japanese knew,
the carriers could have been steaming directly into the path of
Yamamoto's strike force, which had left Japan a few days before.

Fortunately for the Japanese, they weren't. The Japanese
were able to get away with this lapse because their intelligence
failures were overshadowed by the far greater mistakes made by
American intelligence. Those mistakes were all the more astonishing considering that the Americans were perfectly aware of
Japanese intentions, knew that Pearl Harbor was the focus of Japan's intelligence interest, and most intriguing of all, were reading every word Yoshikawa was transmitting to Tokyo.

Beginning in 1919, when construction of the Pearl Harbor naval
base began, the United States operated on the assumption that
war with its Pacific rival, Japan, was inevitable. Pearl Harbor was
intended as a deterrent to Japanese aggression, even though the
U.S. Navy never liked the idea of a base dependent on a 3,000-
mile-long supply line, with only one narrow entrance channel
easily blocked in the event of war, and its ships, fuel storage, and
repair facilities all crowded together in a relatively small area.

The Navy always considered the base vulnerable but assumed that its fleet would be able to steam out to sea in the event
of hostilities and engage the Japanese navy in a massive sea battle.
In such a battle, the Americans assumed, the superior American
battleships and planes would make short work of the Japanese
navy. But by the late 1930s, U.S. intelligence on Japan's military

was seriously out of date; poorly organized and directed, it missed the significant improvements in Japanese military technology.

Among the worst failures was missing the development of Japan's new class of fast battleships with 18-inch guns that completely outranged and outclassed all American battleships. The U.S. ships, designed to withstand the maximum impact of a 16-inch shell, had been rendered obsolete. Other intelligence failures included missing the development of the Japanese advanced "Long Lance" torpedo, far superior than anything in the American arsenal, and most damaging of all, the agile Zero fighter that slaughtered slower American planes until late 1942, when the United States developed new fighters to defeat it. (The Zero intelligence failure is especially hard to understand, since the Japanese plane had first been used in combat in 1937 during the Sino-Japanese War.)

The problem, basically, was that American intelligence was badly fragmented, split among a half-dozen different agencies that did not share intelligence with each other. Like several people working on a jigsaw puzzle who do not cooperate, each agency had a small piece that made no sense unless it could see all the other pieces. It was this fragmentation that would lead to the Pearl Harbor intelligence failure, the worst such disaster in American history.

To understand how that factionalized American intelligence structure failed at Pearl Harbor, it is first necessary to outline the intelligence resources arrayed against Japan before the attack. These consisted of the following.

- ONI "hypo" radio detection stations dotted around the Pacific, which hunted for Japanese naval radio signals with direction-finders and then plotted ship movements. The "hypo" system was supposed to tell the Navy where the Japanese ships were at any given time.

- OP-20-G, an ONI codebreaking unit that attacked Japanese naval codes to divine operational orders from headquarters to ships operating at sea.

- U.S. Army Intelligence wiretapping operations directed against Japanese installations in Hawaii and elsewhere to detect orders to agents that might reveal the focus of Japanese intelligence efforts.

- ONI wiretapping operations against Japanese businesses and diplomatic posts in the United States to detect any orders from Tokyo that would signal imminent hostilities.

- MAGIC, the crown jewel of American intelligence, a U.S. Army cryptanalytic operation that had broken the high-level Japanese diplomatic code and would thus reveal any Japanese government decision to go to war.

At first glance, this is a fairly impressive intelligence array, but there was an obvious lack: no sources in Japan. That meant the Americans had no real insight into Japanese thinking, nor did they have any on-site assets in Japan itself who could provide such elemental intelligence as whether or not the Japanese fleet's sailors were in port on liberty (meaning their ships were not about to sail off into war). With no Japanese sources, American intelligence was reduced to peeking at the Japanese war machine from the outside, hoping that unmistakable clues, primarily electronic, would provide warning of hostile intentions.

They did not, partially because of the very fragmented nature of that system, and partially because at the moment of greatest need, the system broke down altogether.

The first breakdown occurred in U.S. Navy Intelligence. In November 1941 it detected the sudden movement of a large Japanese naval task force from its normal berths to the Kuriles, north of Japan's main islands. Ominously, the force moved under total radio silence (indicating it was not a training exercise), completely blinding the Navy's "hypo" stations that depended on radio signals to make their fix. Within days, naval intelligence lost all track of the task force. The Navy was now paying the penalty for its lack of sources in Japan.

Still, there was hope of discovering what that mysterious task force was up to via the OP-20-G codebreakers who had managed to solve at least part of the main Japanese naval code. Known as JN-25, the code was a very complex system that used 33,000 codewords and a 500-page book of random additives. The Japanese used it to dispatch operational orders from headquarters to ships at sea. The task force, although under radio silence, still had to receive orders. But at this critical moment the Japanese changed the JN-25 code, making it absolutely unreadable. U.S. naval intelligence was blind.

So now there was a major Japanese naval task force loose somewhere in the Pacific at a time of worsening tension between

the United States and Japan. Responding to the Japanese takeover of French Indochina, President Roosevelt had ordered an
oil embargo against Japan. While there were widespread predic-
tions this move made war between Japan and the United States
inevitable, the Americans lacked the kind of high-level sources in
Japan who could have provided some insight into Japanese thinking.

True, there was MAGIC, but even that miracle of cryptography had its limitations. For one thing, the Army kept strict control of MAGIC decrypts, showing them only to a few selected
officials (including Roosevelt). The problem was that unless the
recipients had access to other intelligence, the decrypts often
made no sense. Toward the end of 1941, those decrypts all
pointed to a break in U.S.-Japanese diplomatic relations. Not only
did this represent an unmistakable signal of approaching war, but
the decrypts also laid out a strict timetable for that rupture, indicating that it almost certainly would be accompanied by some
sort of direct military action.

The Army and Navy commanders at Pearl Harbor might
have deduced their base would be the probable target, but since
they were not among the recipients of MAGIC intelligence, they
had no idea that Tokyo and Washington were approaching the
breaking point. Nor were they told that the Japanese diplomatic
posts overseas had been ordered to make plans to destroy their
codebooks and other sensitive papers—another certain indication of approaching war.

Even more significantly, MAGIC was reading the voluminous
intelligence reports being sent to Japan from the Japanese consulate in Hawaii, all of them dealing with Pearl Harbor. When
MAGIC detected the order from Tokyo on December 5 concerning the urgency for detailed intelligence on U.S. ship dispositions
at Pearl Harbor, that would have been a vital clue for the base
commanders. But they weren't told about it, nor were they told
about an even more significant MAGIC decryption, this one reporting on the arrangements by Kuehn, the German asset of Japanese intelligence, to signal progress of an actual strike on Pearl
Harbor.

Similarly, military commanders might have perceived the
imminence of a Japanese strike via important MAGIC decrypts in
November. These revealed the Japanese had set up a system of
coded messages in innocuous-sounding weather reports to signal
diplomatic posts instantly that war was imminent. Among them,

MAGIC revealed, was *higashi no kaze ame* (east wind, rain), meaning war with the United States. Again, however, senior military commanders were not told of this alarm bell, which could have enabled them to put all military installations on full alert the moment it was broadcast.

The last act in this chain of intelligence blunders occurred the night of December 6, 1941, when MAGIC produced a decrypt of an extraordinary 14-part message from Tokyo to the Japanese embassy in Washington. The message ordered two special Japanese envoys to break off peace talks with the Americans, an announcement to be delivered to American Secretary of State Cordell Hull at precisely 1:00 P.M. eastern standard time on December 7. Roosevelt and his advisers pondered the meaning of that curiously specific deadline; why were the Japanese so precise as to which moment the talks would be broken off? Finally, someone remembered that 36 years before, the Japanese had sent a similar message to Russia just before the surprise attack on the Russian fleet at Port Arthur to open the Russo-Japanese War.

"This means war," Roosevelt said, now convinced that the Japanese were about to strike. But where? His advisers brought maps and charts and sketched out the possible targets of a Japanese assault, including the Dutch East Indies and the Philippines. Far down on the list was Pearl Harbor.

Like everybody else in Roosevelt's inner circle, Army Chief of Staff George Marshall, the president's chief military adviser, had no idea which of these possible targets was most likely to be struck. In that intelligence fog, he finally decided that Pearl Harbor, base for the Pacific Fleet, might be a probable target. He sent a telegram to the base commander ordering him to put the base on general alert. But due to a clerk's foul-up, instead of being sent by the high-priority military communications system, the telegram was dispatched via Western Union. It was still lying in an in-box at the Honolulu Western Union office at 7:55 the next morning when the Japanese struck.

The *Kibo Butai* (task force) had taken 10 days to steam across the northern Pacific to a point 250 miles off the coast of Hawaii. Its six aircraft carriers (carrying 432 planes), two battleships, nine destroyers, two heavy cruisers, one light cruiser, eight tankers, and three submarines had sailed several thousand miles completely undetected.

The Japanese planes encountered no opposition from an unalerted Pearl Harbor as they bore in for the attack against the

96 ships anchored in the harbor and the planes parked at Ford Field. "Tora! Tora!" the lead pilot radioed, a coded message that meant the Americans had been caught by complete surprise. In less than an hour, 18 of those ships had been hit, including three battleships. At Ford Field, more than half of the 394 planes parked wingtip to wingtip were destroyed. Nearly 2,400 Americans were killed.

But the Japanese intelligence failures now came home to roost. With no system to tell him the results of the attack and whether or not American reinforcements were on the move, Admiral Chuichi Nagumo, commander of the task force, was operating blind. The pilots from his first-wave attack reported fantastic results, but as Nagumo well knew, pilots tend to exaggerate the results of their own efforts. The pilots in the second-wave attack were confused by the heavy, thick smoke that covered the harbor area, making it almost impossible to spot new targets or determine whether previous targets had been put out of commission. More worrisome from Nagumo's standpoint were the missing U.S. aircraft carriers. He had no idea where they were, and it was perfectly possible the carriers at that very moment were turning into the wind not too far away, preparing to launch a strike that would decimate his task force, whose own planes were preoccupied at Pearl Harbor.

Nagumo faced a critical decision: should he recover his planes, rearm them, and send them back to Hawaii for a follow-up strike? He would have loved some hard intelligence at that point to guide him, but he had none. Japanese intelligence's plan for a signaling system using the German Kuehn had never come to pass; in any event, the Japanese submarine force around Pearl Harbor was otherwise busy, having come under attack by U.S. Navy destroyers (one submarine was sunk). The worst failure, Nagumo was to discover only much later, was that Japanese intelligence, for all its detailed inventory of Pearl Harbor, failed to tell him that the most important targets were not the ships, but the oil storage facility, which contained the entire oil reserve for the Pacific Fleet, and the dockyard facilities. If either of those two targets had been hit, the U.S. Navy would have been in serious trouble: without oil and forced to use the nearest dockyard of similar size three thousand miles away in San Francisco, it would have taken many months to recover.

Nagumo, wary of unseen dangers that might be all around him and convinced he had struck a decisive blow at Pearl Harbor,

An aerial view of Pearl Harbor taken just a few months before the Japanese attack in December 1941. At lower center, looking like four rows of buttons, is the oil storage tank farm—a vital target Japanese intelligence missed. (*United States Naval Institute*)

canceled a follow-up strike and steamed back to Japan. The Japanese would soon learn he had failed. Of the 18 ships hit at Pearl Harbor, 15 were later repaired and sent into action to haunt Japan for the rest of the war. As for the raid's most spectacular result—the sinking of several battleships—that turned out to be an unimportant loss. One of the victims, the *Utah*, was an old ship used only for training; two others, the *Arizona* and the *Oklahoma*, were obsolete, even by U.S. Navy standards. Of the 188 planes destroyed at Ford Field, most were obsolete models.

Untouched were the aircraft carriers, the dockyards, the repair facilities, and the Pacific Fleet's oil supply, the essential ingredients for the U.S. Navy's resurgence. As it happened, only six months later at the decisive naval battle of Midway, the United States sank four of the six Japanese carriers involved in the attack against Pearl Harbor.

During the next three years, Japan would be destroyed in the whirlwind that was spawned at Pearl Harbor, for it would pay a heavy price for its intelligence failures. Those failures involved not only Japan's errors at Pearl Harbor, but even larger intelligence lapses, chief among them a total lack of understanding of how violently the United States would react to such an attack and how it would unleash an industrial might Japan had no hope of matching.

Very few of the Japanese involved in the planning and execution of the Pearl Harbor attack survived the war (its original progenitor, Admiral Yamamoto, was killed in 1943). Among the survivors was Ensign Yoshikawa, who was repatriated to Japan under his identity as Vice-Consul Morimura. He spent the war years at the headquarters of Japanese naval intelligence, fruitlessly trying to divine where the huge American naval armadas would strike next. After the war, he ran a gas station until his death some twenty-five years later.

Just before his death, Yoshikawa quite unexpectedly found himself thrust back in time to 1941 Honolulu, an event precipitated by a strange ghost of Pearl Harbor who appeared in America. The widow of Bernard Kuehn, the hapless German spy for the Japanese, came to claim $25,000 she insisted the U.S. government owed her for its seizure of the Kuehn house in Honolulu in 1941 when her husband was arrested on espionage charges after Pearl Harbor. (Kuehn, blown by the MAGIC decrypts, was sentenced to death, later commuted to life; he was released and deported to Germany in 1945, where he died in 1965.)

The U.S. government, which had seized the Kuehn house under federal forfeiture laws, disposed of Mrs. Kuehn's claim by tracking down Yoshikawa. Imperial Japan's star spy at Pearl Harbor confirmed that the Kuehn house had been purchased with Japanese intelligence funds—a waste of money, Yoshikawa noted sourly, since Kuehn proved to be totally useless. But then, he added, nothing much good came out of Pearl Harbor, anyway.

18

Defeat at the Iron Curtain

The CIA's Underground War
1947–1956

Tragedy in Eastern Europe

It was, they remembered, like a scene out of a nightmare. They could see the men and women huddled together miserably in the bitter winter cold just after dawn, their few meager possessions stuffed into bags and suitcases. The soldiers, armed with clubs, whips, and snarling dogs, herded the people into separate groups of about a hundred.

When the train arrived, the soldiers ordered the groups into boxcars, pushing and shoving them like cattle; anyone who hesitated or resisted was clubbed into unconsciousness, then thrown bodily into the boxcar. Finally, when the boxcars were jammed with humanity, the train left. Another train with a long string of boxcars then pulled up, more people were herded inside, and the process was repeated. Hour after hour this went on until, around sunset, 80,000 human beings had been taken away to their deaths. A terrible atrocity had taken place.

Night now fell on January 14, 1945. The group of Americans who had witnessed this crime at the main railway station in Bucharest, Romania, powerless to stop it, felt sick to their stomachs. But what they had seen that day hardened their resolve: the perpetrators of that crime must never be allowed to have such power over human beings anywhere else in the world. And the men who ordered the crime must be destroyed.

The next day Frank Wisner, head of the OSS mission in Bucharest, whose agents had witnessed the horror at the railway station, wrote a lengthy report to OSS headquarters in Washington. He recited the details of what he and his men had seen the previous morning and went on to provide a lengthy analysis of events in Romania during the previous few months. It amounted to an unrelieved catalog of subversion, political intimidation, assassinations, agitation, and repression—all committed by the Soviet Union in the process of communizing the country.

For all intents and purposes, the Cold War between the Soviet Union and the United States began that day. Wisner's report caused great unease at OSS headquarters, and it soon percolated throughout the rest of the government. To many officials who read it, the report confirmed their worst fears: contrary to the hopes of the Roosevelt administration, the wartime alliance had not moderated Stalin and his henchmen. As events in Romania (and, subsequently, other countries occupied by the Red Army) proved, they were determined to impose Soviet communism on Eastern Europe by force. The United States had a new enemy.

It was an enemy, Wisner decided, not very different from the Nazi enemy then nearing final defeat. What had happened that winter morning at the Bucharest railway station was being repeated, in various forms, all over Eastern Europe as the Russians consolidated their control. The very same trains that had taken the Jews of Europe to the slaughter were now being used by the Soviet Union to transport people by the hundreds of thousands to KGB execution cellars or slave labor camps in Siberia.

Who were these victims? Basically, anyone Stalin decreed a threat, potential or otherwise, to Soviet hegemony. In Romania, he decided that any Romanian citizen with German blood was a threat to the Communist regime he was imposing on the Romanian people. Consequently, all Romanians of "ethnic German origin" between the ages of seventeen and forty-five were rounded up and shipped to slave labor camps in Siberia. Some 80,000 people whose only crime was to have a German grandmother or even a distant German relative were shoved into boxcars without food or water. Days later, when the trains arrived in Siberia, almost half of them were dead. The rest perished in a few months.

Allen Dulles, right, head of the OSS station in Bern, Switzerland, confers with his chief German asset, Gero von Schulze Gaevernitz, in 1945. Dulles, later a director of the CIA, had begun to reorient OSS operations toward the Russians, strongly influenced by early reports from fellow OSS agent Frank Wisner in Romania about Soviet subversion. (*Central Intelligence Agency*)

Through a combination of circumstances, Wisner's OSS team occupied a front-row seat to witness such horrors, the most extensive and long-lasting U.S. cockpit in Eastern Europe to see the Soviet techniques of subversion and domination unfold. What Wisner saw and reported would prove significant, for it would give birth to a vast covert war conducted by U.S. intelligence to check, then defeat, the march of Soviet totalitarianism.

That war would last for more than forty years. The United States would lose it, although in the end final victory was achieved by history. Soviet communism collapsed entirely, along with the Eastern European adjunct Moscow had worked so hard to create.

Frank Wisner did not live to see this historic event. He was one of the early casualties in the war—a man, as things turned out, who was consumed by the very conflagration he had helped light.

On the day Pearl Harbor was attacked, Frank Wisner was a thirty-two-year-old Mississippi-born lawyer working in a Manhattan securities firm. He was a bored lawyer; an energetic, restless man, he became convinced that he was meant to play some important role in the events that were now shaking the world's foundations. He signed up for the ONI, but he quickly discovered that his job in naval intelligence—sitting at a desk collating reports on plans to keep ship convoy intelligence out of the hands of the Germans—was as boring as securities law. Hearing of a new American intelligence agency called OSS that was run by a fellow Manhattan lawyer, the dynamic William (Wild Bill) Donovan, Wisner pressed for a transfer.

He soon found his element, flourishing in the intrigue of such foreign locales as Istanbul. Wisner loved intelligence work, the more difficult the better. In September 1944 Donovan gave him a tricky assignment, one he felt was best suited to Wisner's fondness for intrigue and double-dealing. It would be an assignment that changed Wisner's life.

In August 1944 King Michael of Romania had carried out a coup against the reigning Fascist government and had begun negotiations with the Soviet Union to take Romania out of the war. To prove his intentions, Michael had abruptly ordered all Germans out of the country, allowing them barely enough time to pack their bags. He also contacted the Western allies, inviting them to send delegations to Romania and arrange for the repatriation of nearly two thousand American and British prisoners of war, mostly downed pilots, who had been held by the Germans.

A golden opportunity now presented itself, Donovan concluded. Wisner was assigned to work under cover as chief of the American Air Unit, a group of several dozen military officers who would go to Romania and arrange for the evacuation of American POWs. The rest of the unit would consist of OSS agents under cover. Their function was threefold: (1) get the American prisoners back into Allied hands, (2) grab any German intelligence material that the Germans might have left behind in their hasty evacuation, and (3) keep a sharp watch on the Russians, who would now move in to occupy Romania.

This last task arose out of Donovan's deepening suspicions about Soviet postwar intentions. Now he had the opportunity to monitor what happened when the Russians actually got their hands on a country, especially the covert techniques they might use to subvert the ruling government. Wisner was to proceed cautiously in this area, Donovan warned; he was quietly to collect all the intelligence he could on how the Russians operated, without attempting to interfere with them. The intelligence would be used to buttress Donovan's own memorandums to the upper reaches of the American government warning about Soviet intentions. Similar secret instructions were handed out to other OSS stations and operatives working on the borders of Eastern Europe.

In September 1944 Wisner and his unit arrived in Bucharest, and they immediately struck an intelligence gold mine. As Donovan had predicted, both the German *Abwehr* and SD had left behind mountains of paper they had no time to burn: intelligence reports, names of assets they had recruited in Romania, and invaluable material on what they had learned about Soviet intelligence operations in Eastern Europe. While Wisner negotiated with the Romanian government on the logistics of moving American prisoners to the airport in Bucharest and the arrangements for the landing of transport planes, his men were crating the treasure trove of paper they had found in abandoned German intelligence offices.

That paper, along with 1,888 American prisoners, eventually was flown out of Bucharest, but in the process Wisner made an enemy: the KGB. Soviet agents arrived just behind the advancing Red Army that October, but by that time they found only empty filing cabinets and safes in German offices. Aware that the Germans had no time to burn the files and records, the KGB immediately concluded that Wisner's group had taken them. Wisner claimed to know nothing about any such records, but the Russians knew better. Wisner was a man who bore watching.

Of more significant interest to the KGB, however, was its assigned role in Stalin's plan to get rid of King Michael's caretaker government and its talk of democracy and freedom. The last thing Stalin wanted in Romania was democracy, and Wisner was given a unique view of just how the Russians set about imposing their will.

The first step seemed low-key. When Michael organized a new government, he created a cabinet whose members reflected the various political factions in Romania. Eager not to offend any political group, Michael asked the Communists which post they wanted. Ministry of Justice was the reply, which seemed reasonable enough.

But it was the wedge the native Communists, under orders from the KGB, wanted. First, under the guise of "maintaining order," the ministry created a so-called Guard of Patriotic De-

fense, a left-wing militia that was in fact a collection of thugs assigned to break up "disturbances"—defined as any political demonstration or meeting by anti-Communists.

The Justice Ministry post also allowed the Communists to
take control of Romania's intelligence service. Collaborators with
the Germans were cleaned out, replaced by Communists who
now turned the agency into a domestic spying organization that
collected derogatory information on all non-Communist leaders.

Wisner and his OSS crew recruited a few assets from among
Romania's upper crust to help keep watch on the growing Communist infiltration of virtually all phases of Romanian life. Wisner,
assigned the code name TYPHOID, each night radioed reports
to OSS headquarters. At first these reports were preoccupied with
wartime intelligence about the Germans, but their departure
made any further reporting about them superfluous. Gradually,
the TYPHOID reports came to be concerned with the phenom-
enon that began to occupy Wisner's waking hours, the Commu-
nization of Romania.

It did not require much effort for Wisner's OSS mission to
spot the Soviet involvement in the transformation of the country.
Bucharest was fairly crawling with KGB agents, many of them
functioning as "advisers" to the Justice Ministry. The ministry was
busy expanding its power, and it gradually took control of the
Interior Ministry. With that important government department
in hand, the Communists and their Soviet advisers now moved to
take control of the entire country.

Among the Interior Ministry's tasks was purging all institu-
tions of collaborators with the Germans, a task that served as a
perfect screen to round up and imprison all anti-Communists on
the grounds they were collaborators. Interior Ministry officials
claimed they had secret information "proving" the guilt of those
so accused, information that could not be revealed for fear of
jeopardizing national security. Meanwhile, Soviet troops were busily dismantling the equipment at Romanian oil fields and shipping it to the Soviet Union. They worked unmolested by any remaining German forces in the country; as Wisner was to discover,
Stalin secretly made a deal with German commanders to allow
two German divisions trapped by the Russian advance to escape
the country, in exchange for a German guarantee that Hitler
would not counterattack in Romania. (That December those two
divisions, which the Allies assumed had been wiped out in Ro-

mania, appeared in Belgium to fall upon unsuspecting American troops in the Battle of the Bulge.)

In late 1944 deportations to the Soviet Union began, all legalized by the Interior Ministry on various pretexts, climaxed by the roundup of "Germans" in January 1945. Wisner sensed there was worse to come, and he ordered his agents to recruit more assets to provide information on the Soviet-sponsored efforts to infiltrate the government. But Wisner quickly discovered that the OSS was completely outclassed: the KGB had 1,200 agents in Bucharest alone, had taps on virtually every phone in the city, and had entire battalions of assets recruited among native Communists.

The KGB was perfectly aware of what Wisner and the Americans were up to. The Russians knew that Wisner's official mission—arranging for the transfer of American POWs held in the Balkans—was merely cover for his real mission, collecting intelligence on the Russians and their takeover of Romania. Armed with an understanding between Churchill and Stalin that allowed Moscow a "dominant voice" in Romania and Yugoslavia in exchange for British sway in Greece, Stalin could afford to let the small band of a dozen Americans see whatever they wanted to see. The KGB was content to monitor everything the Americans did and gain control over their assets. And if the Americans saw how, like hungry moles, the Communists were undermining the Romanian government, so what? Who cared about Romania?

Wisner did, and his reports were increasingly alarmist as he watched the Soviet grip tighten. In February 1945 the KGB imported a platoon of professionally trained Communist agitators to organize a huge demonstration under the banner of a new political movement called the "National Democratic Front." Advertised as the "authentic" voice of the Romanian people, it surged through the streets of Bucharest, demanding a say in the government. Shots rang out, and Soviet troops, conveniently bivouacked just a mile away, intervened to stop it. The Interior Ministry embarked on a new wave of arrests, claiming that "antidemocratic" forces tried to break up the demonstration (although in fact the shooting was the work of KGB stooges instructed to precipitate precisely that kind of crackdown).

King Michael had resisted the demand to bring more Communists into the government, but on February 27, 1945, Stalin sent in his chief goon for pressuring recalcitrant foreign leaders, Deputy Foreign Minister Andrei Vyshinsky. In a meeting with Michael, Vyshinsky emphasized that Stalin himself wanted more Communists in the Romanian government. Each time Michael tried to say something, Vyshinsky smashed his fist on the table. Finally, he stalked out of the room, slamming the door behind him so hard, the plaster cracked. Outside the building, Michael could see hundreds of Soviet troops on "routine patrol." The king got the point, and within hours he agreed to let the Communists take over most of the government ministries and departments.

The rest was a slide into tyranny. In March 1945 the Communists took control of the government as Michael fled into exile. The new government, honeycombed with KGB "advisers," began a nightmare of repression. Into a new network of prisons and torture dungeons were dragged thousands of Romanians to confess that their opposition to the Communists was the result only of their being "agents of imperialism." Less than 24 months later, Romania was a Communist state and Soviet satrapy. By that time some 282,000 Romanians had been arrested and deported to Siberia (over 190,000 of them would die there in slave labor camps). For the Romanians who remained, their lives consisted of repression of all "incorrect thought," strict controls on all movements in the country, forced collectivization, and forced labor.

By that time, Wisner had long since left the country. In September 1945 the OSS mission was withdrawn because its ostensible job, repatriating POWs, was over. But his experiences in Romania had effected a powerful change in Wisner. He returned to his law practice after the war, but increasingly preoccupied with an apocalyptic vision of the Soviet juggernaut he had seen in Romania advancing to take over the rest of the world, he simply could not summon any enthusiasm for such esoterica as Securities and Exchange Commission regulations. He wanted to do something about the Communist menace.

His chance came in 1947, when the Central Intelligence Agency was formed. Many of its charter members—among them Allen Dulles, a future director of the agency—had read Wisner's reports on the Sovietization of Romania. "You lifted the scales from our eyes," Dulles told Wisner, in the process of recruiting him for the new CIA. But Wisner was not destined to become simply another agent; the CIA had much grander plans for him.

Basically, those plans amounted to a covert crusade to roll back the Communists in Eastern Europe. Through every means short of actual military intervention, the United States would emulate the Soviet success by infiltrating, destabilizing, and undermining the Communist regimes. The regimes would be destroyed using the very same methods that had originally created them.

To accomplish that goal, the CIA created an organization called Office of Policy Coordination (OPC), a deliberately vague entity that technically was part of the State Department, although its control and funding rested with the CIA. Wisner was named to head OPC, and he immediately set about creating an empire. By 1949 he had 302 people working for him and a $4.7 million annual budget; by 1952 he had 2,812 staffers and an $82 million yearly budget, nearly half the CIA's entire budget.

The exponential growth of OPC underscored its importance in the CIA. Wisner's covert crusade represented the cutting edge of the American counteroffensive against the Soviet Union. In an era of nuclear weapons that had made direct military confrontation between the two superpowers unthinkable, Wisner's operation was America's response to the Soviet menace.

Wisner liked to call it his "mighty Wurlitzer," a full-scale assault involving every technique of covert political action: propaganda, bribery, subversion, disinformation, infiltration of agents, sabotage, and support for anti-Communist exiles (including, unfortunately, a large number of Nazi war criminals). Wisner also organized scores of sleeper underground groups in Eastern and Western Europe that would function as behind-the-lines guerrillas, using secret arms caches Wisner created, to harass Soviet military forces in the event of a Soviet invasion of Western Europe.

The energetic Wisner seemed to work around the clock running this huge enterprise and spinning out still more new schemes (such as his idea for launching a fleet of balloons over Eastern Europe to release millions of propaganda leaflets). But no matter what Wisner tried, nothing seemed to work. Every attempt to destabilize the Communist regimes of Eastern Europe failed, sometimes disastrously so.

In Wisner's conception, OPC's main function was to create a sufficient amount of unrest in Eastern Europe to foment revolts by the people to overthrow the regimes. However, it soon became clear that the hurdles OPC faced—huge internal security apparatuses, a pervasive KGB presence alert for the slightest deviation, and most important of all, the presence of the Red Army—were not about to be overcome as easily as Wisner had hoped.

Romania, Wisner's old stomping grounds, provided the first object lesson. CIA agents in 1947 exerted a great deal of effort to recruit a large network of anti-Communists, the essential prelude for infiltrating the Communist regime and then destabilizing it. The network was detected in short order by the KGB, and within a few months, after feeding the Americans some KGB disinformation, it was rounded up and destroyed.

Similarly, an attempt in Hungary to accomplish the same end also fell victim to KGB counterintelligence; in one day alone, 102 assets recruited by the CIA for an anti-Communist coalition government to replace the Communist regime were rounded up.

As Wisner discovered the hard way, it is not easy to conduct covert actions in a police state, especially one with thousands of KGB agents, a homegrown secret police force, and hundreds of thousands of Soviet troops. That lesson was learned most bitterly in Poland.

In 1950, Poland seemed to represent a real OPC success story. The success went under the name WIN, the Polish acronym for an organization called the Freedom and Independence Movement. Working in cooperation with the main emigré Polish movement in London, the Polish Political Council, WIN since 1947 had been organizing, with the help of OPC, a vast underground movement inside Poland. By 1950 WIN had 500 active agents, 20,000 "partially active" agents, and another 100,000 men who had pledged to fight as guerrillas behind Soviet lines in the event of a Soviet invasion westward.

The group's success, verified by the London Poles who knew the leaders as anti-Communists who had fought as partisans against both the Germans and the Russians before and during World War II, encouraged Wisner to pour more resources into expanding it. Money, military supplies, and radio equipment were smuggled and parachuted into Poland. By 1952 Wisner believed that WIN was very near the point where it could actually overthrow the Communist regime on its own. Then disaster struck.

In December 1952, hardly able to conceal its smug satisfaction, Polish state radio announced that WIN had been a KGB sting operation from the first moment of its existence. In 1947, the radio account revealed, the small WIN movement had been swept up by the KGB. Its leaders, under threat of execution of their families, agreed to cooperate. For the next five years they were to fool OPC completely, even including an elaborate charade that created an entire underground "government" for an OPC agent to see when he slipped into Poland to verify WIN's success.

Stalin's motive for ordering the exposure of WIN was clear: it was used to justify still further repression in Eastern Europe under the guise of "protecting" citizens against the evil foreigners. Still, even the cowed Eastern Europeans could take only so much repression, and when East German workers revolted in 1953, Wisner thought OPC had succeeded at last. But Soviet tanks put down the revolt, an event that underscored the central weakness of Wisner's great crusade: so long as there were large Soviet military forces in Eastern Europe, there was no real hope that any of those regimes would be overthrown from within. The simple fact was that the Soviet Union would never permit it, and it had the military muscle on hand to back up that determination. The Communist subversion of Eastern Europe after World War II succeeded in large measure because there was always a large Soviet military presence to add teeth to the Communist threat.

Regrettably, Wisner failed to comprehend that fact. His efforts were to lead to a tragedy in Hungary. For years, OPC had been active in that most repressive of all Eastern European states, including propaganda broadcasts that encouraged Hungarians to throw off their oppressors. In 1956 they did, a popular uprising that overthrew the Communist government and replaced it with a non-Communist one. But there was no way Moscow would permit such a revolt to succeed and serve as inspiration for the rest of Eastern Europe. Soviet troops brutally suppressed the revolt. Contrary to the expectations raised in the OPC propaganda broadcasts, the United States had no intention of intervening militarily and touching off World War III.

Wisner frantically tried to drum up support for a U.S. military expedition to save the Hungarian revolutionaries, but preoccupied with the crisis in the Middle East (Israel, France, and Great Britain had invaded Egypt) and aware that any military move into Hungary had no chance against overwhelming Soviet military power in that area, the American government decided to do nothing. In rage and frustration, Wisner stood on the Austrian-Hungarian border, watching helplessly as revolutionaries trying to flee to safety were hunted down and machine-gunned to death. It was January 1945 all over again, only worse.

Wisner was shattered by the experience. He suffered a nervous breakdown and did not return to his crusade for six months.

Soviet tanks on the prowl in Budapest in 1956 as the Russians brutally suppressed the Hungarian revolt. The end of the revolt marked a severe defeat for a covert CIA operation to foment such uprisings in Eastern Europe. (*Sovfoto*)

But he suffered another breakdown, and in 1961 he retired from the CIA. No medical treatment, however, could relieve his mind of the terrible guilt and frustration he now felt. He had mounted the great crusade to fight a terrible evil, but at the very moment he thought he had triumphed, it all collapsed.

Increasingly tormented by this burden, Wisner one morning in 1965 took a shotgun and blew his brains out. Before his death, he asked only to be remembered as a "soldier for good," willing to lay down his life for his crusade.

19

The Colonel and the Aviatrix

Spying in The Mandates
1922–1937

An impenetrable paradox

66 Failure," she had written to her husband in what would turn out to be her last letter, "must be a challenge for women." A curiously pessimistic note in an otherwise typically optimistic letter from a woman who had always refused to admit defeat, it would serve as her epitaph.

Amelia Earhart wrote that letter in 1937 shortly before climbing into her plane to begin one of the last legs of her around-the-world flight. She would never complete the flight; somewhere in the vastness of the Pacific Ocean she disappeared—and touched off one of the great mysteries of aviation.

Nearly sixty years after that eventful flight, her fate remains unknown. What happened to her is also an espionage mystery, for Earhart's last flight was shrouded in intrigue. For decades, there have been persistent rumors, hints, and tantalizing clues that she was involved in some way in an abortive American intelligence mission that went terribly wrong.

No one has ever been able to find the definitive answer to this most intriguing aspect of the Earhart mystery, but there is a great deal that can be inferred when looking at the story in a larger context. That context includes the tragic fate of a brilliant

Marine Corps officer, a rich man's yacht, and an abiding obsession of American intelligence.

They were called The Mandates, hundreds of coral atolls and
volcanic islets scattered over thousands of square miles in the
Central Pacific between Hawaii and the Philippines. Originally,
they were known as three separate island groups: the Marshalls,
the Carolines, and the Marianas. Once they represented the high-
water mark of Germany's imperial ambitions, but these distant
colonies were seized by Japan in 1914 after that country declared
war on Germany. It was a brilliant masterstroke: for the expen-
diture of little blood or treasure, Japan in one blow secured a vast
Pacific empire that underscored its own imperial ambitions in
the South Pacific.

And that is precisely what worried the United States, Japan's
great rival for Pacific dominance. The Japanese had secured ap-
proval from the League of Nations to establish a mandate in the
islands, but very few people were fooled: Japan had no intention,
as the mandate required, of ever granting independence to the
inhabitants of those islands at some point in the future.

One glance at a map of the Pacific underscores why the
Americans were so worried about a resurgent Japan gaining control of The Mandates. If the Japanese decided to fortify them and
build military airfields and naval bases, they would control the
approaches to Southeast Asia and the passage to the Indian
Ocean. In the event of war between Japan and the United States,
The Mandates would provide the Japanese with an unsinkable
aircraft carrier from which to seize Hawaii and the Philippines
and threaten all Pacific lines of communication.

Under terms of the League of Nations mandate, Japan was
prohibited from fortifying The Mandates, but the Americans began to hear disturbing news from the islands. Commercial ship
captains reported that the Japanese had instituted tight security,
discouraging all visitors and prohibiting anyone from traveling
around the islands. Natives whispered rumors of extensive construction going on, including dockyards and airfields. Boatloads
of Japanese workers were said to be arriving each day.

By 1920 The Mandates had become a full-blown obsession
of the Office of Naval Intelligence. Convinced that the Japanese
were turning the islands into fortresses, ONI tried recruiting Mi-
cronesians to find out what was happening, but all such operations failed in the face of impenetrable Japanese security. A dark

shroud of mystery settled over such islands as Truk, Peleliu, and Saipan—names that would resonate in history two decades later.

Determined to solve the mystery, ONI began to search for an agent capable of infiltrating The Mandates and finding out what was happening there. The requirements for such an agent were stiff: someone with military expertise capable of spotting and evaluating military installations, along with sound knowledge of the area and an ability to conduct a one-man espionage operation without getting caught. Finally, ONI found its man: U.S. Marine Corps Lieutenant Colonel Earl Hancock Ellis.

In selecting Ellis as its agent, ONI had found a brilliant man—and a very flawed one. These flaws would lead to an intelligence disaster and lay the groundwork for a tragedy.

Called "Pete" by his friends, Ellis was a Kansas farm boy who joined the Marine Corps in 1900 when he was seventeen to escape the dreariness of life on the Plains. By World War I, he was considered among the most brilliant staff officers in the entire American military and was especially noted for his operational planning. He was widely predicted to be a future chief of staff.

After the war, he served in a variety of posts in the Pacific and Japan. He came to love the area and devoted most of his time to studying every aspect of its countries and peoples. But Ellis had a pure military mind, and his studies were filtered through a geostrategic vision that was dominated by the question of a future war between Japan and the United States. A tour of duty in Japan convinced him that the Japanese military intended an eventual showdown with the Americans, so much of his thinking was concerned with how the United States would win such a war.

Ellis came to believe The Mandates would be the key to victory in the future war. That war, he concluded, would turn on which side gained control over The Mandates, meaning that the essential prerequisite for American victory was seizing them from the Japanese. After considerable study, Ellis set down his thoughts in a remarkably prophetic study entitled *Advance Base Operations in Micronesia.* The study outlined an extensive campaign in which the Americans would seize the more important islands, isolating others by air and naval power. Priority would go to taking any islands that brought the Americans to within striking distance of the Japanese home islands. To conduct this campaign, the Americans would have to develop an extensive amphibious warfare capability, landing troops in special tracked landing craft that

U.S. Marine Lieutenant Colonel Earl H. Ellis, the brilliant staff officer who was enlisted for an espionage mission against the Japanese, a mission that was to cost him his life. (*United States Naval Institute*)

could fight ashore. It was an astonishingly accurate blueprint for the American "island-hopping" campaign 23 years later that seized The Mandates and provided the bases to allow attacks on Japan.

Ellis's study brought him to the attention of ONI, which recruited him for a daring mission. Under civilian cover, Ellis would infiltrate The Mandates and carry out a detailed survey to determine the extent of Japanese military improvements. Given his expertise, Ellis would appear to be the perfect choice for so important (and dangerous) a mission.

But in many ways he was also the worst possible choice. Tragically, despite his brilliance, Ellis was an alcoholic. His superiors consistently covered up his affliction so they wouldn't lose the services of his brain. As a result, Ellis only got worse. Moreover, he began to demonstrate symptoms of acute mental instability: in one incident, bored with the conversation during a dinner party in the Philippines, he pulled out a pistol and shot the plates off the table. He also suffered from nephritis, a chronic kidney ailment worsened by his drinking.

Nevertheless, Ellis was sent on his mission. In early 1922 a mysterious new firm appeared in the world of New York import-export companies. Hughes Trading Company, however, was distinctly different. It had no staff, save a secretary who sat around the office all day, reading magazines and answering the occasional telephone ring.

Hughes Trading Company was a thinly veiled front for ONI. Aside from the secretary, the only other employee was a Mr. E. H. Ellis who, according to company records, was in the Pacific arranging copra deals for the company. But Ellis wasn't doing much in the way of copra deals; after arriving in Yokohama, Japan, to take a Japanese passenger ship to The Mandates, he went on a monumental bender and wound up in the hospital. Alarmed, ONI suddenly had second thoughts about the Ellis mission; obviously, his drinking problem had worsened, representing a full-scale security risk.

ONI planned to order Ellis to return to the United States as soon as he recovered, but he slipped out of the hospital. He was next seen, two months later, sailing in a small boat around some of the islands in The Mandates. Although he told everyone he encountered he was in the copra business, that business has only a few full-time traders, and everybody became aware that E. H. Ellis was not who he said he was. So did the Japanese, who began keeping a close watch on him.

In December 1922 a Protestant missionary working on the small island of Jaluit was awakened one morning by local residents to attend a sick American. It was Ellis. The missionary found a doctor, and within a few weeks Ellis recovered. He claimed to be a copra trader, but as the missionary observed, there appeared to be an entire battalion of Japanese agents dogging his every move. Several months later, on May 12, 1923, Ellis was found dead on the island of Palau.

A strange espionage mystery now unfolded. The Japanese waited nine days before informing the American embassy in Tokyo of Ellis's death. Then, to heighten suspicion further, they refused to allow an American ship into waters of The Mandates to pick up Ellis's body. Finally, after extended haggling with American diplomats, they agreed to let a single American go ashore at Palau, disinter Ellis's body from a local cemetery, and bring it back to the United States. Since Ellis's will specified he was to be cremated, the Japanese agreed that the single American would be permitted to cremate the body and bring the ashes out in an urn.

The American chosen for the job was a 17-year veteran sailor whom ONI had converted into a spy. He was ordered to find out how long Ellis had been at Palau, whether he had any documents with him when he died, and anything else of interest. He was also told to keep his eyes open for any signs of construction around the island.

The sailor landed at Palau and began questioning the local residents and the resident missionary. The natives said Ellis showed no signs of illness before his death, and he was under very close surveillance by the Japanese. They suspected that the Japanese had poisoned him. The missionary had even more disturbing intelligence: Ellis had been living on the island, from which he made daily forays in his small boat. Over the months he had amassed a large number of papers, notebooks, and charts that he would not show to anyone. After his death, the Japanese took them all.

Now under tightening Japanese surveillance, the sailor recovered Ellis's body, cremated it, and prepared to carry the urn back to the United States. But just an hour before the ship that was to take him home was scheduled to arrive, the sailor suddenly fell violently ill. The Japanese offered to take the sick sailor to the hospital in Yokohama, where the Americans planned to get a look at him. But just as the sailor was taken to a hospital room, on September 1, 1923, a massive earthquake struck Japan. The hospital in Yokohama was leveled, killing many of its patients. Among the victims was the American sailor who had become mysteriously ill on Palau.

With the death of the two Americans, The Mandates were again shrouded in dark mystery. ONI tried to run several other operations, but the heavy Japanese security prevented the collection of even the most elementary intelligence. Nothing ONI tried seemed to work, further fueling an ONI preconception that the intense Japanese security screen could only mean that they had something significant to hide. For the next ten years, ONI continued to fail. Then the rich man arrived.

Franklin Roosevelt, among his many interests, was a devotee of espionage; he devoured spy novels for relaxation and loved nothing better than to sit around listening to real-life tales from the world of espionage. He was also a secretive man who liked to form various back channels for information that ran parallel to more official channels.

His favorite unofficial channel was something called "The Room," a collection of wealthy friends who dabbled in the world of espionage, gathering intelligence tidbits. Chief among them was the New York financier Vincent Astor (his fortune endowed the famous landmark New York Public Library in Manhattan), who happened to own a large oceangoing yacht, the *Narwhal.*

An acolyte of Roosevelt's and one of his closest friends, Astor was willing to do just about anything Roosevelt asked him.* In 1935 Roosevelt, a former undersecretary of the Navy, had just the favor in mind. Aware that Astor liked to take his yacht on lengthy cruises to various faraway places, Roosevelt suggested his friend visit the Pacific—specifically, the area around The Mandates.

Astor dutifully complied, but the *Narwhal* was an extremely conspicuous way to infiltrate a very security-conscious area. Moreover, Astor was a brilliant financier, but he didn't know much about such things as dockyard construction and military airfields. Even if he had managed to get close to some of the islands in which ONI had the most interest, there is some question as to whether Astor would even have recognized what he was looking at. Clearly, then, some other means would have to be found. In 1937 another opportunity arose. Like the Ellis case, it would end in tragedy.

"I fly better than I wash dishes," Amelia Earhart liked to say by way of flippantly explaining her obsession with flying. Like Earhart herself, the remark was witty and self-deprecatory, two traits of a very remarkable woman.

Like Ellis, Earhart was from Kansas. The daughter of an alcoholic father who drank up the family fortune, she nevertheless managed to triumph over her background and to develop an odd serenity that seemed immune to the vagaries of life.

---

* One favor involved a felony. The Federal Communications Act of 1934 made it a criminal offense to divulge or intercept any telegraphic communications in the United States. The law was a hindrance to American cryptanalysts, who had been routinely tapping into foreign communications that emanated from, or came into, the United States. Additionally, commercial cable companies were providing copies of encrypted telegrams from foreign embassies that used U.S. commercial cable facilities. The companies stopped doing so, and the cryptanalysts appealed to Roosevelt. He in turn asked Astor, a director of the Western Union Company, to make sure the copies kept coming—a violation of the law.

By 1928, a thirty-one-year-old social worker in Boston, she was bored and restless. Her life was transformed one day when she noticed a newspaper advertisement placed by publisher George P. Putnam seeking a woman who would agree to fly as a passenger on a nonstop flight across the Atlantic. Given the crude air technology of the day (Lindbergh had only a cheap compass to guide him), the flight was very dangerous.

Earhart was among two dozen women applying for the flight. Putnam selected her the first moment he laid eyes on her, primarily for marketing reasons. The intention of the flight was to publicize aviation; given Lindbergh's demigod status, Putnam was delighted to see that Earhart not only bore a striking resemblance to Lindbergh, she had the same appealing shyness. His instinct was rewarded when Earhart made the flight successfully and became a national sensation. Occurring only eight years after women had managed to achieve the vote, Earhart's flight came to symbolize a new dawn for women in America.

The translatlantic flight hooked Earhart on aviation, and she immediately took up flying lessons. In 1931 she flew the Atlantic solo, an accomplishment that made her an international sensation and the inspiration for an entire generation of women. Among her most fervent admirers was George P. Putnam, the man who had introduced her to aviation. They fell in love and Earhart accepted his proposal of marriage, but only after he agreed to sign an agreement that allowed her to leave the marriage if she found "the wedded state unbearable."

Earhart went on to achieve a series of aviation firsts, making her the most famous aviatrix of all time. In 1937 she planned an unprecedented feat: flying around the world with only a navigator as her crew, a voyage of 27,000 miles to be accomplished in grueling, multi-thousand-mile stages. She would fly a twin-engined Lockheed Electra, at that time the world's best all-around airplane.*

In light of what happened later, it is interesting to note the extraordinary help Earhart got from the White House for this ostensibly commercial flight, essentially a publicity stunt to demonstrate the feasibility of long-range aviation. For the cross-Pacific phase of the flight, Roosevelt ordered that a special airfield be

---

* Intriguingly, the plane was configured for the Earhart flight by a brilliant young Lockheed engineer named Clarence (Kelly) Johnson, who later designed the U-2 and SR-71 spy planes.

The famous aviatrix Amelia Earhart at the controls of her Lockheed Electra during her around-the-world flight in 1937. Earhart disappeared during one of the Pacific legs of the trip, touching off aviation's greatest mystery—and a tantalizing espionage puzzle. (*Library of Congress*)

constructed on Howland Island along the flight path, and he ordered Coast Guard units to provide radio beacons and other aids.

The reason for Roosevelt's unusual aid was only partially related to Eleanor Roosevelt's close friendship with Earhart; the hidden purpose had to do with Earhart's navigator, Fred Noonan. A former Pan Am navigator who had been fired for drunkenness, Noonan was among several Pan Am employees who had done occasional favors for ONI during flights over the Pacific. Now he was asked for another. The specific details of that assistance have never become public, but it apparently had something to do with the flight's projected path across the South Pacific, which skirted some Japanese-held areas in which ONI had a continuing interest.

Whether Earhart was aware of this private intelligence arrangement is difficult to ascertain. In any event, she took off from Lae, New Guinea, on July 2, 1937, on a 2,556-mile flight to Howland. But she never made it: some 15 hours after she left, Howland heard her last radio transmission, which indicated she was having trouble spotting the island (a small speck only 15 feet above sea level). Nothing more was heard. Earhart and Noonan had disappeared.

The largest sea search in history was ordered by Roosevelt. Navy ships and planes combed some 200,000 square miles of the Pacific but found nothing. Finally, after a full week of looking without spotting anything, the search was called off.

In subsequent years there were only tantalizing clues to her fate—and its possible connection to espionage. "The real story," Admiral Chester W. Nimitz said many years later, "would stagger the imagination." Nimitz would not elaborate, nor would Roosevelt's secretary of the treasury Henry Morgenthau enlarge on his statement one day to Eleanor Roosevelt, "I hope I've just got to never make it public. It isn't a very nice story." Earhart's mother in 1948 said her daughter had told her she was involved in a "secret mission" for Roosevelt, but she did not elaborate.

Putnam himself became involved in the mystery in 1944 when, as an Army Intelligence officer, he was asked to listen to the tapes of Tokyo Rose, the Japanese propaganda broadcaster, in an attempt to determine if the voice could be his wife's.

What could have inspired such a bizarre assignment? It came about when U.S. forces captured Japanese-held islands in The Mandates during the war and encountered native islanders who told strange stories about a white woman and a man being held captive by the Japanese in 1937 and later taken to Japan. For their part, the Japanese denied any such incident had taken place.

The war established the sadly ironic truth about The Mandates. All that Japanese security before the war was to protect *weakness,* not strength. Japan did not fortify the islands, but it wanted to conceal that fact from the Americans; serious military construction in The Mandates did not begin until after Pearl Harbor. American intelligence was unaware of that construction, one that later took a heavy toll in American lives. The Americans invaded almost completely blind.

The heavy cost exacted at such bloody specks as Tarawa and Peleliv demonstrated anew the truth that the price of intelligence failure is almost always paid in blood.

SPECTACULARS

"You can't hide a hippopotamus with a handkerchief" is an old saying in the espionage trade. It refers to the difficulty of keeping a large-scale intelligence operation secret, especially one that involves many people and extends over a wide geographic area.

This principle is especially true in the case of successful operations. Although intelligence agencies prefer to operate in the dark away from the glare of attention, they are, above all, government bureaucracies subject to the same battles over budgets as are all other such organizations. Having learned early in the game how favorable publicity about a great intelligence success can help loosen budgetary purse strings, spy agencies usually arrange to have such news find its way into the public spotlight. (They are much less forthcoming about failures.)

Then too, the people who run intelligence agencies share the common human trait of wishing to ensure their place in history. Entire forests have fallen in the name of producing memoirs by chiefs of intelligence agencies, books that have a recurring theme: I was directly responsible for our spectacular successes, while failures were the responsibility of those boobs who wouldn't listen to me. Interestingly, this theme has been repeated in the new flood of memoirs unleashed by the fall of the Soviet Union. It is astounding how much some of the senior officials of Soviet intelligence know about the more spectacular successes of the KGB and the GRU, yet they seem to know nothing about any failures or abuses by those agencies.

The three following case studies involve spectacularly successful operations whose details became known for all the reasons such successes usually emerge into the daylight:

215

(1) they were triumphs for the agencies and intelligence officers who organized them; (2) those involved wanted history to recognize their contribution; (3) the other side uncovered them; and (4) they were simply too large in scope to keep secret (the hippopotamus effect).

Two of the case studies concern operations run by Soviet intelligence. One of them is one of the century's greatest intelligence operations, the KGB's patient recruitment and nurturing of the "Ring of Five" in Great Britain. The second involves a spectacular KGB operation in the United States, the Walker spy ring.

The third case study concerns a brilliantly run operation by Israeli intelligence, noted for a string of intelligence spectaculars. The case cited here involves high seas piracy, and there aren't many intelligence agencies, rumors notwithstanding, that can boast of having that kind of talent.

20

The Cambridge Comintern

The Ring of Five
1934–1951

Stalin's Englishmen

The German Communist playwright Bertolt Brecht, this century's great cynic, in 1951 took a look around the wreckage of European idealism and was willing to admit that for his generation, communism had turned to ashes. Still, he was not ready to concede that there existed any superior alternative.

"The East and West," he said, "are both whores. But my whore is pregnant."

For lack of anything better, this will serve as the epitaph for a tall, gangly Englishman who left none of his own. At the very moment Brecht uttered these words, the man code-named HOMER was seated at a table in a Moscow conference room sipping a glass of vodka. Around the table were gathered the top officials of the KGB, celebrating their triumph of triumphs.

A toast was proposed. Everyone stood to raise glasses in honor of HOMER, the KGB's greatest English spy. Then there was another. And another. Finally, with great solemnity, one of the KGB officials pinned a medal to the Englishman's lapel, shook his hand, and kissed him on both cheeks.

With that, the ceremony was over. Donald Stuart Maclean—the HOMER who for nearly twenty years gave the KGB every im-

portant secret of his native land, the superspy who was most responsible for the Iron Curtain and the stalemate of the Korean
War—had now come in from the cold. His remarkable career as
a spy was over.

He had fled to the Soviet Union one step ahead of the net
drawing around him. Now, he believed, he would settle into a
comfortable existence in the Communist paradise to which he
had devoted most of his life, secure in the belief that he had
contributed more than any single person to the survival of the
Soviet Union. The Russians had told him repeatedly that HOMER
was their glittering star, the crown jewel in their greatest espionage triumph, the "Ring of Five"—five English Communists who
on behalf of the Soviet Union infiltrated their government's
nerve center and betrayed it.

There was no reason for Maclean to disbelieve such praise.
The material he had provided the Soviet Union nearly filled an
entire wall of filing cabinets in KGB headquarters, evidence of an
espionage career that has seldom been equaled. And it was all
the purest gold, the actual documentary evidence of the inner-
most secrets, thoughts, and plans of the Soviet Union's enemies.
None of the other members of the KGB's great spy ring—H. A. R.
Philby, Anthony Blunt, Guy Burgess, and John Cairncross—had
managed to provide so valuable a treasure trove of secrets.

But Maclean's triumph soon turned to ashes. He would try
to become a good Communist in a state that no longer had any
use for such idealism. Suffocated by the deadening hand of Soviet
communism, Maclean would end his days a bitter and wrecked
man in a system he knew had failed. And in an irony that perhaps
only Bertolt Brecht could have appreciated, Maclean in the end
was betrayed by the system for which he had betrayed so much
and so often.

It was an irony lost on the KGB, which was dominated by
men of narrow vision preoccupied with the minutiae of operations. Instead, they liked to ponder a curious operational irony
about their Ring of Five: of the network's members, Maclean was
the one the KGB had initially most doubted, the one his handlers
were convinced would never achieve greatness.

It would not be the first time that people had badly misread
Donald Maclean.

Like the other members of the Ring of Five, Maclean was born
into wealth and privilege. His father, Sir Donald Maclean, was a

distinguished, wealthy barrister who had been elected to Parliament in 1906 and knighted in 1917. Maclean hated the stern, authoritarian father who had imposed on him an upbringing of emotionless stoicism in an attempt to produce a clone of himself. The elder Maclean decreed his son would attend a private school so strict that boys' pants pockets were sewn shut so that they would never be tempted to touch themselves.

Maclean's transformation came in 1931 when, at age eighteen, he entered Cambridge University. There, he was introduced to drink and sex (he discovered he was bisexual, a circumstance that was to torment him with guilt the rest of his life), and he drifted into the exciting world of extreme left-wing politics. His initiators into both sex and politics were Anthony Blunt, a fellow at the university, and Guy Burgess, a flamboyant homosexual student. They formed themselves into a secret club, later joined by John Cairncross, a homosexual student seduced by Burgess, and "Kim" Philby, another student whose politics had veered sharply leftward.

They were bound by a shared determination to do something about the terrible inequities their devotion to Marxism convinced them were the result of a capitalist system that had to be destroyed. In depression-era Great Britain, those inequities were especially striking, but aside from Maclean getting arrested in a melee that broke out during a demonstration by the unemployed, there wasn't much they were doing about it.

At this point, there were three volatile elements in these young radicals that set them slightly apart from the normal run of English Communists whose Marxism tended to be of the drawing room variety: a fervent belief in communism, a determination to wreck the hated capitalist system and change the world, and an uncritical belief in the Soviet Union as the beacon for mankind.

Credit for exploiting these elements on behalf of the KGB goes to two of its most skilled agents, Arnold Deutsch, an Austrian Communist, and Theodore Maly, a Hungarian ex-priest who embraced communism with the same devotion he had once embraced Catholicism. In a move that was to prove very significant, the two men decided to look among the young Communists in Cambridge and elsewhere to find willing recruits from a class of people destined later to enter the British establishment. Their strategy was to work carefully and patiently, clothing their approach in the name of seeking "fighters" for the underground struggle against fascism. Deutsch and Maly never mentioned the words "KGB" or "Soviet intelligence." Instead, they appealed to their recruits' idealism and willingness to sacrifice in the name of a higher cause. They would carry out secret work, the students were told, for the Comintern, the international Communist organization.

Deutsch and Maly, two urbane and sophisticated veterans of a dozen underground struggles, were role models to the young Cambridge radicals. They were calm, assured men who projected an air of wisdom; they had seen the future, and it worked.

Maly concentrated on Maclean, convincing him that he should abandon his postgraduate plan of teaching English in the Soviet Union. Like his fellow starry-eyed idealists, Maclean pictured himself in workingman's clothes teaching factory workers such things as split infinitives; later, they would join together singing the "Internationale" and return to the production lines to turn out the tools for building the great communal society. Instead, Maly urged, Maclean should subvert his true political feelings and join the Foreign Service, there to let the Soviet Union know of any evil plans by the capitalist enemies and their stooges.

It remains a mystery why Deutsch and Maly succeeded so well in converting the idealism of the Cambridge students into espionage. The story is a strange one, having much to do with the culture and morality of England's interwar generation. Perhaps, as some have speculated, what they did was only partially a political act; the scarlet thread that united the Ring of Five was hatred of their parents and all they represented. There is reason to consider this motive, for they all maintained a curious distance from the reality they were so actively seeking to change.

Consider, for example, the elder statesman of the ring, Anthony Blunt. Many years later, having confessed his treason, Blunt was trying to explain why he and his fellow ring members felt compelled to work for the KGB. "You don't understand the 1930s," he sneered at his MI5 interrogator.

What a joke: the MI5 man had been born in England's working class and very well remembered his father thrown out of work in the terrible 1930s' economic depression, unable to get a job, finally destroying himself with drink in despair. Blunt, meanwhile, was living in ease at Cambridge on a generous allowance from his family, spending languid summers at their country estate. So, too, Maclean: he never had to worry about money while at Cambridge, where every need was taken care of by his family.

His summers also were spent lolling around the family country estate.

The fact is that none of the Ring of Five ever did a hard day's work in their lives. For all their talk of injustice and the plight of the workingman, these were political abstractions to them. Worse, their politics were blind: they loved to talk about the danger of "imperialism," but it was a category in which they never included the Soviet Union's invasion of Poland in 1920 and, later, the Soviet seizure of the Baltics, the invasion of Finland, and the cynical deal with Hitler to partition Poland.

Graham Greene, the chief apologist for the Ring of Five, was to compare their betrayal to apostate Jesuits executed for their refusal to bend to prevailing orthodoxy. The Jesuits' virtue, Greene claimed, was disloyalty, and in an age of victims, disloyalty was a necessity. It was a colossally wrong reading of the Ring of Five, for the facts belie Greene's tortuous justification. Three of the ring—Philby, Burgess, Maclean—fled to the Soviet Union rather than answer for their supposedly virtuous disloyalty, while the others remained behind. Blunt could not bring himself to abandon his career as an art historian and the comfort of an English upper-class life, complete with London club. Cairncross could not break away from the comforts of his villa in the south of France. "Stalin's Englishmen" were no Jesuit martyrs—or martyrs of any kind, for that matter.

Maclean certainly did not regard himself as a martyr. He once told Philby that his work for the KGB was akin to "cleaning out a toilet: it's a dirty job, and someone has to do it." He made the same statement to his original recruiters, Deutsch and Maly. They were sophisticated enough to pretend they hadn't heard it, but when Maclean repeated the sentiment to an agent from the new KGB, Anatoli Gromov, he was upbraided sharply. Gromov made it clear that the job of obtaining *razvedka* for the sake of the Motherland was not to be compared to cleaning toilets.

Gromov and Maclean had their little tiff in 1940, when Maclean, who had been serving in the British embassy in Paris, was evacuated to London. By then he had been a star KGB asset for five years after joining the Foreign Office in 1935, fresh out of Cambridge. He began by providing the KGB with everything that came across his desk. In 1938, assigned to Paris, he rewarded the KGB's investment by providing information on the British and French eagerness to appease Hitler (no small factor in Stalin's decision to seek a separate deal with the German dictator) and revealed French-British contingency plans for intervening in Finland.

Maclean's return to London meant that he passed to the control of Gromov, who was *rezident* at the London embassy under the alias Gorsky and cover as second secretary. Maclean did not particularly like him. Humorless and a stickler for even the minutest details of KGB tradecraft, Gromov was very different from the more informal Maly, for whom Maclean had developed a deep fondness. But Maly, along with an entire generation of foreign-born KGB operatives, had been swept up in the Stalin purge that, among other things, sought to "Russianize" the KGB.

Gromov was appalled when he got his first look at the Ring of Five. Contrary to established espionage practice, all the members of the ring knew each other intimately (Gromov was offended to discover that Blunt and Burgess often slept together), seemed to take few security precautions, and drank too much for their own good. Gromov tried to whip the ring into shape, but they ignored his detailed instructions for clandestine meetings and didn't want to bother with such things as dead drops, preferring instead the informal practice they established with Deutsch and Maly of simply meeting in a public park.

Gromov despaired of ever getting the Ring of Five to observe even elementary security precautions. Convinced they would be arrested at any moment, he resolved to split Maclean, the most valuable member of the ring, from the others so the KGB would at least save him. But Maclean had his own problems. Inept mechanically, he could not learn how to operate the miniature spy camera Gromov gave him to photograph documents. Finally, Gromov gave up. Maclean would be permitted to follow his usual procedure, which was simply to steal secret documents, bring them to Gromov for copying, then return them. In the event of especially sensitive documents that were too risky to take out of the building, Maclean, blessed with a phenomenal photographic memory, would memorize what he had read and later repeat it word for word.

The KGB was willing to tolerate this violation of its tradecraft because of the sheer quality of what Maclean was producing. Named as British liaison to the Combined Policy Committee, he was able to tell the Russians about the secret British Tube Alloys Project (the atomic bomb) and the American decision to begin the Manhattan Project, along with an astonishing range of diplomatic secrets. It was as though the Russians were able to sit in on the most secret British and American councils.

World War II was the golden age for the Ring of Five. Blunt had joined MI5, where he was in charge of secretly opening diplomatic bags and spying on exile governments; Burgess had gotten into MI6, which also recruited Philby; and Cairncross joined GCHQ, where he passed on ULTRA decrypts to the KGB. But the star remained Maclean. In 1944 he was transferred to Washington, D.C., where he opened an intelligence oil gusher.

Maclean was highly popular at the British embassy, and no wonder: he was always willing to fill in for a sick or vacationing colleague, put in long hours, and work on weekends. His colleagues considered him an ambitious workaholic, not realizing that he was poking into every secret corner. There was no secret Maclean did not encounter at some point, and the very value of his material forced the KGB to devise a highly secure way to get it from him. Gromov was transferred to Washington for the sole purpose of handling Maclean, but he was concerned that the city wasn't safe for KGB operations. Assuming that all Soviet diplomats were under FBI surveillance, Gromov then set up a special system: he moved to New York, where Maclean would travel regularly to leave material at a series of dead drops. One of those visits would prove very costly for Maclean and the KGB.

In 1945, British and American cryptanalysts, reoriented toward a new enemy, began attacking a huge pile of intercepted Soviet enciphered communications, including an unusually large amount of traffic that had been transmitted from the Soviet consulate in New York. What could the Russians have been transmitting in all those hours of traffic? Slowly, as the cryptanalysts began to make progress, they realized that there was a major KGB asset code-named HOMER who had been providing volumes of intelligence for transmission to Moscow.

While the cryptanalysts slowly made progress, HOMER was giving away the company store. Thanks to his job as British liaison on a joint committee with the Americans deciding atomic energy matters, Maclean was able to provide the KGB with the priceless intelligence that the American postwar nuclear arsenal was a hollow shell: the Americans, contrary to Soviet belief, were not producing nuclear weapons and had only a few in inventory. In 1948, when President Truman dispatched B-29s to Europe as a means of dampening Soviet aggression, Maclean revealed that although Truman was trying to create the impression that the planes were

armed with atomic bombs, in fact they carried only conventional
bombs. An undeterred Stalin built the Iron Curtain.

In 1950, named head of the embassy's American Department, Maclean encountered an intelligence blockbuster. He
learned that the Truman administration had decided to keep the
war in Korea limited; no nuclear weapons would be used, and
there would be no invasion of Manchuria. As Chinese Field Marshal Lin Pao, commander of Chinese forces in Korea, later confirmed, China would not have risked its army in Korea without
solemn assurances from Soviet intelligence that there was no
chance of an American counterstroke against China itself.

But at this moment of his greatest triumph, Maclean learned
his days were numbered. His fellow asset, Philby, had been assigned in 1949 as MI6 chief of station in Washington, in which
post he served as British intelligence's liaison with American intelligence. Philby was ushered into a great secret: Operation
BRIDE, the cracking of Soviet intelligence communications, had
uncovered HOMER. An original list of over a hundred suspects
had been narrowed to just six. One of them was Maclean. As
Philby told his KGB control, Maclean was rapidly assuming the
status of major suspect, since his trips to New York coincided so
perfectly with sudden jumps in Soviet transmissions to Moscow.
Soon, the list of suspects narrowed to two, then one, when cryptanalysts broke a Soviet telegram that discussed a trip by HOMER
to New York one day in 1945 to visit his pregnant wife. On that
day, Maclean had gone to New York to see his pregnant wife.

As the net closed, Maclean began to crack. "I am the English
Hiss," he blurted to a friend. Gromov became increasingly worried: Maclean was about to be arrested, and once in the hands of
counterintelligence interrogators, he almost certainly would fall
apart, revealing the entire Ring of Five. Something would have
to be done.

The solution was to evacuate Maclean to Moscow, using Guy
Burgess as his escort. The plan worked perfectly, except that to
the KGB's shock, Burgess on the spur of the moment decided to
defect, too. That act exposed his friend Philby to suspicion; his
effectiveness was finished.

And so was the Ring of Five. With Maclean and Burgess
gone, and Philby under suspicion (he would flee to the Soviet
Union in 1963), that left only Blunt and Cairncross. But Blunt
had retired from espionage, preoccupied with his career as an
art historian and Surveyor of the Queen's Pictures, and Cairn-

cross had joined the Treasury Department, where his access to any kind of valuable intelligence was limited (in any event, he had decided to give up spying).

In the Soviet Union, meanwhile, Maclean entered the stifling, stagnant world of Soviet communism, just then beginning the dry rot that would ultimately cause its collapse. Adopting a new name of Mark Petrovich Frazer (after the author of *The Golden Bough*), he found himself shunted off to the miserable industrial city of Kuibyshev to work on an economic magazine. Depressed, he asked to have his family join him. When the Soviets refused, Maclean tried to commit suicide. The KGB, now concerned that a depressed Maclean might redefect, arranged for his wife Melinda and their three children to join him in the Soviet Union and moved the family to Moscow.

Burgess was also living in Moscow at the time, but Maclean deliberately avoided him. He was repelled by the sight of Burgess (now using his new identity of Jim Andreyevitch Eliot, after George Eliot, the pen name of Victorian novelist Marian Evans). Burgess had become a hopeless alcoholic. But Maclean himself was disintegrating. Disillusioned about life in the Soviet Union and increasingly ambivalent about his decision many years before to become a Soviet spy, he began drinking heavily and would erupt in wild rages. His marriage collapsed; his wife would later leave him to marry Philby after he arrived in the Soviet Union in 1963. Shortly after Philby's arrival, Burgess died of acute liver failure. Neither Maclean nor Philby attended his funeral. A year later the last of the Ring of Five, Blunt and Cairncross, were publicly exposed. Blunt confessed and gave up Cairncross, who also confessed.

Maclean would live for another twenty years, but they were not happy ones. He was a man caught between two fires: anger at the fossilized Soviet communism that had betrayed the revolution and fury with a capitalist system he could not abide. He was haunted by every person's nightmare—that he had wasted his life.

Maclean died in 1983, his funeral unattended by Philby, who would survive him by five years. Maclean's estate was less than $10,000, sufficient to fulfill one surprising instruction in his will: he wanted to be cremated and have his ashes buried in England beside his parents.

His wishes were carried out, and there was a short burial service in England attended by only a handful of people. The vicar who presided mentioned nothing about Maclean's role in the Ring of Five and his place in the annals of espionage. Instead, he read from the thirteenth chapter of First Corinthians: "Love keeps no score of wrongs, does not gloat over other men's sins, but delights in the truth."

21

The Family That Spied

The Walker Spy Ring
1967–1985

America as an open book

The spy was cautious, carefully checking for any surveillance
by counterintelligence agents. Approaching the dead drop at
night on the deserted country road, he slowed his van to 20 MPH,
then suddenly accelerated to 70 MPH. For four hours he circled,
doubled back, stopped, slowed, and accelerated, checking for any
sign the enemy was watching him.

Finally, certain there was no surveillance anywhere, he approached the dead drop. He spotted the upright 7-Up soda can,
signal that the dead drop was ready to be serviced. He drove
another five miles and stopped before a utility pole with a NO
HUNTING sign on it. He got out of his car and put a paper bag of
documents inside a plastic garbage bag and left it beside the pole;
to anyone driving by, it appeared to be an ordinary bag of trash
someone had thrown on the side of the road.

Now the spy moved to the second phase of the dead drop
operation, driving another mile to a point beside the road. Another upright soda can signaled there was a package of money
waiting for him to pick up. The can was there, but to his distress,
he couldn't find the package of money. He doubled back to the
site where he had left the bag of documents. They were gone.

The spy was concerned; perhaps there had been a foul-up. Not likely, he thought. His controllers were thorough professionals who didn't make mistakes.

It was now near midnight. Uncertain what to do, the spy decided to check into the local motel. He would spend the night there, and the next morning, in daylight, he would recheck the dead drop area to see if the missing package had been mistakenly put in the wrong site.

At 3:30 A.M., the front desk clerk woke him to say that his van had been hit by a drunken driver; could he come to the front desk to fill out an accident report? The spy went to the window and looked outside. His van was parked there, and from his point of view, he couldn't see any damage.

Maybe it was a trap. He considered the idea of burning his written instructions for the dead drop. No, the instructions, very complicated, were difficult to memorize. He would need them again in a week's time: the procedure worked out with his controllers was to repeat a dead drop contact precisely one week after the first contact was aborted.

Taking out his gun, he slowly opened the door to his room. The hallway was clear. There was no sound, except the steady hum from a small room at the end of the hall that contained the ice machine. Keeping his back to the wall, the spy carefully inched his way down the hall. When he reached the end, he placed his ear on the metallic door. It was cold. He could hear no sound on the other side, except the hum of the ice machine.

He carefully opened the door. No one was in the room. So far, so good, but he was still wary. He concealed the dead drop instructions behind the ice machine, then returned to his room. Still no sign of anything amiss; maybe somebody really had hit his van. He would go downstairs and check.

Still holding his gun, he approached the elevator bank. As he touched the "down" button, two men suddenly appeared behind him. "Stop! FBI!" one shouted.

The spy whirled, pointing his gun. The two men had guns leveled at him. "Drop the gun!" one of them commanded.

For a millisecond, the spy considered trying to shoot his way out of the trap, but he realized there was no point. The two men were only a few feet from him; at that distance, even if he managed to shoot one of them, the other would kill him. He dropped his gun with a soft thud onto the hallway carpet.

The two men pushed him against the wall, ripping the hairpiece from his head, then yanking the thick-soled shoes off his feet. A half-dozen other men now materialized as if out of nowhere. They shoved him into a room beside the elevator bank.

"Take your clothes off," one of them commanded the spy. He started to strip; as each article of clothing was removed, it was seized and subjected to minute examination. The spy noticed that the men carefully scrutinized every stitch of the seams and the buttonholes. Someone tore the wire-rimmed glasses from the spy's head and minutely examined them.

"Fucking traitor," the spy heard one of the men in the room say. Now, for the first time, he felt fear; perhaps these angry-looking agents would beat him to within an inch of his life, or kill him. He was still fearful when he heard somebody start to recite the Miranda warning, "You have the right to remain silent. . . ."

"I choose to remain silent, gentlemen," the spy said with a careful politeness he hoped might mollify their anger.

"Sit down," one of the agents commanded, as two others pushed him into a chair. "We've got some interesting things to show you."

First, the spy was shown the dead drop instructions that had been recovered from behind the ice machine. "These instructions," an agent said, "were prepared by the embassy of the Soviet Union. Unless you and the KGB are engaged in some sort of treasure hunt, these are detailed instructions for a *treff* [Russian for secret rendezvous]. You know what *treff* is, don't you?" The spy remained silent.

"But there's more," the agent said, as another brought a plastic garbage bag into the room. Opening it, the agent found a paper bag with documents. He pulled out a typed letter, signed by the spy, that reminded his controllers he was to receive $1 million over the next ten years for material similar in quality to the papers in the bag. One by one, the agent removed the documents. There was no sound in the room other than the documents slapping onto a table. Each was stamped TOP SECRET and dealt with U.S. Navy cryptographic procedures, regulations for conducting nuclear war, and operational procedures for the nuclear aircraft carrier USS *Nimitz*.

"You're under arrest for violation of the Espionage Act of the United States," the agent said.

The spy had blanched when he saw the plastic garbage bag; somehow, the material he had left at the dead drop had been picked up by the FBI. How could it have happened? He felt himself trembling again.

The agents stared at him, hardly able to believe that this bald, unprepossessing man sitting there trembling in fear and squinting nearsightedly at them was the great KGB spy. He was that rare espionage category known as superspy, a man who for 18 years had wreaked an almost breathtaking demolition of vital American military secrets, penetrating even the most elaborate security precautions. He had organized a spy ring that probed deeply into American secrets, and he had managed to evade suspicion and detection for a long time. Indeed, he would not have been caught were it not for a fortuitous break for the FBI.

The fact that John Anthony Walker, Jr., didn't look like a superspy—or any kind of a spy, for that matter—was one of the secrets of his success. Another was his political coloration: a member of the John Birch Society and a fervid supporter of Ronald Reagan, he appeared to be such a true-blue American that no one could have suspected he was a Soviet spy. But the chief reason for his success was a pure amorality. A man bereft of conscience, Walker sold out his country strictly for money. He recruited his own family and closest friend to work for the KGB, and he felt not the slightest compunction in giving the Russians every vital secret he could get his hands on.

As a result, the KGB was able to reap the rewards of one of the more successful operations it had ever run in the United States—one that provided so much insight into American military plans, the Soviet Union would have won any showdown during the 18-year period Walker was their star asset. Even a partial listing of Walker's treasures conveys the scope of his importance to the KGB:

- All American troop and air movements to Vietnam from 1971 until the U.S. withdrawal in 1973.

- The exact times and planned targets for U.S. air strikes against North Vietnam during the height of the American bombing campaign.

- The secrets of all U.S. Navy cryptographic machines.

- Authentication codes for U.S. nuclear missiles.

- Technical details of missile defense systems aboard U.S. warships.

- Technical details of the Tomahawk cruise missile.

- U.S. Navy contingency plans for attacking the Soviet Union in the event of all-out war.

- The locations of secret U.S. Navy underwater microphones used to track Soviet nuclear submarines.

- Vulnerabilities of American spy satellites.

- Locations and procedures for American nuclear submarines on station to launch nuclear missiles against the Soviet Union in the event of nuclear war.

It all amounted to quite an achievement for a failed high school dropout who everybody predicted would never amount to anything.

John Walker, the son of an alcoholic father, was ten years old in 1947 when his family moved to Richmond, Virginia. Not too long afterward, Walker started to get into trouble. It began as petty mischief, but by the time Walker was a teenager, he had a police record for thefts and burglaries. In 1955, after still another arrest for burglary, a local court gave Walker a choice: jail or join the military. Walker, who had dropped out of school the year before, opted for the Navy.

Although his family had long written him off as a bad seed, Walker demonstrated surprising industry and diligence in the Navy. He studied hard and was steadily promoted. In 1964 he faced a watershed in his career: hoping for a promotion to warrant officer, he needed a top secret clearance for the rank. But there was his juvenile criminal record. Normally an impediment for a security clearance, Walker's criminal past was waived by Navy investigators, who finally decided that his excellent performance of duty since joining the service showed that he had "straightened out." He was granted the security clearance and a promotion to warrant officer. It would turn out to be one of the worst mistakes the Navy ever made.

By 1967, married and the father of two small children, Walker seemed established in his naval career. He had specialized in electronic communications and was among a handful of Navy people who knew the ins and outs of its highly advanced com-

munications systems. In April of that year he was assigned as a
watch officer for the headquarters of the Atlantic Fleet in Norfolk, Virginia, which put him in the very nerve center of one of
the greatest collections of secrets in the world. Through the headquarters communications center flowed top secret messages to
and from nuclear submarines, operational orders to the fleet, and
naval intelligence reports arriving every hour.

The communications moved through banks of state-of-the-
art cryptographic machines provided by the NSA, technological
wonders that could encrypt or decrypt messages in seconds. The
systems that ran the machines, generated by supercomputers that
produced ciphers of complexity approaching mathematical infin-
ity, were absolutely unbreakable—unless an enemy somehow got
its hands on the machines.

Walker carried out his task with brisk efficiency, even though
his mind was increasingly preoccupied with an off-duty activity:
he had opened a bar in Norfolk, hoping his Navy connections
would bring in a lot of business. But the bar was failing. Walker,
watching his modest life savings disappear into the bar, was becoming desperate for money.

On the night of December 22, 1967, in an act he later said
was "strictly spur of the moment," he copied the top secret manual for the KL-47 cryptographic machine, one of the oldest in
the Navy inventory, on the office copying machine. He stuffed
the pages into his pants pocket and strolled past the armed Marine guards at the high-security installation.

The next day he drove to Washington, D.C. He looked up
the address of the Soviet embassy in the telephone book and took
a taxi to 16th Street NW. He stood in front of the building, uncertain how to get inside. Fearful that the FBI might be watching
him, Walker noticed the gate swing open to allow a car to exit.
He slipped inside as the gate was closing and said to a startled
guard, "I want to see the security manager."

Taken inside the embassy, he was ushered into the office of
a well-dressed young man he assumed to be a KGB agent. The
Russian asked him why he was there. "I am interested in pursuing
the possibilities of selling classified U.S. government documents
to the Soviet Union," he said, handing over the papers from his
pocket.

The Russian said nothing and excused himself for a moment. When he returned, he handed Walker an envelope containing 20 fifty-dollar bills. Then he gave Walker a receipt to sign.

(The receipt was standard tradecraft: it satisfied government accountants and provided documentary proof that an asset had been recruited—a possible lever later if the asset balked at further service or tried to deny it.)

Several burly Russians suddenly arrived. One handed an overcoat and broad-brimmed hat to Walker. So dressed, he was taken outside and pushed into the backseat of a car that then roared out of the embassy gates. Any watcher would have found it impossible to identify the man bundled up in overcoat and hat in the backseat. The Russians drove into Virginia and a half hour later stopped and wordlessly shoved Walker out of the car. Then the car sped away.

And on that note of typical KGB procedure, John Walker became a spy for the Soviet Union. Subsequently, he was contacted by a Russian near Norfolk, who gave him a miniature spy camera, along with elaborate instructions for a dead drop in the countryside outside Washington. Walker soon began filling it with treasures from the communications center, including details of ORESTES, America's most advanced cryptographic machine. With Walker's material, consisting of construction diagrams and operating manuals, the Russians were able to build their own version of ORESTES, allowing them to read all American top-grade military communications.

By 1968, Walker was earning $4,000 a month from the KGB and had managed to survive an incident that should have brought an end to his espionage career. One morning his wife, Barbara, found a metal box secreted in the bottom drawer of his desk. Opening it, she found several rolls of film, along with photographs of what appeared to be country roads and a note that read, "Want information on rotor." At the bottom of the note was a notation: "Please destroy this note."

Confronted by his wife, Walker simply replied, "I'm a spy." Uncertain what to do and convinced her family would be broken up if she went to the authorities, Barbara Walker decided to do nothing.

Having survived this close call, Walker now sought to expand his operation. Transferred to San Diego, he befriended a Navy radio expert, Chief Petty Officer Jerry Whitworth. Walker recruited him carefully, finally learning that Whitworth was desperate for money. Walker, aware that Whitworth was pro-Israel, used a so-called false flag recruiting pitch, claiming he was stealing classified material for the Israelis. Whether or not Whitworth be-

lieved this lie is debatable, but he began handing over details of
the Navy's highest-grade radio communications systems.

In 1971, under pressure from the KGB to obtain more cryptographic material, Walker volunteered for duty aboard the USS
Niagara Falls, then in the waters off Vietnam. As Walker was aware,
the supply ship was serving as a major communications center
for all U.S. armed forces in Vietnam. Even better, when he arrived, he was named as CMS (classified materials system) custo-
dian, thus obtaining legitimate access to just about every single
classified message passing between American forces in Vietnam
and command centers in the United States. And just to top all
that off, Walker was occasionally assigned as a special courier to
take highly classified material by hand to U.S. headquarters in
Saigon.

Walker selected the best nuggets from this flourishing supply and dropped them off to the KGB during various home leaves.
In return, the Russians lavished money on him, and it was not
hard to see why. Thanks to Walker's material, the Russians
learned of the encryption system that contained operation orders
for Air Force and Navy air strikes against North Vietnam, along
with the system used to direct B-52 strikes. Although the Americans began to wonder why the North Vietnamese always seemed
to know the specific targets of American strikes and why their
forces in South Vietnam had an uncanny ability to evacuate areas
scheduled to be hit by B-52s, no one deduced that the enemy was
reading American signals. It was considered impossible that the
Vietnamese would have developed the capability for such a feat;
little thought was devoted to the more logical alternative that the
Russians were reading the signals and tipping off the North Vietnamese.

At the same time, the U.S. Navy began to wonder how the
Russians always seemed to know about deployments of American
warships. Even the most secret exercise would suddenly be interrupted by the appearance of a Russian ship. Again, compromise
of the encryption systems was considered the most unlikely possibility; the keys for those systems were constantly changed, and
the NSA experts were convinced that even the most dedicated
Russian attack would not have made any crack in the systems.

By this time, Walker had earned nearly a half-million dollars
from espionage, but his string of success was running out. Scheduled to retire in 1974, he was determined to keep the money flow
from the KGB coming. To fill the gap, he recruited his own son,

A nasty surprise: the Soviet guided missile cruiser *Frunze* suddenly appears beside a U.S. Navy task force that had secretly been deployed in the Indian Ocean in 1985. Navy officials who wondered how the Russians seemed to know the sailing orders of American warships would learn later that thanks to John Walker, the KGB's prime asset, the Russians had access to U.S. Navy encrypted communications. (*United States Navy*)

Michael, who had joined the Navy. Then, when his friend Jerry Whitworth claimed he was burned out and no longer wanted to steal top secret documents, Walker recruited his brother Arthur, a retired Navy lieutenant commander who was working as a staff engineer at a defense contractor. As he did with Whitworth, Walker claimed that he was gathering material for the Israelis.

Arthur Walker provided material of only limited value, but Michael Walker proved to be another gold mine. As per his father's instructions, he worked hard to get into naval communications. Fortuitously, from his father's standpoint, he was assigned to the *Nimitz*, whose communications center soon provided Walker with a wealth of top-grade material. Young Walker's assignments included the "burn center," where copies of top secret messages and other classified material no longer needed was to be shredded and burned. Walker would steal whatever appeared to be interesting and store it beneath his bunk.

By then, John Walker had become the bright star in the KGB galaxy, accorded the rare honor of direct meetings with KGB officials in Vienna. "Of all our spies in America, John," one KGB man told him, "you are the best!" However, he went on to express concern about security, hardly able to believe that Walker had gotten away with it for so long. Walker laughed, noting there wasn't the slightest suspicion attached either to himself, his son, Jerry Whitworth, or his brother. And, he added, there probably never would be. In retirement, he was running a private detective agency in Virginia, occasionally appearing on local television to discuss surveillance and bugging techniques. A Birch Society member, he was a rabid supporter of Ronald Reagan. Walker tried to explain to the puzzled Russians why a Birchite and Reagan supporter would never be suspected by fellow Americans of being a Soviet spy.

Walker did not mention to the Russians one imperfection in his cover: his wife, Barbara. When she had first discovered his espionage sideline several years before, she had decided not to turn him in. But they had since gotten divorced. She moved to Maine, but despite all the money Walker was making, he evaded making his alimony and child support payments. Barbara Walker was living in near-poverty, a miserable life worsened by a growing drinking problem. At some level, Walker was aware that she might end his life in espionage with a single phone call to the FBI, but he put it out of his mind; even if she did, she was such a hopeless drunk, who would believe her anyway?

That is exactly what happened. On November 23, 1984, shortly after Walker received $100,000 from a grateful KGB for details on the American KL-36 cryptographic machine, his ex-wife called the local FBI office in Maine and told the agents her husband was a Soviet spy. Her account was rambling, disconnected, and full of venom for her former husband, leading the agents who met her in person to conclude she was making up a story to get back at him. She was also, obviously, a drunk.

But their report, routinely forwarded to the Norfolk FBI office, caused two counterintelligence agents based there to wonder. They were struck by her description of the photos and note she found in her husband's metal box some years before. It sounded to them like typical KGB tradecraft, the kind of thing Barbara Walker could not have made up. It was time to take a look at John Walker.

The FBI immediately hit pay dirt when agents interviewed Walker's daughter, who revealed that her father tried to recruit her shortly after she enlisted in the Navy. She said she turned him down. It was sufficient to get a warrant for the bugging of Walker's phone, which quickly produced another lead: agents heard a tearful conversation between Walker and his daughter-in-law, during which she pleaded with him to tell his son to "stop spying."

That was enough to get Walker's son removed from any access to classified material, but the FBI still faced a major problem: it needed much firmer evidence to arrest and convict John Walker of espionage. The solution was a radical plan, one that had never been tried before. Called Operation WIND FLYER, the idea was to find out Walker's next scheduled appointment with a dead drop, then monitor the drop and catch him red-handed—along with any KGB agents who happened to be around.

An FBI black bag job on Walker's house turned up, astonishingly enough, the detailed dead drop procedures the KGB had provided him, along with instructions to destroy them after he had committed the details to memory. Walker and the KGB were now about to pay a high price for his gross operational error in leaving such incriminating material lying around his house. The FBI analyzed the snapshots of the dead drop site the KGB had given Walker and finally narrowed it down to a rural Maryland road.

The dead drop was staked out, and on the night of May 19, 1985, a huge FBI surveillance operation that extended for miles around spotted a car with diplomatic license plates slowly cruising the area. A quick check revealed the car was assigned to the Soviet embassy and registered to Aleksei Tkachenko, officially third secretary, but known to the FBI as a senior KGB operative. Obviously, Tkachenko was not out for a pleasure drive so late at night at the extreme end of the 25-mile radius that was imposed on Soviet diplomats.

Despite careful KGB countersurveillance, the FBI had no trouble spotting Tkachenko putting an upright soda can by the side of the road (the signal to Walker that the dead drop was ready to be serviced), then leaving an ordinary garbage bag next to a utility pole some miles away. At that point the FBI pounced, grabbing Tkachenko and two other KGB agents, all of whom immediately flashed their diplomatic credentials and claimed diplomatic immunity. FBI agents opened the garbage bag and found $100,000 in cash.

Several hours later, Walker arrived to wander into the FBI trap. Even his arrogant self-confidence could not withstand the unimpeachable evidence that now confronted him: the documents he left at the dead drop, the KGB instructions found in his possession, and the tapes of his phone conversation with his daughter-in-law.

The Russians were not about to go to jail—they were declared *persona non grata* and thrown out of the country—but Walker was in deep trouble. Any slender hope he had of beating the case disappeared when Arthur Walker, approached by the FBI, instantly confessed, giving his interrogators 35 hours of details on how his brother had recruited him for espionage. John Walker caved in; he would plead guilty, in exchange for a relatively lenient sentence of 25 years in prison for his son. Walker himself got no mercy, receiving life in prison. Jerry Whitworth got 365 years in prison; Arthur Walker got life.

While the American military frantically scrapped and rebuilt their entire communications systems—at a cost to the taxpayers of nearly $1 billion—a KGB defector named Vitali Yurchenko arrived to tell the Americans about the honors and promotions that were lavished on the KGB agents involved in the Walker operation. (Even though, Yurchenko added sourly, none of the agents had actually recruited and nurtured him; he was a simple walk-in who dropped a treasure in their laps.)

Yurchenko claimed the operation was considered the greatest KGB American operation in history, even better than the World War II atomic bomb espionage operation. "You know," Yurchenko said, "if you had gone to war with us during the time of Walker, you would have lost, just as you did in Vietnam. We would have wiped you out."

His American listeners nodded solemnly, aware that he was absolutely right.

22

The Pirates of Tel Aviv

Operation PLUMBAT
1965–1968

The supreme Israeli triumph

The police in the Norwegian resort town of Lillehammer needed only one look to conclude that something very terrible and dangerous had come to afflict their peaceful country. The body of the Arab sprawled in a pool of blood, his body torn apart by the fire of two machine guns, was mute testimony to the arrival in Norway that summer of 1973 of a vicious underground war, a deadly struggle from which the Norwegians prayed they could remain aloof.

But testimony from eyewitnesses confirmed the police's worst fears. The victim, a Moroccan waiter at a popular restaurant who had no police record or known political affiliation, was cleaning up the restaurant's outdoor dining section just before closing time when a car containing five white men roared up. Two of them jumped out and riddled the victim with the fire of two submachine guns. The men got back into the car and sped off.

A professional hit, obviously, but why would anyone want to kill an obscure Moroccan waiter in Lillehammer, of all places? Based on what they had heard from their colleagues in a half-dozen other European police agencies, the Norwegians instantly deduced that the waiter was the latest victim in a no-quarter strug-

gle between Black September, the most radical Palestinian terrorist group, and Israel's *Mossad* (*Mossad Letafkidim Meyouch-
hadim*). Ever since the terrorists had murdered Israeli athletes at
the 1972 Olympics, *Mossad* hit squads had roamed through the
Middle East and Europe, relentlessly hunting down, then killing,
those believed responsible. In retaliation, Black September had
murdered several *Mossad* agents.

Although the waiter seemed to have no connection with the
Black September-*Mossad* war, police theorized he might have
been a high-level terrorist leader working under deep cover—
although there did not appear to be any rational reason why such
a man would be operating in Lillehammer, far from such known
centers of terrorist intrigue as Paris (where there was a large Arab
immigrant population) and Cyprus (operating headquarters for
Palestinian terrorism). Nevertheless, one police team went to
work on the dead man's background to discover his presumed
Black September connections, while a second concentrated on
tracking down the killers.

This latter task turned out to be surprisingly easy. Thanks to
a fairly large number of eyewitnesses, police had good descriptions of the two men who actually did the shooting, along with
descriptions of the car, including the license plate. In short order,
police found six foreigners who had entered the country shortly
before the murder. One of them, a woman, had rented the car.
Careful checking of their passports, three of them Danish, revealed they were clever forgeries. More significantly, the leader
of the group, a man named Dan Aerbel, claimed to be a Danish
businessman but spoke with a pronounced Israeli accent and, it
was learned, held dual Israeli citizenship. So did the other five.
A few more clues convinced police they had ensnared one of the
fabled *Mossad* hit teams.

Under arrest for murder, the six Israelis at first were reluctant to talk, but police reminded them they were in a rough spot,
then dangled a prospect of salvation: if they agreed to be coop-
erative, then perhaps something could be worked out. The police
were sympathetic; certainly, they hinted, anyone could understand why the Israelis would want to eliminate the terrorists who
had been slaughtering their people. Norwegian courts might also
be sympathetic—provided, of course, the Israelis made a clean
breast of things.

Aerbel began to waver. He was exhausted, having spent several grueling months in hit-team operations. Nevertheless, he

could look back in satisfaction, having achieved in Lillehammer his main goal of eliminating Ali Salameh. Known as the "Red Prince," Salameh was one of the world's most notorious terrorists, the man involved in a long list of bombings, airplane hijackings, and his crowning achievement, planning the 1972 Olympics assault in which the Israeli Olympic team was killed. Salameh was adept at disguises and a master of underground warfare, Aerbel told his Norwegian interrogators, but *Mossad* had finally tracked him down. Salameh, it was discovered, had adopted the cover of an Arab immigrant waiter in Lillehammer. His death elated the Israelis; at last the 1972 slaughter had been avenged.

In Aerbel's calculation, this account of terror and retribution would play well in a Norwegian court. True, there had been a cold-blooded murder committed on Norwegian soil, but when the circumstances became known, there was no doubt the court would be prepared to be lenient.

Aerbel's confidence was rattled when police broke the bad news: a detailed investigation of the dead waiter revealed that he was exactly what he claimed to be, a Moroccan immigrant waiter who worked hard, had no political affiliations whatsoever, and dutifully sent most of his salary back home to his family. He bore a striking physical resemblance to Salameh, but that was the only possible connection.

Slowly, the horrifying truth dawned on Aerbel: *his team had shot the wrong man.*

How that had happened no one knew, but Aerbel realized he and his team were now in serious trouble. Facing a murder charge backed by eyewitness testimony, they were in the classic position that arrested spies have faced since time immemorial: officially, the Israeli government knew nothing about hit teams and had never heard of Dan Aerbel and his fellow defendants. They were figuratively adrift in the open sea, surrounded by sharks. As Aerbel was the first to realize, they needed a lifeboat. Just as he and his cohorts were about to be dragged into court, he thought of one. He offered a trade: in exchange for "consideration" by the authorities, Aerbel would reveal Israel's greatest secret and the most audacious (and consequential) intelligence operation in its history.

What the Norwegian authorities subsequently heard—and passed on to a number of intelligence agencies with which they did business—was an espionage story so fantastic, it made spy fiction pale by comparison. Aerbel, as the man who headed the operation, knew all the details. He was justifiably proud of his role, for he had accomplished what had long been thought impossible: he gave his nation the atomic bomb.

For the first time, the secret world heard about an amazing espionage coup code-named PLUMBAT.

The story began in 1965, when the Israeli government, in deepest secrecy, decided that the beleaguered Jewish state had to develop nuclear weapons. Called the "Samson option," the idea was to build a nuclear arsenal to be used if Israel's basic security were ever threatened by an Arab invasion. If it appeared that Israel was about to lose a war, the weapons would be used as a strategic trump card against its enemies. Additionally, the arsenal would serve as a deterrent against Egypt and Syria, Israel's main enemies, who were suspected of pressuring Moscow, their sole arms supplier, for access to nuclear weapons. As the Israelis envisioned it, when they succeeded in developing and building their nuclear arsenal, word of the existence of such ultimate weapons would be leaked, making it clear Israel was prepared to use them in the event the Arabs did.

But developing such weapons faced formidable obstacles. Above all, Israel needed access to sufficient supplies of uranium oxide ore, the essential ingredient for a nuclear research and development program. And that is precisely what it didn't have, nor was there any reasonable prospect of getting any.

The problem was that the production and sale of enriched uranium was tightly controlled by the "club" of world nuclear powers, especially the United States. The material was handled only in small amounts and under the strictest supervision, a procedure that sought to guarantee that no country, outside of the nuclear club, could gain access to sufficient amounts of the precious metal to develop and build nuclear weapons. U.S. officials made it clear they would never permit nuclear weapons to enter the Middle East powder keg.

The *Mossad*, assigned the job of getting the raw material for the Israeli atomic bomb, was thwarted in every attempt. Finally, one of its veteran operatives, Dan Aerbel, came up with an idea. Aerbel, born of a family of Danish Jews, had been working under commercial cover as a Danish businessman for a number of years, in the process developing a wide range of contacts in the European business community. In that community, Aerbel realized, lay the solution to Israel's problem. Somehow, *Mossad* must penetrate one of the companies that mined and processed uranium, then divert its production to Israel. Given the tight controls of uranium production, however, that task looked impossible.

Aerbel's solution was at once simple and brilliant. After searching among European chemical companies that had any business with uranium (most often for use in nuclear power plants), he fastened upon a small West German company called Asmara Chemie. As Aerbel was aware, one of Asmara's partners, Herbert Schulzen, a Luftwaffe pilot during World War II, had often expressed great guilt for his role, however small, in the war, when his country bore the responsibility for the murder of 6 million Jews.

Aerbel, who had lost a number of family members in the Holocaust, established a relationship with Schulzen, claiming to be a buyer for the Israeli government who arranged manufacturing contracts with foreign firms for various Israeli agencies. Aerbel moved carefully: he saw to it that Asmara was awarded a modest contract to make chemical decontamination kits for the Israeli army. Schulzen noticed that the Israelis paid Asmara far above prevailing rates for such work; grateful to be earning a handsome profit while helping people for whom he had great sympathy, he became a close friend of Aerbel's. In many long conversations, Aerbel played on Schulzen's guilt about the Holocaust, telling him about family members gassed at Auschwitz and survivors who had found sanctuary in Israel. Of course, Aerbel noted, Israel had many enemies, and the threat of a new Holocaust always loomed. It was rare, he noted, for anyone those days to do business with the Israelis. The idea that a German would work with the Jewish state was certainly cause for hope in a very dangerous world.

Schulzen had been hooked, and now the *Mossad* moved to bring him into the net. Aerbel invited him to Israel, where he was lavishly wined and dined by Israeli businessmen—actually *Mossad* agents—who told him about how many of their family members had been murdered by the Nazis. Even two decades later, the Israelis said, the threat that had almost destroyed them still loomed. For example, Schulzen was told, the Arab boycott and hostility of major nations made life very difficult for Israeli businessmen. The worst problem, they said, was in obtaining "certain critical materials for our survival." Nothing more specific was said on this subject, but Schulzen appeared to be sympathetic.

The next step in Schulzen's seduction began after he returned to Germany. He was showered with Israeli procurement contracts that turned his small outfit into a booming enterprise. Judging the moment had come, Aerbel moved in for the kill: Schulzen was asked if he could help the Israelis obtain 200 tons of uranium oxide, a critical nuclear material. Aerbel claimed his country needed so large an amount to power their new nuclear reactor and research center called Dimona, in the Negev. (He didn't bother to mention that the Israelis had constructed a three-story-deep secret underground facility at Dimona to develop nuclear weapons.)

Whether Schulzen believed Aerbel's fairy tale is not known, but he agreed to help. In March 1968 his company ordered the uranium ore from a Belgian mining concern. Asmara was carefully checked out by both the mining concern and the International Atomic Energy Agency, which monitored all deals involving bomb-grade uranium. Nothing seemed amiss: Asmara appeared to have a legitimate need for a shipment that size for a new petrochemical process to produce soap; it was a legitimate, thriving enterprise; and it had a robust financial profile, proven by over $5 million on deposit in Swiss banks.

Actually, Asmara had no plans to make soap, and all those millions in Switzerland had been secretly deposited by the *Mossad* to boost the West German company's profile. It was *Mossad* that also wrote up the detailed plan Asmara submitted to regulators on how it would handle the uranium ore. Addressing the strict European controls on any overland movements of nuclear materials, the Asmara proposal called for the radioactive ore to be picked up by ship in Antwerp, then taken to a processor in Milan, Italy, and finally moved to the Asmara plant, also via ship.

What the regulators did not know was that the Italian firm knew nothing about any uranium. At *Mossad*'s instigation, Schulzen had contacted an old friend and asked to use the Milan firm's name as a mere bureaucratic formality involving some irksome customs regulations for a shipment of "metals." Since Schulzen had an unblemished reputation, the friend agreed. The regulators approved the deal.

With all the regulatory paperwork now in place, the *Mossad* could put the rest of its intricate plan into motion. *Mossad* agents set up a phony shipping corporation in Switzerland under a Liberian flag of convenience, which they used to buy a 2,260-ton rust bucket of a West German merchant ship named *Scheersberg A*.

In November 1968 the ship hired a crew, then sailed to Antwerp to begin loading the ore. The workers who loaded several hundred steel drums were puzzled to notice that each drum had the word "plumbat" stenciled on it. The ship's crew was also puzzled, but things soon grew even more strange.

Assuming they were headed for Milan to deliver their cargo, the crew settled down for a routine sail down the coast of Western Europe. But only 24 hours later, the ship suddenly changed course and docked at the West German port of Hamburg. The crew was informed that the ship had been sold to a new owner, who wanted a new crew. The old crew was thanked for their efforts and given lavish payments in satisfaction of their contracts. By now totally puzzled about this curious turn of events, the old crew was further baffled when the new crew arrived and didn't even exchange a word of greeting to their predecessors, a very odd occurrence in the close brotherhood of seamen.

On November 17, 1968, the *Scheersberg A* departed Hamburg, informing port authorities that it was headed for the Italian port of Genoa. Genoese authorities were dutifully notified to expect the ship in a few days' time. But Genoa waited in vain, for the *Scheersberg A* never arrived. In fact, the ship didn't appear anywhere. It had disappeared into thin air.

At first, authorities assumed the ship had sunk, but there were no reported sinkings anywhere along the shipping lanes to Genoa. Curiously, the owners of the ship had not reported her overdue and missing, and no families of the missing crew members called to report them gone.

While authorities in Europe were trying to find the *Scheersberg A*, she suddenly appeared 15 days later in the Turkish port of Iskenderun. Mysteriously, the ship's captain and crew were totally different from the crew that had boarded her some weeks before in West Germany. Turkish authorities, unaware that the ship was reported missing in Europe, accepted the ship captain's story that he had just sailed from Naples, was putting in at the port for replenishment, and would return to Italy in a few hours. Since the ship was not conducting any unloading operations and was riding high in the water, indicating empty holds, the Turks didn't bother to inspect her. They did carefully inspect the supplies being loaded on board, though. Satisfied that all was in order, they allowed the *Scheersberg A* to go on its way.

The next appearance of the mystery ship came several weeks later in the Sicilian port of Palermo, where the new captain and his crew simply walked off the ship and disappeared. Still another new crew was hired by the ship's owner, and the *Scheersberg A* sailed for Antwerp. Its arrival precipitated a full-scale investigation, for port authorities determined that the ship's holds were empty. Nuclear regulators went into shock: what happened to the 200 tons of uranium ore?

Schulzen claimed to know nothing; he had simply arranged for shipment of the ore to the Italian processing plant. But officials at the plant said they knew nothing about any uranium ore. The ship's owners might have been of some help, except they had disappeared, leaving behind an empty office in Switzerland and no trace they had ever been there.

A tight lid of secrecy was clamped on the matter of the *Scheersberg A* and the missing cargo, for it was clear that the uranium ore somehow had been stolen. By whom was not known, but there was no way nuclear regulators were about to let the world know that enough material to make 10 atomic bombs had slipped through what was supposed to be a tight control system designed to prevent just such an incident.

The mystery of the *Scheersberg A* was not cleared up until several years later when *Mossad* agent Dan Aerbel began talking to the Norwegians in the hope of mitigating a murder charge. He revealed the arrangement with Schulzen, the creation of the Switzerland-based shipping company, the setup with the Italian processing plant, and the substitute crews (Israeli sailors) as all part of the elaborate *Mossad* operation to hijack the uranium ore. The actual theft took place on the high seas; several days after the *Scheersberg A* left Hamburg on November 17, 1968, it rendezvoused in the Mediterranean near Cyprus with a fleet of small Israeli vessels. The uranium was unloaded, and the ship sailed on to Turkey.

The uranium enabled Israel's nuclear weapons program to perfect an atomic bomb five years later. Eventually, the Israelis were able to build a small, but credible, nuclear arsenal, along with nuclear warheads for a surface-to-surface missile called *Gabriel*. The Israeli nuclear deterrent was an open secret by design, for its unmistakable message was that no enemy could hope to defeat Israel totally. How much of a role that deterrent played in the eventual political settlement with Israel's Arab enemies has yet to be determined.

Nevertheless, there is no doubt that the PLUMBAT operation played a vital role in the building of that deterrent. Even for an intelligence service known for spectacular operations, *Mossad* surpassed all its other achievements with the uranium theft—even though PLUMBAT has never been officially acknowledged.

Much more is known about some of the key players in the PLUMBAT episode. Dan Aerbel, having provided the Norwegians with a solution to the *Scheersberg A* mystery, got a relatively mild prison sentence of 19 months for the murder of the innocent Moroccan waiter. He gave a full confession, a document that interestingly contains not a single word about PLUMBAT. What he had to say on that score was classified and forwarded to friendly intelligence services, who thus learned how the Israelis had stolen 200 tons of uranium ore. The news was upsetting enough, but there was a general consensus that it could have been worse: suppose a group of terrorists had stolen the stuff?

The other members of Aerbel's hit team, who also confessed, received equivalently light sentences. They and Aerbel returned to Israel after being released from jail and disappeared into the thick fog the *Mossad* settles around its agents.

Herbert Schulzen, the West German businessman who played a pivotal role in PLUMBAT, was never charged with any crime. Somewhat bemusedly, he watched the frantic overhaul by nuclear regulators of statutes covering the shipments of bomb-grade material—an attempt, so it was said, to ensure that another PLUMBAT would never happen. It amounted to a perfect example of locking the barn door after the horse was stolen.

Oh, and the *Scheersberg A*? The Israelis sold the ship to a Cypriot shipping outfit. Very few people realize that the old, tired rust bucket—renamed the *Kerkya*—slowly chugging around the Mediterranean these days delivering loads of cement is the ship that played such an important role in this dramatic espionage operation.

EPILOGUE

Espionage as Opera Bouffe

Operation CORNFLAKES
1944–1945

An OSS curiosity

No account of espionage would be complete without reference to the tendency of all human endeavors to descend into pure folly; or, as Marx's famous dictum has it, history repeats itself first as tragedy, then as farce.

Espionage normally is a very serious business that involves very serious people. Yet, there are moments when all sense seems to leave even these sober-minded people. They will formulate operations that are so divorced from reality and common sense, it is difficult in retrospect to understand how any intelligent person could have thought of such insanity.

There are any number of such follies, but there is one supreme example that remains an almost completely forgotten footnote to history. It was a World War II operation called Operation CORNFLAKES, a purely lunatic intelligence enterprise that used vast resources to accomplish absolutely nothing. The operation was conceived and run by the American OSS, which apparently did not devote a single moment of intelligent thought to whether all the trouble was worth it. The result, of course, was failure. But since the operation was so badly conceived, no real harm was done. No lives were lost as a result of Operation CORNFLAKES, a rarity in ill-conceived intelligence enterprises.

Although Operation CORNFLAKES was an American conception, its real birth was in British intelligence. As part of their extensive propaganda operations against Nazi Germany, the British had devised a plan to disrupt German morale by using the mails.

The plan, of doubtful utility, called for the British, using international mail to Germany from neutral countries, to slip in some distinctly unauthorized postal matter. After gaining access to the list of German subscribers to newspapers from neutral countries, MI6 operatives hired a master forger to produce a series of cleverly forged stamps that were stuck on envelopes addressed to Germans from nonexistent companies in neutral capitals. At a quick glance, the envelopes appeared normal, but the stamps actually were parodies of real issues. For example, one stamp substituted a portrait of Heinrich Himmler for Hitler as a means of sowing dissension inside Nazi Germany—part of a whispering campaign organized by British intelligence to spread rumors that Himmler was poised to take over the government.

Busy postal clerks, without the time to examine the stamps carefully on every envelope, would routinely cancel such envelopes and send them on their way. Similarly, even busier censors would hardly bother looking at the envelope, preferring to spend their time checking the contents (which were always innocuous-appearing business or personal letters).

The effect was negligible, at best. In the first place, most of the Germans who had the wherewithal to subscribe to foreign newspapers—an expensive proposition in wartime Germany—were largely businessmen or Nazi party functionaries whose morale hardly would be rattled by a propaganda stamp. Secondly, the MI6 operation failed to take into account the realities of Nazi Germany, where the omnipresent Gestapo and its vast network of domestic informants made every German extremely circumspect in what they said, wrote, or did—and what was in their mail. The overwhelming majority of Germans who received a mysterious letter from a person or business in a foreign country they had never heard of either assumed there was some mistake or that the letter amounted to some kind of provocation. In either case, frightened of having evidence lying around that might put them under suspicion, the recipients tended to burn such mail.

Oddly, the American OSS seemed to have learned nothing from the British failure. In early 1944 they began to organize an even more elaborate operation. Ultimately, it would cost the

American taxpayers millions of dollars, occupy several thousand people, and have no impact whatsoever on the course of World War II.

The operational concept, which sprang from the fertile minds within the OSS who were assigned the job of dreaming up dirty tricks against the Germans, was very ambitious. Called Operation CORNFLAKES, it proposed a massive infiltration of Allied propaganda into the German postal system as a means of undermining German home front morale by degrading confidence in Hitler and creating a sense of defeatism inside Germany.

It was a tall order, and to carry it out, the OSS borrowed the MI6 idea of infiltrating propaganda via the mail system and expanded it into something much grander. Instead of a few letters from neutral countries, the OSS plan was to inject many thousands of propaganda letters by a much more direct route. Allied planes who routinely shot up German trains would carry sacks of faked mail; after they had strafed a train that had a mail car attached, the sacks would be dropped around the train wreckage. As the OSS was aware, it was standard practice of the German postal service to recover sacks of mail from train wrecks and arrange other means of delivery.

Beginning early in 1944, OSS agents began combing prison camps for German POWs who had ever worked as mail clerks. The puzzled German clerks were called in for extensive interrogations and, seduced by meals and drink far above the normal standard of prison rations, encouraged to discuss the minutiae of how the German postal system worked. Ex-postal workers, flattered that the enemy would take so avid an interest in their lowly civilian occupations (and eager to keep this good fortune going), were expansive about how mail was collected, canceled, and delivered in Germany.

Armed with that knowledge, the OSS then rounded up brigades of German exiles and put them to work formulating letters to German citizens. Utilizing German telephone directories obtained at great risk and cost from inside Nazi Germany, the exiles selected people at random, writing these strangers personal letters full of family gossip about relatives who did not even exist. The letters were strictly domestic mail that was not subject to censorship.

A team of master forgers produced perfect copies of genuine postage stamps for these letters, including a few deliberate parodies designed to rattle German morale. The most striking was a parody of a standard German definitive that featured a portrait of Hitler. The OSS version, however, altered the portrait to show part of his skull and included a new inscription that read, in colloquial German, "German Reich shot to hell."

Still other groups of forgers worked to produce precise replicas of the kind of paper Germany used for normal postal stationery, along with exact copies of standard German mail sacks. Another group of forgers made precise copies of German postal cancellations to authenticate the thousands of "letters" being produced by the OSS writers, who spent day after day scribbling heartfelt personal missives about how Dietrich's infected foot was feeling much better, how Aunt Helga was still running around with that idiot, and by the way, wasn't it terrible how the government was going to cut food rations further? (The writer claimed a friend high in the government as a source for this disquieting news.)

Several thousand people were involved in this operation, but all their work was rendered useless in August 1944, when the OSS discovered the Germans had changed the cancels used on domestic mail. Samples of mail using the new cancels were secured, and Operation CORNFLAKES went back to the drawing board. The thousands of envelopes already written were thrown out, and a whole new batch was prepared.

The next month all was ready to go when another disaster struck: due to wartime problems, the German postal system decreed that henceforth only business mail would be forwarded when mail sacks were recovered from train wrecks. The OSS went back to work, devising a whole new batch of fake envelopes, all of them now from real German businesses culled from the phone directories.

At last, in February 1945, Operation CORNFLAKES was ready to go. There were eight separate drops made of fake sacks of mail by strafing planes that shot up trains with mail cars. As the OSS hoped, the fake sacks, virtually indistinguishable from the real thing, were picked up and included with the genuine ones for forwarding to addresses all over Germany.

Some of the envelopes, in addition to a personal letter, also contained copies of the OSS's chief propaganda vehicle, a one-page newspaper called *Das Neue Deutschland* (*The New Germany*). Prepared by anti-Nazi German exiles who had once worked for German newspapers and magazines, the paper was a perfect parody of the official German Nazi newspaper—except that the OSS

A brainstorm of Operation CORNFLAKES was the use of altered German
postage stamps. This issue, a propaganda parody of a regular issue of Nazi
Germany, shows Hitler with part of his face eaten away to reveal his skull. The
normal *Deutsches Reich* inscription on the bottom of the stamp has been
altered to read *Futsches Reich* (roughly, "Reich shot to hell"). (*Author's
Collection*)

version contained the kind of news the official paper never
printed. Among such items were details on the 1944 attempted
coup against Hitler, the enrichment of top SS officials while most
Germans were living on near-starvation rations, and the realities
of Germany's military position.

The OSS expectantly waited for an anticipated tremor in
German morale. But there wasn't any. The problem was that the
OSS had used city telephone directories to find addresses, but it
had somehow overlooked the fact that German cities by 1945
were largely in shambles. Badly out of touch with the realities of
life in 1945 Germany, the OSS failed to realize that almost all
essential services in those cities, including postal delivery, were
virtually nonexistent. The main problem was that because of Allied bombing, many Germans had lost their homes; millions of
them had moved or were living with relatives. In such chaos, very
few people had the time to fill out change-of-address cards. Postal
deliverers, confronted with an address that was now a pile of
rubble, simply threw the mail away if they couldn't find the
recipients.

But there was a more serious problem, and that had to do
with the very nature of Nazi Germany. Like MI6, the OSS failed

Two issues of *The New Germany*, a newspaper produced by Allied propaganda in 1944. These issues were mailed to German citizens at random during Operation CORNFLAKES. (*Author's Collection*)

to consider the reaction of typical Germans who receive an envelope from a company with which they have never done any business. Inside, they found a personal letter alluding to relatives and events that had no connection with reality. They could only conclude that either the letter had been misaddressed to them, or that something was seriously wrong. If the envelope contained one of those OSS-produced propaganda newspapers, that was cause for alarm, for even to be seen in possession of such a subversive piece of paper was enough to get the holder executed. Similarly, if the envelope contained one of those OSS propaganda parodies, that was also cause to be worried. The recipients could only wonder if they had been singled out for some sort of provocation designed to test their loyalties.

In any event, the effect was almost always the same: the Germans hastily burned such material, hoping no one had noticed they were the recipients of subversive mail. For that reason, the impact of Operation CORNFLAKES was something less than a snowflake on the ocean.

However, there were a few unanticipated exceptions. Several fervent Nazis who somehow found themselves recipients of Operation CORNFLAKES mail and received copies of the OSS German newspaper instantly realized they had been provided with an insurance policy. After the collapse of Nazi Germany, they came forward waving copies of the newspaper, insisting its mere possession certified that they had been anti-Nazis all along.

Other German recipients of Operation CORNFLAKES mail in future years would rue the day they had ever burned those envelopes. The stamps on the envelopes, few of which survived the war, came to be worth a lot of money to collectors, especially any so-called entires (a genuinely used entire envelope including the OSS forged stamp). According to philatelic experts, only two such genuine examples survived the war, and they are today worth a fortune.

It was philately that was to expose the existence of Operation CORNFLAKES. After the death of President Roosevelt, an avid stamp collector, his famous collection was put up for sale. Experts hired to evaluate the huge collection were puzzled when they encountered copies of strange-looking parodies of German stamps that showed part of Hitler's skull and others that substituted Heinrich Himmler in place of Hitler. They also encountered copies of German wartime postage stamps that were so expertly forged, only detailed analysis revealed the forgery. Obviously, these forgeries had been carried out by people using top-grade engravers, paper that had been laboriously prepared to mimic perfectly the genuine article, and production processes that duplicated the genuine printing methods.

In other words, obviously only a government would have had the capacity for so expensive and technically proficient an operation. But since counterfeiting is a serious crime under American law, it seemed inconceivable that the American government was involved in such a thing. Moreover, what would have been the point? Counterfeiters don't bother taking the considerable legal risk of making fake money to produce one-dollar bills. By the same token, a forger would not bother to invest so much time, effort, and money to produce ordinary postage stamps. In wartime Germany, the stamps most commonly used on domestic mail cost somewhere around two cents in American money, clearly not much of a motive to inspire counterfeiting.

The answer, the experts became convinced, had to lie elsewhere. It took them some time, but finally they found among

Roosevelt's papers correspondence between himself and the head of the OSS, General William Donovan. At some point, apparently, Donovan—aware of Roosevelt's philatelic passions—had forwarded to him some of the OSS forgeries and propaganda parodies that had been produced for Operation CORNFLAKES. Other correspondence outlined the scope of the operation.

The OSS was not especially happy that their operation had come to light during the sale of the Roosevelt collection; the organization at that time was in a fight for its life. President Truman was not enthralled with the OSS, concluding that it was overstaffed, spent too much money, and had a very spotty record, at best. He wanted to disband the agency on the grounds that in the postwar retrenchment, the country could not afford such expensive entities. The brief spurt of publicity over Operation CORNFLAKES was not helpful to the OSS at this point. The newspaper stories contained only sparse details about the operation, but they were enough to make the point that it was badly conceived, spent a lot of money to no particular purpose, and wound up having virtually no impact on German morale, its stated purpose.

It would take the declassification of secret OSS records many years later for the full story of Operation CORNFLAKES to emerge. But those details did not change the initial conclusion by Truman (and others) that the operation was fundamentally a tribute to folly.

As Truman himself put it, "Wasn't anybody thinking over there?"

Index

Abakumov, Viktor S., 158–59
Abwehr, xxiii
   Allied invasion of France and, 27–28,
      29
   Egyptian operations of, 84–91
   infiltration operations of, 37–40,
      43–44
   penetration of, 40, 44–46
   Romanian evacuation and, 197
   U.S. operations of, 50–58
Acosta, Juan, 16, 18–20
Additives, 64
Advance Base Operations in Micronesia
   (Ellis), 207
Aerbel, Dan, 240–44, 246–47
Agent, definition of, xix
Agent of influence, definition of, xix
Agent provocateur, definition of, xix
Albert, Heinrich, 121, 123–24
All This and Heaven Too, 57
Almasy, Laszlo von, 85, 86–87
Al Mukharbarat, xxiii
Aman, xxiii
Ames, Aldrich
   betrayal of Dmitri F. Polyakov by, 132,
      134–35
   CIA career of, 132–33
Ames, Carleton, 132
Amt Ausland Nachrichten und Abwehr. See
   Abwehr
Angleton, James Jesus, 137, 140–44,
   146–48
Angola, Cuban operations in, 21
Arrow Cross, 152, 155, 156
Artamanov, Yuri, 3–5, 10, 11
Artuzov, Artur, 9
ASCHE. *See* Thilo-Schmidt, Hans
Asmara Chemie, 243–44
Aspillaga, Florentino, 17, 24
Asset, definition of, xix
Astor, Vincent, 211
AT&T, 75
A3725. *See* Schmidt, Wulf

Atomic bomb technology
   Israel and, 242–47
   MAGIC operation and, 81
   Nazi Germany and, 94, 96, 99–104,
      108–11
   Soviet attainment of, 105–15
   traitors and, 93, 94, 107
Australian Secret Intelligence Service
   (ASIS), xxii

Bacon, Francis, xvii, 75
Berg, Moe, 111
Beria, Laventri, 144, 158
BERNHARD, 88
Bertrand, Gustave, 61–63, 65–67
Biuro Szyfrow 4, 66
BLACK, 86, 90
Black bag job, definition of, xix
Black Chamber, 76–77, 78
Blackmail
   honeypot operations and, 94
   KGB use of, 144, 169–70, 174, 175
   William Sebold and, 50
Black propaganda, definition of, xix
Black September, 240
Black Tom, 116–25
Blunt, Anthony, 218–25
BODYGUARD, 30–36
Boeckenhaupt, Herbert W., 130
Bolshevik revolution, 3–7, 9–10
Book code, 42, 87–88
Born, Max, 97, 98
Bossard, Frank, 130
BOURBON. *See* Polyakov, Dmitri F.
Boy-Ed, Karl, 120, 121, 124
Bradley, General Omar, 45
Braun, Wehrner von, 100
Brecht, Bertolt, 217, 218
BRIDE, 224
Britain
   attitude toward Joseph P. Kennedy in,
      170–71
   Bolshevik revolution and, 9

CORNFLAKES operation and, 249–50
GRIFFIN operation and, 95–104, 110
history of intelligence gathering in,
    xiv
homosexuality in, 68, 71–72, 219
Iran-Iraq War and, xii
Nazi agents in, 27–28, 32, 40–47
North African campaign of, 83–84, 86
Ring of Five operation and, 216,
    217–26
smuggling of Jews by, 98, 104
Soviet agents in, 130
torpedo attacks by, 182
Trust operation and, 11, 13
ULTRA operation and, 31–32, 33, 35,
    40, 44–45, 67–72
World War I code breaking and, 60,
    74
British Security Service. *See* MI5
Bronze Goddess, 61, 69
BRUTUS, 45
Bundes Nachrichten Dienst (BND), xxiii
Bundesamt für Verfassungsschutz (BfV),
    xxiii
Burgess, Guy, 141, 218–25
Bush, George, xii-xiii

Cairncross, John, 218–25
Canadian Car and Foundry Company,
    bombing of, 123
Canadian Security Intelligence Service
    (CSIS), xxii
Canaris, Admiral Wilhelm
    Allied invasion of France and, 27–28
    FBI sting of, 57–58
    Hitler's planned invasion of Britain
        and, 43–44
CANDY operation, 105–15
Casey, William, 24
Castro, Fidel
    Cuban double agents and, 16, 19–20,
        24
    Ignacio Rodriguez-Mena and, 20
CD-501 transmitters, 22
Central Intelligence Agency (CIA)
    Aldrich Ames and, 132–35
    Angolan operations of, 21
    Cuban double agents and, 16–25
    Eastern European Communist
        infiltrations by, 200–204
    East German operations of, 163–66
    founding of, 141
    Iran-Iraq War and, xi-xiii
    KGB mole war and, 139–48
    TOP HAT operation of, 126–35

CHEKA, 5–12
China
    CIA and, 163–64
    KGB assets and, 161–63, 165
    Korean War and, 224
    Soviet intelligence on, 131
Churchill, Winston
    assassination plots against, 71
    BODYGUARD operation and, 30, 31
    Double Cross System and, 46
    Enigma and, 67–68
    Joseph P. Kennedy and, 171
    MAGIC operation and, 81
    Nazi intelligence on, 167, 168, 172–74
    Soviet takeover of Romania and, 199
"CIA War Against Cuba," 17, 25
Cipher system, definition of, 63–64
Code breaking
    book codes and, 87–88
    BRIDE operation and, 224
    CANDY operation and, 113–14
    Enigma and, 61–72
    Federal Communications Act of 1934
        and, 211
    MAGIC operation and, 73–82, 187–89,
        192
    Nazi successes at, 70–71
    radio transmissions and, 60
    techniques for, 64
    Hugh Trevor-Roper and, 41–42
    ULTRA operation and, 31–32, 33, 35,
        67–72
    Walker spy ring and, 230, 232–34, 236
Code, definition of, 63–64
Cohen, Lona, 105–7, 114
Cohen, Morris, 106, 114
Colby, William, 147
Cold War
    CIA-KGB mole war during, 139–48
    Ring of Five operation and, 223–25
    Soviet takeover of Romania and,
        193–200
    TOP HAT operation and, 126–35
    Walker spy ring and, 227–38
Communications Security Establishment
    (CSE), xxii
Compartmentalization, 54
Computers, Alan Turing and, 66, 68, 71
CORNFLAKES operation, 248–55
Counterfeiting, 88, 254
Cramer, General Hans, 32–33
Credulity, deception operations and, 1
Cryptanalysts. *See* Code breaking
Cuba, double agents employed by, 16–25

Dangle, 160, 164
D-Day invasion, 34–35, 46, 81
Deception operations, rationale for, 1
Defections
    of Cuban agents, 16–17, 24
    false, 143
    penetration operations and, 137–38
Defence Signals Directorate (DSD), xxii
Del Monte, Antonio, 173
Desert Storm. *See* Gulf War
Deutsch, Arnold, 219–22
Deuxieme Bureau, 61, 65
Dienst III-B, 120, 121
Diesel Research Company, 54, 55
Direccion General de Intelligencia (DGI),
    xxii
    Maria del Rosario and, 133
    use of double agents by, 16–25
Direction de la Surveillance du Territoire
    (DST), xxiii
Direction du Renseignements Militaires
    (DRM), xxiii
Directorate Generale de la Securite Exterieure
    (DGSE), xxii
Discard, definition of, xxi
Disease warfare, 121
Disinformation, definition of, xxi
Doenitz, Admiral Karl, 71
Donovan, William (Wild Bill), 196–97
Double agents
    BODYGUARD operation and, 32, 35
    Cuban use of, 16–25
    Hu Simeng Gasde and, 160–66
    KONDOR operation and, 89–91
    Ring of Five operation and, 216,
        217–26
    ULTRA and, 70
    See also Double Cross System
Double Cross System, 32, 37–47
Drummond, Nelson, 129–30
Dryden, John, 93
Dulles, Allen, 195, 200
Dunlap, Jack E., 129, 130
Dzerzhinsky, Feliks, 7–13, 15

Earhart, Amelia, 205, 211–14
East Germany
    Chinese assets of, 161–66
    CIA and, 163–66
    Soviet involvement in, 203
Eichmann, Adolf, 154–55, 158
Einstein, Albert, 97, 110
Eisenhower, Dwight D., 46
Eliot, Jim Andreyevitch. *See* Burgess, Guy

Elizabeth I, xiv
Ellis, Earl Hancock, 207–11
Enigma
    British intelligence on, 41
    decryption of, 66–72
    French intelligence on, 61–63
    invention of, 64–65
    Japan and, 78–79
Eppler, Johann, 84–91
Estikhabarat, xi, xxiii

False flag recruiting, 233
Farouk, King, 91
Fathmy, Hekmet, 85, 87–89, 91
Federal Bureau of Investigation (FBI)
    Aldrich Ames and, 135
    counterintelligence and, 52–53
    creation of, 124–25
    Tyler Kent investigation by, 174–75
    Pearl Harbor attack and, 180
    Ring of Five operation and, 223
    sting of Nazi assets by, 54–58
    TOP HAT operation and, 126–31
    Walker spy ring and, 228–30, 236–38
Fermi, Enrico, 100, 111, 112
Flap, definition of, 177
Flat Earth Society, 143
Foley, Francis, 95, 98–102, 104
Ford Motor Company, Nazi assets in, 51,
    55
Forschungsamt, 70–71
France
    history of intelligence gathering in,
        xiv
    World War I code breaking and, 60
Frazer, Mark Petrovich. *See* Maclean,
    Donald Stuart
Friedman, Elizabeth, 75–77
Friedman, William F., 73–80, 82
Front, definition of, xxi
Fuchs, Klaus, 113, 114
Fuller, Colonel Bonner, 86

Gaevernitz, Gero von Schulze, 195
GARBO, 45, 46
Garby-Czerniawski, Roman. *See* BRUTUS
Gasde, Horst, 161–63, 165–66
Gasde, Hu Simeng, 160–66
Geheime Staatspolizei. See Gestapo
Gehlen Org, xxiii
Gerd, Hans, 84–89, 91
Germany
    Black Tom munition bombing and,
        116–25

loss of The Mandates by, 206
reparations paid by, 125
scientific reputation of, 96–97
World War I code breaking and, 59, 60
See also East Germany; Nazi Germany; West Germany
Gestapo, xxiii
  CORNFLAKES operation and, 249
  FBI and, 53
  recruitment of William Sebold by, 48–51
Ghafer, Hussein. *See* Eppler, Johann
Goddard, Robert H., 51, 52
Goerdler, Karl, 154
Gold, Harry, 114
Golitsin, Anatoli, 142–48
Gordievski, Oleg, 134, 159
Gouzenko, Igor, 114
Government Communications Headquarters (GCHQ), Enigma and, 65, 67
GPU (*Gosudarstvennoye Politicheskoye Upravleniye*), 12–15
Greek city-states, *proxenos* and, xiv
Greene, Graham, 221
Greenglass, David, 113
GRIFFIN. *See* Rosbaud, Paul
GRIFFIN operation, 95–104, 110, 111
Gromov, Anatoli, 221–24
Grotjan, Genevieve, 80
Groupement de Communications Radioelectriques (GCR), xxiii
Groves, General Leslie, 110, 111
GRU (*Glavnoye Razevedyaltelnoye*)
  atomic weapon technology and, 108, 112, 114
  memoirs of, 215
  TOP HAT operation and, 126–27, 129–31
GT/ACCORD. *See* Polyakov, Dmitri F.
Gulf War, xii-xiii
Guojia Anqouanbi, xxii

Hahn, Otto, 97, 99, 100
Harriman, Averell, 147
Harvey, William K., 56
Hebern, Edward, 64
Heine, Edmund, 55
Heisenberg, Werner
  assassination plot against, 111
  career of, 97, 109
  internment of, 114–15
Held, Martha, 121, 123, 124

Helms, Richard, 147
Himmler, Heinrich, 249, 254
Hiroshi, Oshima, 81
History of intelligence gathering, xiii-xiv
Hitler, Adolf
  Abwehr operations and, 43, 50–51, 84
  Allied invasion of Europe and, 28–30, 34
  appeasement of, 221
  atomic bomb technology and, 109
  CORNFLAKES operation and, 249–54
  Enigma and, 65
  German opposition to, 154
  Hungarian Jews and, 152, 154
  MAGIC operation and, 81
  Soviet takeover of Romania and, 198
  traitors and, 96
  ULTRA operation and, 61, 70
  Franz von Papen and, 125
  See also Nazi Germany
HOMER. *See* Maclean, Donald Stuart
Homosexuality
  Ring of Five and, 219, 222
  Alan Turing and, 68, 71–72
Honeypot operations, 94, 169
Hoover, J. Edgar
  Abwehr and, 58
  creation of FBI and, 124
  William Harvey and, 56
  Tyler Kent investigation and, 174
House on 92nd Street, The, 55
Howard, Edward Lee, 134
Hughes Trading Company, 209
Hull, Cordell, 189
Hungary, CIA involvement in, 202, 203–4
Hussein, Saddam, xii-xiii

Illegal (in Soviet intelligence), definition of, xxi
Ilovaiskaya, Tatiana, 169
Intelligencers, xiv
Iran-Iraq War, xi-xii
Irish-Americans, German recruitment of, 121–22, 125
Israel, atomic bomb technology and, 242–47

Jahnke, Kurt, 123
Japan
  MAGIC operation and, 78–82
  occupation of The Mandates by, 206–10, 214
  Pearl Harbor and, 177, 179–92

Jilinsky, General Yakov, 59
JN-25, 187
Johnson, Clarence (Kelly), 212
Johnson, Herschel, 155

Kalaris, George, 148
Kazui, Kamaga, 82
Kennedy, John Fitzgerald, 146, 170–71
Kennedy, Joseph P., 167–68, 170–74
Kennedy, Joseph P., Jr., 170–71
Kent, Tyler Gatewood, 167–75
KGB (*Komit Gosudarstvennoy Bezopasnosi*)
    Aldrich Ames and, 133–35
    atomic bomb technology and, 105–6,
        108, 109, 111–14
    Chinese assets and, 161–63, 165–66
    Cuban double agents and, 21, 22, 23
    execution cellars of, 194
    Kennedy assassination and, 146
    Tyler Kent and, 168–70, 174–75
    memoirs of, 215
    mole war of, 139–48
    purge of, 222
    Ring of Five operation and, 216,
        217–26
    Romanian operations of, 197–202
    TOP HAT operation and, 126, 131,
        133–35
    Walker spy ring and, 216, 227–38
    Wallenberg family and, 153–54,
        156–59
    WIN sting of, 202–3
Kheifetz, Gregory, 112
Khomeini, Ayatollah, xii
Khrushchev, Nikita, 144
Knight, Maxwell, 167–68, 171–73, 175
Koch, Paula, 84
Kolesnikov, Pavel P. *See* Stetakiewicz,
    Viktor
Komit Gosudarstvennoy Bezopasnosi. *See*
    KGB
KONDOR operation, 83–91
Korean War, 224
Kuehn, Bernard, 184, 188, 190, 192

Lang, Hermann, 55
Langer, Gwido, 66–67
Langfelder, Vilmos, 157, 159
Leal, Eduardo, 24
Le Carre, John, 137
Legal (in Soviet intelligence), definition
    of, xxi
Legend, definition of, xxi
Lehigh Valley Railroad, 118, 119

Lenin, Vladimir, 3, 4, 7, 11
Letterbox, definition of, xxi
Liddell, Guy, 167
Lindbergh, Charles, 212

Maclean, Sir Donald, 218–19
Maclean, Donald Stuart
    CANDY operation and, 112
    defection of, 141
    Ring of Five operation and, 217–26
MAGIC operation, 73–82, 187–89, 192
Maly, Theodore, 219–22
Mandates, The, 205–14
Manhattan Project
    creation of, 110
    security for, 105–6
    Soviet intelligence on, 112–14, 222
Marshall, George, 189
Martynov, Valeri, 134
Masterman, J. C., 43
MATEO. *See* Acosta, Juan
May, Alan Nunn, 111, 112, 114
Meitner, Lise, 97
Meldekopf, 54
Memoirs of intelligence chiefs, 215
Menzies, Stewart, 40
Mexico, German revolutionary plans in,
    124
MI5
    Double Cross System and, 40–47
    Tyler Kent and, 167–68, 171, 173–75
    Ring of Five operation and, 220, 223
MI6
    CORNFLAKES operation and, 249–50,
        252
    GRIFFIN operation and, 98, 101, 103,
        104
    KGB moles in, 141–42
    recruitment of Soviet agents by, 134
    Ring of Five operation and, 223, 224
MI8, creation of, 74
Michael, King of Romania, 196, 197,
    199–200
Michniewicz, Wladyslaw, 13–14
Miller, Joan, 172–73
Moles
    CIA-KGB struggle over, 139–48
    definition of, xxi
Monarchist Association of Central Russia
    (MOTsR), 6
    Trust operation and, 8, 10, 12, 13
Monkaster, Peter. *See* Gerd, Hans
Morgenthau, Henry, 214
Morimura, Ito (Takeo Yoshikawa),
    179–81, 183–85, 192

Mossad Letafkidim Meyouch-hadim, xxiii, 240–47

Motorin, Sergei, 134

Nagumo, Admiral Chuichi, 190

Nasser, Gamal Abdel, 91

National Dock and Storage Company, 116–18

National Geographic, BODYGUARD operation and, 32

National Security Agency (NSA), 82, 129

Navarre, Henry, 61–63

Nazi Germany
  Allied invasion intelligence of, 26–36
  atomic bomb and, 94, 96, 99–104, 108–11
  CORNFLAKES operation and, 249–55
  counterfeiting operation of, 88
  Double Cross System and, 37–47
  Enigma and, 61–72
  Hungarian Jews and, 149–50, 152–56
  Joseph P. Kennedy and, 171, 172
  MAGIC operation and, 80–81
  science in, 97–103, 108–9
  traitors to, 94, 95–96
  U.S. spy operations and, 167–75

Neue Deutschland, Das (The New Germany), 251–54

97-shiki-O-bun In-ji-ki (alphabetical typewriter 97), 79

Nimitz, Chester W., 214

Nixon, Richard M., 131

Noonan, Fred, 213–14

Norden Bombsight, 51–52, 55

Nosenko, Yuri, 139–40, 144–48

Oberkommandos der Wehrmacht (OKW). *See* Wehrmacht

Office of Naval Intelligence (ONI)
  Japanese occupation of The Mandates and, 206–10, 213
  Pearl Harbor attack and, 180, 186–87
  Frank Wisner and, 196

Office of Policy Coordination (OPC), 201–3

Onetime pad, definition of, xxi

Oppenheimer, Robert, 97, 107, 112

OP-20-G, 76, 186, 187

ORESTES, 233

OSS
  James Angleton and, 141
  atomic bomb technology and, 110, 111
  CORNFLAKES operation and, 248–55
  Romanian operations of, 194–200

Oswald, Lee Harvey, 145–46

Our Hearts Were Young and Gay, 42

Ovakimian, Gaik, 113

OVERLORD, 29–31

Palestinian terrorists, 239–41

Pao, Lin, 224

Patton, General George, 33–35

Pearl Harbor
  intelligence errors and, 177, 179–92
  MAGIC operation and, 81

Penetration operations, 137

Penkovsky, Oleg, 93

Perception, intelligence and, xii–xiii

PERSEUS, 106, 113

Philby, Harold Adrian Russell (Kim)
  James Angleton and, 140–42
  William Harvey and, 56
  Ring of Five operation and, 218–25
  Wallenberg family and, 154

Physics, German innovations in, 97

Pilsudski, Marshal, 14

Playback, definition of, xxi

PLUMBAT operation, 239–47

Poland
  CIA involvement in, 202
  Trust operation and, 13–14

Politics, espionage and, xiv

Polyakov, Dmitri F., 126–32, 134–35

Polygraph testing
  of CIA agents, 134, 135
  of U.S. assets, 21, 24

Pontecorvo, Bruno, 112, 114

Popov, Dusko. *See* TRICYCLE

Proxenos, xiv

Publicity about intelligence operations, 215–16

Pujol, Juan. *See* GARBO

PURPLE, 78, 80–82, 180

Putnam, George P., 212, 214

Quingbao, xxii

Rebecca, 86, 87

Reilly, Sidney, 13

Reuper, Carl, 55

Right Club, 171–73

Ring of Five, 216, 217–26

Ritter, Nikolaus, 51–58

Robertson, Thomas A., 42–45

Rodriguez, Antonio, 16–17

Rodriguez-Mena, Ignacio, 20–21, 24–25

Romania
  CIA involvement in, 202
  Soviet takeover of, 193–98

Romanov, Grand Duke Nikolai, 7
Rommel, Field Marshal Erwin
  Allied invasion plans and, 31
  Enigma and, 69
  KONDOR operation and, 83–91
Roosevelt, Eleanor, 213, 214
Roosevelt, Franklin D.
  assassination plots against, 71
  Vincent Astor and, 210–11
  CORNFLAKES operation and, 254
  Amelia Earhart and, 212–14
  Hungarian Jews and, 155
  Japan policy of, 188, 189
  Joseph P. Kennedy and, 170, 171,
    173–74
  MAGIC operation and, 81
  Manhattan Project and, 110
  Nazi intelligence on, 167, 168, 172–74
  U.S.-Soviet alliance and, 194
Rosario, Maria del, 133
Rosbaud, Paul, 96–104, 110
Rosenberg, Ethel, 93, 113, 114
Rosenberg, Julius, 93, 113, 114
Rowlett, Frank B., 73–74, 78
Russia, Tannenberg battle and, 59
Russo-Japanese War, 189
Rybkin, Boris, 153

Sadat, Anwar, 85, 88, 89, 91
Salameh, Ali, 241
SAPPHIRE, 142
SASHA, 143, 147
Satellite reconnaissance
  Gulf War and, xii
  Iran-Iraq War and, xi
Savama, xxiii
Savinkov, Boris, 13
Scheersberg A, 244–47
Schindler, Oskar, 150
Schmidhuber, General August, 149–50
Schmidt, Wulf, 37–41, 44–47
Schulzen, Herbert, 243–44, 246–47
Schutzstaffel (SS), 149
Scud missiles, Iraqi deployment of, xii,
    xiii
Sebold, William, 48–51, 53–58
Sergeyev, Lily. *See* TREASURE
Shirinsky-Shikhmatov, Kirill, 5
Sicherheitsdienst (SD), xxiii
  Tyler Kent and, 170
  Romanian evacuation of, 197
  turf wars involving, 28
Signal Intelligence Service (SIS), MAGIC
    operation and, 73–82

Simeng, Hu. *See* Gasde, Hu Simeng
Sino-Japanese War, 186
Sleeper, definition of, xxi
Soviet Union
  atomic bomb and, 105–15
  Chinese intelligence and, 162
  CIA operations in, 126–35
  GRIFFIN operation and, 103
  KGB privileges in, 144
  Korean War and, 224
  Lenin's economic policy and, 4
  Donald Maclean and, 218
  monarchist underground in, 3–7
  recruiting of American Communists
    by, 113
  takeover of Romania by, 193–200
  treason and, 93
  Trust operation and, 3–15
  Walker spy ring and, 230–31
  Wallenberg family and, 150–51, 153
SPARROW, 157
Spy dust, 145
SS. *See Schutzstaffel*
Stalin, Josef
  assassination plots against, 71
  atomic bomb technology and, 107,
    109–10
  BODYGUARD operation and, 30
  Hungarian peace overtures and,
    156–57
  KGB purge and, 222
  MAGIC operation and, 81
  Ring of Five operation and, 221, 224
  takeover of Romania and, 194,
    197–200
  treason and, 93
  Trust operation and, 11, 14, 15
  Raoul Wallenberg and, 158
  WIN sting and, 203
  See also Soviet Union
Station, definition of, xxi
Stein, Lily, 55
Stengel, Casey, 116
Stetakiewicz, Viktor, 11
Stimson, Henry, 76
Strassman, Fritz, 99, 100
Substitution systems, 64
Suicide of agents, 89, 130, 204, 225
Supreme Monarchist Council (VMS), 3,
    5

Tannenberg battle, 59
TATE. *See* Schmidt, Wulf

Technology
  CIA use of, 22–23, 131–32
  code breaking and, 60, 64–65, 77–79
Te Wu, xxii
Thilo-Schmidt, Hans, 61–62, 65–67
Tinker, Tailor, Soldier, Spy (Le Carre), 137
Tito, Marshal, 143
Tkachenko, Aleksei, 237
TOP HAT. *See* Polyakov, Dmitri F.
TOP HAT operation, 126–35
Traitors. *See* Treason
Transposition, 64
Treason
  atomic bomb technology and, 93, 94,
    107
  perspectives on, 93–94
  TOP HAT operation and, 128
TREASURE, 45, 46
Tres, 4, 5
Trevor-Roper, Hugh, 41–42
TRICYCLE, 45, 46
Trotsky, Leon, 4, 15
Truman, Harry S., 177, 223–24
Trust operation, 3–15
Tube Alloys Project, 110, 111, 113, 222
Turing, Alan, 68–69, 71–72
TYPHOID. *See* Wisner, Frank

ULTRA, 61–72
  Allied invasion of France and, 31–32,
    33, 35
  code breaches and, 86
  Double Cross System and, 40, 44–45
  KONDOR operation and, 87
  Ring of Five operation and, 223
United Nations (UN), foreign agents in,
  126–27

Vietnam War, 230, 234
VMS. *See* Supreme Monarchist Council
Von Bernstoff, Count Johann, 120–21,
  124
Von Der Goltz, Horst, 120–21
Von Papen, Franz, 120–22, 124, 125
Von Roenne, Colonel Alexis, 26–30,
  32–34
Von Rundstedt, Field Marshal Gerd, 31,
  32, 33
Vyshinsky, Andrei, 199–200

Wagner, Honus, 116
Walker, Arthur, 235–36, 238
Walker, Barbara, 233, 236
Walker, John Anthony, Jr., 227–38

Walker, Michael, 234–38
Walker spy ring, 227–38
Walk-in, definition of, xxi
Wallenberg, Jacob, 151, 153–54
Wallenberg, Marcus, 151, 153–54
Wallenberg, Raoul, 149–59
Walsingham, Francis, xiv
Wehrmacht
  Allied invasion of France and, 26–27,
    35, 36
  Enigma and, 70–71
Welland Canal, 122
West Germany
  Hu Simeng Gadse and, 166
  reparations paid by, 125
  Soviet operations in, 129
Whalen, William H., 129, 130
White, Dick, 43
Whitworth, Jerry, 233–36, 238
Wilson, Harold, 147
Wilson, Woodrow, 117, 124
WIN, 202–3
WIND FLYER, 237
Wiretapping operations, 186–87
Wisner, Frank, 194–204
Witzke, Lothar, 123
Wolkoff, Anna, 171–75
Wolkoff, Nicholas, 171–72
World War I
  Black Tom munition bombing and,
    116–25
  radio communications during, 59–60
  U.S. communications intelligence
    during, 74
World War II
  BODYGUARD operation and, 26–36
  CANDY operation and, 105–15
  communications intelligence and, 60
  CORNFLAKES operation and, 248–55
  Double Cross System and, 37–47
  GRIFFIN operation and, 95–104, 110,
    111
  KONDOR operation and, 83–91
  MAGIC operation and, 73–82
  Pearl Harbor intelligence and, 179–92
  Ring of Five operation and, 221–23
  TRAMP operation and, 48–58
  ULTRA operation and, 31–32, 33, 35,
    61–72
  Wallenberg family and, 150–51,
    153–58

Yakushev, Aleksandr
  monarchist underground and, 3–6
  Trust operation and, 8–11, 13, 15

Yamamoto, Admiral Isoroku, 181–83, 185, 192
Yardley, Herbert O., 74–75, 76, 78
Yatskov, Anatoli, 113
Yoshikawa, Takeo. *See* Morimura, Ito
Yurchenko, Vitali, 134, 238

Z operation, 179–92
Zarubin, Elizabeth, 112–13, 114
Zarubin, Vassili, 112–13, 114
Zimmermann, Arthur, 124
Zionists, British intelligence and, 89